The Human Side of Cyber Conflict

Organizing, Training, and Equipping the Air Force Cyber Workforce

Panayotis A. Yannakogeorgos, PhD
John P. Geis II, PhD, Colonel, USAF, Retired

Contributors

Stephen Hagel, Colonel, USAF, Retired
Chad Dacus, PhD
John L. Conway III, Colonel, USAF, Retired
Adam B. Lowther, PhD
Steven Drinnon, Lt Colonel, USAF

Air University Press
Air Force Research Institute
Maxwell Air Force Base, Alabama

Project Editor
Jeanne K. Shamburger

Copy Editor
Carolyn Burns

Cover Art and Book Design
Daniel Armstrong and L. Susan Fair

Composition and Prepress Production
Michele D. Harrell

Print Preparation and Distribution
Diane Clark

AIR FORCE RESEARCH INSTITUTE

AIR UNIVERSITY PRESS

Director and Publisher
Dale L. Hayden, PhD

Editor in Chief
Oreste M. Johnson

Managing Editor
Dr. Ernest Allan Rockwell

Design and Production Manager
Cheryl King

Air University Press
600 Chennault Circle, Bldg 1405
Maxwell AFB, AL 36112-6026
afri.aupress@us.af.mil

http://aupress.au.af.mil/
http://afri.au.af.mil/
Facebook:
https://www.facebook.com/AirUnivPress
and
Twitter: https://twitter.com/aupress

Library of Congress Cataloging-in-Publication Data

Names: Yannakogeorgos, Panayotis A., author. | Geis, John P., II, author.
Title: The human side of cyber conflict : organizing, training, and equipping the Air Force cyber workforce / Panayotis A. Yannakogeorgos, John P. Geis II ... [and five others].
Other titles: Organizing, training, and equipping the Air Force cyber workforce
Description: Maxwell Air Force Base, Alabama : Air University Press, Air Force Research Institute, [2016] | Includes bibliographical references.
Identifiers: LCCN 2015045544 | ISBN 9781585662593
Subjects: LCSH: United States. Strategic Command (2002-). Cyber Command. | United States. Air Force—Recruiting, enlistment, etc. | United States. Air Force—Officers—Training of. | United States. Air Force—Personnel management. | Cyberspace operations (Military science)—United States.
Classification: LCC U163 .Y358 2016 | DDC 358.4—dc23
LC record available at http://lccn.loc.gov/2015045544
ISBN: 978-1-58566-259-3

Published by Air University Press in June 2016
Second Printing March 2017

Disclaimer

Opinions, conclusions, and recommendations expressed or implied within are solely those of the authors and do not necessarily represent the official policy or position of the organizations with which they are associated or the views of the Air Force Research Institute, Air University, United States Air Force, Department of Defense, or any other US government agency. This publication is cleared for public release and unlimited distribution.

Dedicated to those bold, silent Airmen, military and civilian, who employ cyber capabilities to project power and ensure freedom of action to achieve national security objectives in or through cyberspace sans honor, decoration, or recognition.

Education is not what it is said to be by some, who profess to be able to put knowledge into a soul where it is not present, as though putting sight into blind eyes.

—Plato
The Republic

Contents

List of Illustrations	*vii*
Acknowledgments	*ix*
Executive Summary	*xi*

1 Introduction: Project Context and Methodology 1
   Tasking 1
   Definitions 1
   Tasks and Timelines 2
   Phases 1 and 2: Defining the Problem, Exploratory Research, and Analysis 3
   Phase 3: Analysis and Vetting Findings with OCRs and against Data 9
   Phase 4: Roll Out Project Findings to CSAF, Key USAF Stakeholders, and Project Participants 11

2 Connecting Technology and Policy 13
   Comparing Information Technology and Operational Technology 15
   Core and Peripheral Technologies 23
   Peripheral Technologies That Will Benefit from Core Technology Trends 33
   Air Force Acquisition and the Cyber Workforce 36
   National Initiative for Cybersecurity Education 39
   Summary 45

3 Recruit, Retain, Regain 51
   Recruit 52
   Retain 65
   Regain 67
   The Air Force Warrant Officer and Cyber Technology: A Good Fit? 70
   Summary 73

4 Understanding the Impact of Millennials on the Cyber Workforce 77
   Who Are the Millennials? 78
   Maturational Theory versus Generational Theory 79

	Traditionalists, Boomers, and Xers	80
	Adapting to Millennials	82
	Summary	86
5	**Force Development**	89
	14N Intelligence Officer	91
	17 Series—Cyberspace Warfare and Network Operations Officers	96
	1B4 Enlisted Cyberspace Defensive Operations	106
	Enlisted Cyberspace Intelligence Analyst	114
	13NXXX Cryptologic Language Analysts and Foreign Language Requirements for the Cyber Mission Force	117
	3DXXX Career Fields	122
	Summary	126
6	**The Air National Guard, the Air Force Reserve, and Cyber**	137
	Cost as the Overarching Factor	138
	Civilian Cyber Skills in the Reserve Components	139
	Summary	143
7	**Educating and Training Cyber Forces**	147
	Education versus Training	148
	Levels of Education within the USAF Cyber Workforce	153
	Cyber Advanced Courses in Engineering: In-Sourcing Educational Force Multipliers	162
	Air University and Education at the Operational Level	168
	Air University: Education at the Operational and Strategic Levels of Cyber Conflict	171
	Toward an Air Force Cyber Operational History	175
	Training Cyber Forces	177
	Training Issues	178
	Summary	184
8	**Concluding Thoughts**	189
	Appendix: Overall Recommendations and Status	195
	Abbreviations	207
	Bibliography	215
	About the Contributors	235

Illustrations

Figure

1	Cyber operations definitions	1
2	Tasks and timelines of research phases	2
3	Organizations visited and consulted	9
4	Technologies and policies affecting cyberspace operations	14
5	Spectrum of operations in cyberspace	17
6	PG&E gas transmission pipeline explosion	21
7	NICE framework	41
8	Age groups of cybercrime perpetrators	58
9	Percentage of SMART funds awarded by discipline	63
10	Notional 14N (cyber) career development pyramid	97
11	Breakdown of the 17D community	98
12	Inventory and sustainment of 17D career field	99
13	Developmental timeline for some cyberspace specialties	104
14	17D career pyramid	106
15	1B4 enlisted cyberspace defense operations career development	112
16	Proposed 1N4X1A fusion analyst / digital network analyst career pyramid	115
17	Air Force NMT/CST language requirements	118
18	Career development path of 1B4 and 3DX enlisted AFSCs	124
19	Generic career pyramid for 3DXXX career fields	125
20	FEMA regional headquarters	141
21	Cyber tasks at levels of Bloom's Taxonomy	149
22	Cyber in foreign military doctrine and strategy	150
23	2014 ACM programming competition	152
24	Informatics Olympiad medal totals, 1988–2014	152

ILLUSTRATIONS

25	17D overall degrees	154
26	Top-ranked cyber programs worldwide	155
27	USAFA cyber major preference for 17D	156
28	USAFA nonrated preferred AFSC and GPA	156
29	USAFA cyber majors' first-choice nonrated AFSCs	157
30	Timeline of AFRL ACE and AFIT ACE development	165
31	ABET-accredited program graduates from top-producing colleges	167

Table

1	Key recommendations	xviii
2	IT system and ICS comparison	18
3	UCT Phase 1	101
4	UCT Phase 2	102
5	Enlisted cyber support AFSCs	108
6	1B4X1 course of instruction for cyberspace defense operations	109
7	Intermediate Network Warfare Training	111
8	3DXXX career fields	122
9	17D bachelor's degrees	153
10	17D master's degrees	153
11	Cyber-educated accessions from top universities	155
12	Average GPAs of USAFA cyber major vs. all USAFA cadets	156
13	USAF cyber accessions from the top 10 schools	161
14	ROTC cyber degree production by school and ABET accreditation status	162
15	Average yearly unemployment rate and percentage of 17D/33S cyber degree holders accessed from OTS	166
16	Percentage of Airmen by career field and educational level	168

Acknowledgments

This book was a collaborative effort. John Geis and Stephen Hagel have worked with me throughout this project and were instrumental not only in recruiting participants and reading, reviewing, and revising chapters but also in their contributions of significant chapters. In bringing this volume to print, we would like to thank several people who were invaluable in the genesis, production, and completion of the project. We sincerely appreciate the belief of Gen Mark A. Welsh III, US Air Force chief of staff, in the importance of the research topic and his appreciation of the complexity of the subject matter. Lt Gen Allen G. Peck, USAF, retired, director of the Air Force Research Institute, contributed many improvements to the research, and we thank him for his constant and generous support in recruiting Department of Defense and national senior leadership participation in the study.

We would like to express our gratitude to Adm Michael Rogers, USN; Gen Hugh Shelton, USA, retired; Gen John E. Hyten, USAF; Lt Gen Edward Cardon, USA; Lt Gen Michael J. Basla, USAF, retired; Lt Gen Burton M. Field, USAF; Lt Gen Robert J. Elder, USAF, retired; Lt Gen Jon Davis, USMC; Lt Gen Harry Raduege, USAF, retired; Maj Gen Suzanne Vautrinot, USAF, retired; Lt Gen Jeff Lofgren, USAF; Maj Gen Earl D. Matthews, USAF, retired; Maj Gen Burke E. Wilson, USAF; Mr. Robert Joyce; Mr. Russell Fraz; and Mr. Frank DeGiovanni. We are grateful to all for taking the time to provide senior leader perspectives on their organizations and for encouraging their overburdened staffs to spend some time with the research team as we tried to untie the Gordian knot of cyber workforce development.

Dr. Kamal Jabbour, Col William Young, USAF; Col Jodine K. Tooke, USAF; Col Kimberlee Joos, USAF; Lt Col Stephen Bailey, USAF; CMSgt Robert B. Jackson, USAF; CMSgt John Sander, USAF; Capt Jonathan Williams, USAF; Dr. Roger Hurwitz, Dr. Vint Cerf, Dr. Martin Libicki, Dr. Hal Arrata, Dr. Bob Mills, Dr. Tom Mabry, Mr. Hal Flynn, Dr. Eneken Tikk-Ringas, Mr. Chris Spirito, and Mr. Xeno Kovah provided valuable information and perspectives on current education, training, and workforce development practices. Their input gave our research team a solid foundation for addressing how the Air Force and nation can resolve the challenges of developing the cyber workforce.

Without the guidance and expertise of all of the above and countless others, this project could not have come to a successful conclusion.

ACKNOWLEDGMENTS

Finally, it is necessary to commend Maj Jonathon Burson, USAF, and Maj Lacy Croft, USAF, who helped shepherd this manuscript through the publication process, as well as Jeanne Shamburger and Demorah Hayes, who worked tirelessly to guide this project through the editorial and quality review processes.

                              PANO YANNAKOGEORGOS, PhD
                              Air University
                              Maxwell AFB, AL
                              June 2016

Executive Summary

On 18 March 2013, the chief of staff of the Air Force tasked the Air Force Research Institute (AFRI) to review the training and development of the USAF cyber forces to take stock of current Air Force cyber force development. AFRI was to determine whether structural changes were required to ensure the successful organizing, training, and equipping of the Air Force's cyber workforce. This study is the culmination of research AFRI conducted to examine the USAF's cyber human capital planning and management strategies and to recommend improvements where needed.

The goal of this study was to examine how we should recruit, educate, train, and develop cyber operators from the time they are potential accessions until they become senior leaders in the enlisted and officer corps. Guiding the research were these key questions:

- What is a "cyber force"?
- What must the Air Force do to organize, train, and equip Airmen who can plan and execute Air Force and joint missions in cyberspace?
- What force structure is needed to operate the Air Force's defined mission sets?
- Should the Air Force cyber force remain a traditional force or be modeled on a nontraditional personnel structure?

To explore facets of cyber workforce development, the research team collaborated with six directorates of Headquarters Air Force and the Twenty-Fourth Air Force, Twenty-Fifth Air Force (then the Air Force Intelligence, Surveillance, and Reconnaissance Agency [AFISRA]), Air Force Space Command (AFSPC), Air Force Personnel Center (AFPC), Air Education and Training Command (AETC), National Security Agency (NSA), Central Intelligence Agency (CIA), Air Force Research Laboratory (AFRL), Air Force Wargaming Center (AFWC), Air Force Institute of Technology (AFIT), United States Cyber Command (USCYBERCOM), US Navy, US Army, US Marine Corps, and many other organizations across the government, the private sector, academia, and civil society. The intent was to create a set of recommendations not only to meet Air Force mission requirements but also to fit the manpower demand of USCYBERCOM's Cyber Mission Force, currently in the process of expanding.

EXECUTIVE SUMMARY

The study surveyed technological trends that will affect the workforce. Cyber—a dynamic domain of warfare—will change. Personnel planners must not focus solely on accessing operators with knowledge, skills, and abilities (KSA) to harness today's technology but also must consider future technologies when they forecast manpower requirements. Otherwise, we may be investing in skill sets needed in today's computing environment but perhaps not in the midterm as trends such as cloud computing begin more widespread adoption worldwide and the inevitable transition to Internet Protocol version 6 (IPv6) commences in earnest.

Our summary of conclusions for senior leaders is broken out along the lines of the organize, train, and equip construct.

Organize

Recruiting. The research team found that discovering people with an aptitude for cyber operations is essential—a majority of recruits should be deeply experienced in the fields of science, technology, engineering, and mathematics (STEM). However, we are concerned that placing too high a value on STEM degrees may create barriers to entry in the cyber field, thereby excluding some very talented operators and depleting the pool from which operators are drawn. In addition, we concluded that the USAF needs cyber operators with not only a proclivity toward cyber operations but also a grasp of legal, policy, and ethical issues related to cyber operations and national security. However, this cadre is shallow and needs to be grown. We therefore urge the addition of "arts" to STEM—creating "STEAM." STEAM will assure that the USAF has a team of social/behavioral scientists, lawyers, and instructors who have a sound understanding of the technology but specialize in crafting policy. These team members will work alongside their STEM counterparts to integrate cyber power in service to the nation.

Proper accessions will require more targeted recruiting and training. Models predicting cyber success are useful in selecting people for cyber training and reducing washout rates. We recommend (1) continued utilization of a cyber test to identify high-potential recruits—both within the service and from the general US population—with an aptitude for cyber and a grasp of basic principles of information technology, (2) ongoing investment in screening, and (3) consideration of adjusting the test to include variables that can discover innovative, autodidactic team players who do not limit themselves to the tactics, techniques, and procedures (TTP) checklists.

This study confirmed that hacker stereotypes are often inaccurate. Many hackers we interviewed did not align with the caricature of couch potatoes living in their parents' basement; they included marathon runners and patriotic citizens with outside-the-box ways of critically analyzing problem sets but who felt disinclined to enter government service. Therefore, senior leaders who perpetuate a stereotype of hackers as "a certain kind of individual" do a disservice to attracting talent into the military and government.

Contributing to negative perceptions of the hacker community is the tendency to focus on destructively inclined individuals, thus tainting how inquisitive hackers are viewed. A major recruiting challenge we discovered was the impact of criminal records on the ability to obtain security clearances. This situation is partly due to the strict criminalization of hacking activity in the United States, including that of the inquisitive hacker types (discussed later in this study). We found that the USAF would benefit from leveraging games and competitions to serve as an outlet for inquisitive hacking skills and to instill our core values into individuals who aspire to join the ranks of those defending the nation. Legitimate hacking competitions provide legal outlets for students with creative computer skills. From these competitions and through its sponsorship of and advertising at these competitions, the USAF can and should recruit only those personnel who clearly adhere to its core values.

We also found that not all officers with computer science (CS), computer engineering (CE), or electrical engineering (EE) degrees enter the 17-series cyber operator career field once they join the Air Force. Anecdotal stories of people who have a proclivity to hack but are initially assigned outside cyber suggest that the Air Force should identify a path for Airmen to transfer into the 17X/1B4/3D series or cyber-related civilian career fields later in their careers. The cyber test could be one way to allow Airmen from other Air Force specialty codes (AFSC) who are interested in cyber—or with CS, CE, or EE degrees—to demonstrate their aptitude to be cyber warriors.

We found that any reliance on Officer Training School (OTS) to produce cyber accessions is problematic. A statistical analysis of OTS accessions shows that when the US economy is robust, OTS has a greatly diminished capacity to recruit or access cyber officers. Furthermore, because of the Air Force's current disinclination to direct

EXECUTIVE SUMMARY

US Air Force Academy (USAFA) cadets to certain majors and career fields, the USAFA cannot be counted upon to deliver more cyber-educated graduates. Thus, we recommend that ROTC be the primary accession source for educated cyber warriors and that ROTC budgets be bolstered to recruit STEAM-qualified 17D- and 17S-series officers. We also recommend targeted recruiting and scholarships at high-ranking state colleges as the most cost-efficient methods of attracting top cyber talent for the lowest tuition expenditures.

Retention. The study also focused on retaining our investment in cyber operators. While retention is generally high at present, there is cause for long-term concern. The Air Force is seeking to recruit and retain skills in high demand in industry. Despite this trend, research shows that statistically the Air Force has very high retention rates for personnel serving on national mission–related teams because those Airmen have extremely high job satisfaction. However, the quality of those individuals who departed—described anecdotally as top performers—is not quantifiable. At the juncture where an Airman is asked to leave one of these teams for instructor or field duty, retention is a problem; we heard several anecdotal stories of senior noncommissioned officers departing the service within two years of retirement. In most cases, they were hired by contractors to continue doing the same job they were doing before, often at higher pay and without having to change duty locations. To retain the flexibility to reliably move Airmen as needed, we recommend that the Air Force explore the legalities of including noncompete clauses to restrict contractor competition for cyber Airmen who have not yet reached retirement age.

We further recommend that the USAF examine possible paths for regaining individuals who separated from the service to practice cyber operations in the private sector but might later want to return to government work to apply lessons learned in industry to USAF missions.

Educate/Train

The Air Force accesses an officer and enlisted corps that generally has no understanding of cyber hygiene; this practice threatens the security of our networks, given that we do not acquire systems with mission assurance designed into our systems and platforms. Contrary to intuition, most of our new Airmen do not understand why or how many types of cyber intrusions happen. They cannot comprehend how to recognize even the more commonly found types of malware or phishing. The core of this problem is not the proverbial "dumb users" but poor system design and engineering rooted in how the software and hardware industries create their products. Fixing this problem at the core requires technological solutions by implementing either better system design or information assurance measures to prevent social engineering and other unintentional insider threats. To ameliorate this situation, we recommend that the Air Force establish a short course in cyber hygiene with course objectives of achieving analysis-level understanding of common cyber threats as a part of all officer and enlisted accessions programs. We stress, however, that this is a short- and midterm objective as the cyber acquisition process evolves and as cost-effective strategies for "baking in" security based on mission priorities and requirements are developed and implemented.

The USAF needs to better emphasize cyber education. To compete with nation-state adversaries, the Air Force and Department of Defense (DOD) at large require a cadre of operators that have the foundational skills of mathematics and computer programming to react to novel threats in novel solutions. A significant area of concern that we discovered during our research is Air Force efforts to ramp up the cyber workforce with trained operators who are commercially certified rather than with educated officers who can apply their knowledge to address unique threats. We concluded that education (learning how to think) is as valuable, or more so, than training (learning how to do). This finding leads to recommendations to expand the intake of new graduates to include the arts—or the STEAM concept—and emphasize the AFRL/AFIT advanced cyber engineering and cyber education programs as well as advanced academic degrees (AAD).

We found few personnel with AADs across the cyber AFSCs. The historic difficulty in finding AADs for cyber billets compelled leaders to remove requirements from the personnel rosters so their vacant billets could be filled by AFPC. Doing so leaves a dearth of education and creative thinking in our cyber forces. We therefore recommend that cyber leaders recode billets they believe should have an AAD assigned as "AAD required." AFPC should then take those requirements and create a glide path for the cyber career fields to grow their AAD population to meet that demand. A cyber graduate program similar to that offered by the School of Advanced Air and Space Studies (SAASS), alongside the AFIT cyber operations master's degree program, is a logical piece of the solution to the AAD shortage. Until the right number of AADs is created, AFPC should still fill AAD-required billets

EXECUTIVE SUMMARY

with the best people available so as to not penalize commanders for making their needs known.

A gap currently exists in the production of planners and strategists who have operational- and strategic-level familiarity with the cyber domain. To help bridge this gap, we recommend that Air University be leveraged to gather critical, strategic thinkers from across the government and private sector to advance thought in our newest domain of cyberspace. We also recommend that the USAF establish a Center for Advanced Cyber Thinking and Strategy (C-ACTS) at Air University to promote new concepts of how cyber can perform or enhance the USAF's core missions. These ideas can then be used to educate planners and strategists through the existing Cyber Horizons program.

Related to the above recommendations, our study noted that many people within the Air Force perceive cyber as a new domain yet neglect our service's nearly 30-year history of operations within it. Consequently, Airmen fail to understand past problems and lessons learned that could be harnessed to propel our cyber policies and TTPs into the future. We recommend that the Air Force Historical Research Agency be commissioned to collect official cyber unit histories and oral histories of the pioneers of the Air Force cyber mission for use as the basis of follow-on studies with appropriate lessons learned.

Because cyber workforce development is a whole-of-government problem, the president has directed a whole-of-government educational solution in which the Air Force should play its part. Led by the Department of Homeland Security (DHS), the National Initiative for Cybersecurity Education (NICE) will standardize both cyber functions and the education requirements to perform those functions across the entire US government workforce. We recommend that the Air Force begin to align the key KSAs in which cyber operators are educated and trained to the NICE framework, which, as of this writing, the Office of Personnel Management is scheduled to implement in 2018.

Although the cyber career field evolves rapidly, the research team found that the cyber curriculum does not always keep pace. Systematic procedures for updating curricula add rigor to the USAF's education and training programs but may create a lag time before courses reflect real-world capabilities. Thus, we recommend that all cyber-related schools be tasked with keeping their curricula fully current as changes occur in cyberspace.

Equip

Equipping the schoolhouse and training ranges is one area that should receive priority to enhance the cyber workforce. Cyber-range facilities in which to practice cyberspace operations are presently inadequate. Most of these ranges are funded out of hide or with fallout money. To assist in keeping curricula up to date, we recommend that this haphazard method of funding cyberspace training and education cease. Specifically, cyber ranges should be included in the program objective memorandum (POM), with all monies and personnel needed for operations and maintenance explicitly present in the annual budget in exactly the same manner we create a POM for ranges in the other two domains (air and space).

Cyberspace is evolving rapidly in terms of applications and threats. The core of the digital network environment, however, is on the cusp of changing for the first time in history with the shift from IPv4 to IPv6. The Air Force has a tremendous opportunity and responsibility to lead the DOD and the nation in the transition to IPv6. Such a shift will help reduce existing attack vectors into US systems while enabling the Air Force to better accomplish its mission. It will require the service's cyber operators to keep pace with technological change. The Air Force's cyber schoolhouses offer some general background on IPv6, but it is insufficient. Detailed, specific training on IPv6 should be required. We recommend that our senior leaders make IPv6 migration a primary focus area and give IPv6 education and training sufficient commitment to spur the necessary transition. Harnessing IPv6 is critical if the Air Force is to remain the best-equipped, best-trained, and most lethal force on the planet.

Nonstandardized equipment and inadequate contractor performance have facilitated recent adverse cyber events. This study finds that the Air Force can hold vendors financially liable for inept software designs and/or coding that leave systems vulnerable. The research team concedes that efforts are under way to pursue such action. Any revenue arising from these efforts should be directed to addressing the specific problem created by the vendor and then to enhancing software assurance so the same thing does not happen again. Finally, since fixing poor programming can be more difficult and costly than writing it properly in the first place, the DOD and Air Force should provide adequate incentives for secure programming that far exceeds the level necessary to avoid liability.

EXECUTIVE SUMMARY

This study's discoveries, analyses, and recommendations are aimed at guiding staff officers and senior leaders alike as they consider how to create a cyber workforce that better supports both Air Force and US Cyber Command missions across the range of military operations. Our overarching recommendations are summarized in table 1. For an expanded list of recommendations and their statuses, see the appendix.

Table 1. Key recommendations

KEY RECOMMENDATIONS		
Organize	Educate/Train	Equip
Use economic indicators with existing manning and retention statistics to adjust selective reenlist bonuses to mitigate manning crisis levels. (AFPC)	Examine/implement reforms to the Instructional Systems Development process with career field to ensure that education and training are attuned to the operational environment. (AETC/AFPSC)	Mandate IPv6 transition for the USAF's operational benefit. (HAF/A6/AFNIC)
Recognize cyber as a separate domain with separate language / social science requirements, and catalog personnel identified/recruited.	Map curriculum to NICE's KSAs to ensure interagency relevance. Investigate use of cyber competitions for recruiting.	Actively contribute to Internet governance. (A6/AFRL/AFIT)
Incorporate DHS-NICE framework across cyber career fields. (A6S)	Enhance the IPv6 networking and software programming in the curriculum. (AFSPC/AETC)	Equip schools consistent with POMed (requested in program objective memorandum) lab/range equipment, including software/hardware.
Create electronic position description/tracking mechanism mapped to NICE. Investigate the use of the special experience identifier (SEI) to track specialized cyber skills for assignments. (A1)	In lean years, give the 1B4 career field priority for tuition assistance and other like programs in cyber-related fields.	Integrate acquired systems to avoid a "patchwork quilt" of systems and software. (AFSPC, SAF/AQ, AFMC)

Table 1 (*continued*)

KEY RECOMMENDATIONS		
Organize	Educate/Train	Equip
Mandate that cyber units code their billets for AADs.	Fully fund the AFIT/AFRL distinct ACE programs (change AFIT program name); estimated cost is $1.6M.	Emphasize software assurance, and incentivize contractors to use best practices.
USAFA customers should create demand signal to cadets that there are good jobs for them as 17D/Ss. Create a summer course for cadets as a means of enticing them into the career field. (USAFA)	Ramp up cyber AAD production (including AFIT) to meet identified demand. Create a cyber hygiene curriculum for accessions programs. (AETC)	Develop technical cyber acquisition certification similar to that for engineering.

Notes

(All notes appear in shortened form. For full details, see the appropriate entry in the bibliography.)

    1. Yannakogeorgos, "Rise of IPv6," 103–28.
    2. National Defense Authorization Act for Fiscal Year 2013, Public Law 112-239, sec. 933.
    3. Dacus and Yannakogeorgos, "Designing Cybersecurity into Defense Systems."

Chapter 1

Introduction: Project Context and Methodology

Tasking

The chief of staff of the Air Force (CSAF) charged the Air Force Research Institute (AFRI) with reviewing and recommending actions for the development of USAF cyberspace forces in the areas of education, training, and assignment and then identifying a cybersecurity human capital planning and management strategy. This book is the culmination of our findings. The appendix provides a comprehensive list of near-term recommended tasks and the offices of primary responsibility.

Definitions

Before delving into the cyberspace career field, the research team sought to clarify the terms *cyberspace* and *cyber operations*. This project was more a personnel than a cyber study; thus, resolving the question of what cyberspace is, which continues to vex the nation and world, was beyond its scope. The team therefore used the Department of Defense (DOD) definitions of cyber-related terms in Joint Publication (JP) 3-12 (R), *Cyberspace Operations*, to focus the study (fig. 1).

> **Cyberspace Operations:** "The employment of cyberspace capabilities where the primary purpose is to achieve objectives in or through cyberspace."
>
> **Offensive Cyber Operations (OCO):** The projection of power "by the application of force in and through cyberspace" to deny the adversary freedom of action.
>
> **Defensive Cyber Operations (DCO):** Ensuring freedom of action via active/passive defense to "preserve the ability to utilize friendly cyberspace capabilities and protect data, networks, net-centric capabilities," etc.
>
> **DOD Information Networks (DODIN):** "Actions taken to design, build, configure, secure, operate, maintain, and sustain DOD communications systems and networks in a way that creates and preserves data availability, integrity, [and] confidentiality."

Figure 1. Cyber operations definitions. (Developed from JP 3-12 (R), *Cyberspace Operations*, 5 February 2013, v, vii, II-2.)

The research team also utilized the CSAF's determinations at the June 2013 Corona about which career fields, functions, and highly specialized skills comprise USAF cyberspace operations. Cyberspace career fields currently fall broadly into three categories: OCO, DCO, and cyberspace infrastructure maintenance—the DODIN. The personnel required to conduct operations in these broad categories include the enlisted career fields 1B4 (cyberspace defensive operations), 1NX (highly specialized cyberspace intelligence analyst), and 3D (cyberspace support); the officer 17 series (cyberspace warfare and network operations) and 14N (intelligence) career fields; and a myriad of other active duty and civilian occupational codes. To reduce the complexity of the study, the team focused on career fields of core cyberspace operators who will serve on US Cyber Command (USCYBERCOM) cyber teams.

Tasks and Timelines

Figure 2 depicts the tasks and timelines of each research phase:

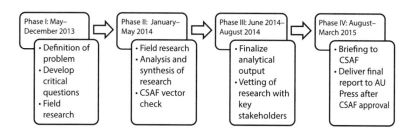

Figure 2. Tasks and timelines of research phases

One should note that throughout the research phase, the Air Force was making continuous progress to refine how it organizes, trains, and equips for conflict in cyberspace. As the research team interacted with stakeholders in cyber force development throughout the service, solutions to identified problems were either already being discussed or spurred by the research team's insights and inquiries. Additionally, as researchers identified areas that needed to be broadcast to a wider audience, they published results, produced working papers, and made presentations regarding the current state of their research and received feedback.[1]

Phases 1 and 2: Defining the Problem, Exploratory Research, and Analysis

Hypothesis Testing

The study's thesis question asked whether the current system of accessing, educating, and training cyberspace operators to prepare them for the roles and missions they will perform for combatant commanders is optimal. The study's hypothesis asserts that this supposition is true. The tasking letter, however, clearly presumes this hypothesis to be false based on the charge to develop a new plan for cyberspace human capital management. This tasking also reflects an Air Force senior leadership view that improvements need to be made in accessing, educating, and training cyberspace operators. Preliminary interviews supported Air Force leadership beliefs, corroborating that the hypothesis appeared to be false. Participating organizations at this stage were Twenty-Fourth Air Force (24th AF), Headquarters Air Education and Training Command (AETC), Headquarters Air Force Space Command (AFSPC), Headquarters Air Force A3/5 (HAF A3/5), and the Air Force Secretariat Office of Information Dominance and Chief Information Officer (SAF/CIO A6).

In parallel to this study, the entire Air Force cyber workforce management enterprise was also working to address the CSAF's concerns. By developing a collaborative relationship with Air Staff members, the AFRI research team assured that its efforts were included. Further, we shared discoveries about various stovepipes for the Air Staff's consideration as it worked tirelessly to implement change in the cyber workforce.

To fully evaluate the thesis question and substantiate the preliminary interviews, the team designed this study as an inductive synthesis of the Air Force and national cyberspace enterprise. This approach allowed the research team to develop a set of forward-looking requirements for the cyberspace force and a plan that meets these requirements. The plan addresses the CSAF's concern that the Air Force has become the "universal donor" of cyberspace personnel to USCYBERCOM and others within the national cyberspace enterprise. Therefore, a significant consideration in this study was the level of demand for cyberspace operators—both now and in the future—from agencies within the national cyberspace enterprise.

Bounding the Area of Study

By its very definition, this study was vast. It touched on every aspect of the cyberspace community from the accessions process for junior Airmen and lieutenants to the development of our most senior generals. Nonetheless, the research team established boundaries for the study so that "mission creep" would not create an unmanageable project. Team members established parameters defining the boundaries of each of the key and contextual questions during the exploratory research phase of the project. Setting such limits helped to avoid wasting resources researching irrelevant areas; however, the parameters were relaxed enough to allow for deeper investigation of crucial aspects of the cyber workforce.

The AFRI research team began the research process with an expansive scope of questions pertaining to cyberspace operator force development, with the goal of learning more about individuals in cyber operations career fields. These individuals are in diverse Air Force units, including the Air Force Personnel Center (AFPC), AFSPC, Twenty-Fourth Air Force, AETC, and HAF/A6SF. Cyberspace operations have a wide spectrum of issues across numerous disciplines. For example, cyberspace force development not only must include curriculum development and personnel reform but also must consider the environment in which future cyberspace warriors will have to operate. This environment includes the technical complexity and rapidly changing aspects of the domain, the threat landscape, actor motivations, and emerging as well as future targets.

Identifying Key Questions

The research team conducted a series of group discussions to identify what questions the study would examine. The sessions, held by the research team at the outset of phase 1, were helpful in recognizing some of these key questions and guiding the interview process.

> **Outputs from This Activity**
> - Expert relationships developed through outreach and interview processes; ability to hold follow-up discussions with experts
> - General understanding of the key force development issues throughout interview process

To further refine the study questions that guided the remaining phases of the project, team members held discussions with key stakeholders after the initial key questions were developed.

Broad questions that guided the research team as it conducted the study were key, and they contained subcomponents or subquestions requiring analysis. Where possible, each subquestion was addressed by at least two methodological approaches, and, when appropriate, quantitative analysis and statistical modeling provided rigor to qualitative assessments.

Identifying Experts and Conducting Structured Interviews

At the study's onset, one of the primary goals was to analyze the issues efficiently and thoroughly. For the research team, this step meant traveling to relevant sites to talk with key cyber workforce stakeholders. The organizational complexity of the study made in-person, structured interviews essential. Additionally, such interviews helped the research team build working relationships with key stakeholders, thereby gaining their trust and confidence so they would be willing to share the information required by the research team.[2]

Structured interviews were identified as an appropriate qualitative research tool to enable researchers to gain insights into specific areas where information was limited in existing literature.[3] Other than Air Force strategy and doctrine, no published works directly addressed developing the USAF's human capital required for conducting cyberspace operations. Thus, in this study, a significant portion of the data on cyberspace operator development came from interviewing informed experts because their thoughts on the subject were not in any written source.

To conduct the networking and structured interview process, the research team took the following steps. First, it developed a structured interview guide during a brainstorming session during which a series of open-ended and direct questions about the study were crafted and then peer-reviewed with cyber experts. Researchers used the guide to prompt interviewees to provide meaningful responses to topics of interest, including their general understanding of cyber issues as well as their perspectives of specific aspects being investigated. Asking all interviewees the same series of questions also assured consistency. The interview guide was crafted across the spectrum of expertise, including the military/government, the intelligence community, academia, the private sector, and hackers to avoid asking experts irrelevant questions about areas they were unfamiliar with.

Once the team identified an expert, members contacted that person via the most prudent form of communication (e.g., a phone call or an e-mail). In the contact process, researchers provided an overview of the project, a description of how they found the expert, an explanation about why the researcher thought this expert could provide relevant information to help the project, and, finally, a copy of the interview guide to allow the expert to begin thinking about the questions prior to the appointment.

The research team started the structured interview process with managers and experts at AFSPC, Twenty-Fourth Air Force, HAF/A6, and AETC to quickly learn about the nature of problems associated with cyberspace force development.[4] These experts were helpful in several ways:

1. They provided information that helped researchers build a basic understanding of the topic.
2. By sharing their own hypotheses about the topic, they showed researchers alternative ways of looking at the issue.
3. They suggested other individuals, organizations, and written sources to tap for additional relevant information and opinions.
4. Their development of a trust-based relationship with the research team early in the research process led to increased stakeholder buy-in throughout the study.

AFRI initiated the networking process by identifying personnel in relevant Air Force organizations who might have an understanding of, or specific knowledge about, force development issues in the cyberspace career fields. They included military members ranging from enlisted personnel to flag officers, DOD civilians, and contractors from AETC, AFPC, Twenty-Fourth Air Force, and AFSPC. These exchanges yielded a list of 43 other offices to be included in the study process (not including offices recommended or directed by the CSAF and other general officers). Outside the Air Force, several interagency partners were also incorporated into the study—such as the Defense Information Systems Agency (DISA), Department of Homeland Security (DHS), National Security Agency (NSA), and Central Intelligence Agency (CIA)—to help guard against myopic conclusions. Additionally, several civilian information technology (IT) firms and the National Academy of Science were consulted to provide broader viewpoints on the subject.

Researchers found the interviews with informed experts extremely useful to the study since they provided direct answers to their questions. During these interviews and discussions, researchers used a structured interview guide to ask experts questions tied to their specific areas of expertise. This structured interview process gave the research team relevant, current information to analyze and often led to specific areas requiring further research.

The team ensured thoroughness in the interview process by having one cyber subject-matter expert and one researcher familiar with the Air Force personnel system present for each interview. The research team decided to conduct the interviews in this manner because the study was both technically complex and highly personnel-related in nature. Early evidence clearly demonstrated that significant data would have been missed without the perspectives of both researchers during the interviews.

Additionally, the interview process during the initial phase allowed the research team to build a repository of individuals who were consulted for their expertise throughout the later phases. As the research team identified various issues with the cyberspace force, it contacted applicable experts in its contact list. Oftentimes, the Air Force was able to resolve these issues relatively quickly either through informing the researchers of ongoing processes or commencing processes if feasible. The relationships that the team developed with the network of experts throughout the study thus allowed it to iteratively refine its knowledge of specific issues, keep the contents of the study current, and facilitate connections within the cyber workforce bureaucracy to help the Air Force resolve career field issues.

During the initial phase, the research team reviewed written sources to find cyberspace experts outside the realm of normal Air Force thinking. It identified a number of interesting thinkers with a variety of perspectives and initiated contact with them in hopes of illuminating ideas and perspectives that challenge current assumptions about cyberspace force development.

Outputs from This Activity

- List of key sources on professional development of cyber forces, future threat environments, and cyber policy
- General understanding of topic, developed through research into written sources and interviews/site visits
- Input and buy-in from all project stakeholders
- Set of key questions about the development of USAF cyber operators that should be included in developing the model

While cyberspace experts form a relatively tight-knit community, the research team discovered that they are generally happy to share their unique information and experience. Interviewees from this community discussed with researchers specific problems they would like addressed in the study and suggested others who could provide relevant information about the Air Force's cyberspace force development issues. Thus, this study was not limited only to Air Force experts. To gain a broader understanding of a subject, researchers engaged with experts outside the Air Force—including stakeholders from sister services, interagency partners, the private sector, hacker communities, academia, and international partners.

Identifying Sources for Exploratory Research

The team conducted exploratory research concurrent with the interview process and development of the network of experts. Researchers examined doctrinal, policy, academic, and media literature concerning issues related to developing the USAF's cyberspace operators. A breadth of written sources was surveyed to uncover information about past efforts, current practices, and anticipated best practices as well as any differing opinions among key authors about the issues being investigated. This data helped the team evaluate its own assumptions and biases and build its own analysis of the issue.

The research team consulted a wide variety of resources to augment interviews and discussions with leaders in the cyber arena. These included Air Force, DOD, and intelligence community policy and doctrine; books and academic journals; newspaper and magazine articles; blogs and Internet sites; and industry reports. Overall, this exploratory research yielded insights along a curve of diminishing returns. Although initial research returned a host of new insights, team members found fewer novel ideas and observations as their research continued. They determined that they were nearing completion of this research phase when findings became redundant and new avenues stopped appearing. Organizations visited and consulted during the course of the study include but are not limited to those found in figure 3.

PROJECT CONTEXT AND METHODOLOGY | 9

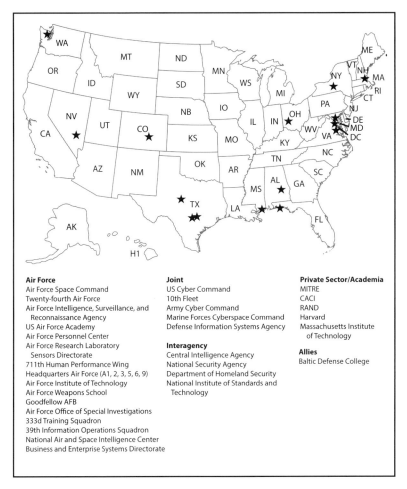

Figure 3. Organizations visited and consulted

Phase 3: Analysis and Vetting Findings with OCRs and against Data

This step of the research involved vetting preliminary findings and conclusions on the key questions with interested agencies and stakeholders.[5] The purpose of this process was to ensure peer review by outside experts and to uncover stakeholder sensitivities or other issues of importance to them.

Where the vetting process found controversy in the preliminary findings or recommendations, those areas were further researched, revised as appropriate, and used for subsequent vetting. This iterative process was similar to an informal Delphi approach that allowed the findings to improve over time and produce a quality, peer-reviewed final report. In some cases, this process uncovered bureaucratic sensitivities not related to errors of fact in the analysis. The causes of these objections were recorded alongside the rationale. If these objections could not be resolved in the research process, they are noted in this book and were disclosed to the CSAF.

A Cyber Advisory Group (CAG) was formed to vet findings and gather data during the conclusion of the research project. This group consisted of a wide range of experts consulted throughout the research process, including key stakeholders, operators, policy makers, Air University (AU) faculty, and strategic thinkers across the Air Force. One goal of the meeting was to refine our final analytical product by bringing together policy makers and practitioners with whom the research team engaged over the past year of our study to judge the feasibilities of our proposed recommended solutions. Another aim was to specify how existing responsibilities or authorities should be modified to improve the management of cyber career fields within the military to support US national security applications of cyber power.

The event gave participants an opportunity to engage in practical, forward-looking discussions to shape our final cyber workforce development report to the CSAF. Our aim was to break down stovepipes that AFRI discovered by bringing together the individual skills of participants from multidisciplinary backgrounds to contribute toward developing a more effective cyber workforce. This forum helped to generate rapid insights into key areas related to developing the future cyber workforce and the sharing of expectations and experiences on viable, near-term strategies for transforming that workforce. To obtain the best balance between the needs for focused and explorative discussions, the team limited attendance to 20 people. Participants were chosen from across the interagency on the basis of their expertise or involvement in cyber workforce development. The output from the advisory group formed a significant basis for study conclusions.

> **Output from This Activity**
>
> The final version of the cyber force development study on developing long-term cybersecurity human capital planning and management strategies

Phase 4: Roll Out Project Findings to CSAF, Key Air Force Stakeholders, and Project Participants

The last step of the project was to deliver the final study results to the CSAF and other stakeholders within AETC, AU, and the Air Force chain of command. This step is crucial to presenting relevant information about the cultures of cyberspace operators examined in the case studies and assuring that our insights continued to be relevant for the CSAF. These results are also a way to build excitement around, and belief in, the power and usefulness of cyberspace operations as an aspect of national power.

The research team briefed the CSAF in March 2015, presenting the study's overall findings and recommendations. This larger volume captures the research, findings, and recommendations in greater detail than was possible in discussions with the chief.

Notes

(All notes appear in shortened form. For full details, see the appropriate entry in the bibliography.)

1. Yannakogeorgos, "Rise of IPv6," 103–28; Yannakogeorgos, "USAF Cyber Education"; Lowther, "Rise of the Millennials," 97–105; and Dacus and Yannakogeorgos, "Designing Cybersecurity into Defense Systems."

The AFRI team's presentations of its findings during the course of the study included the following individuals: CSAF, assistant vice-chief of staff, and deputy chief of staff for intelligence, surveillance, and reconnaissance (HAF/A2), 3 March 2015; Maj Gen Burke E. Wilson (commander, Twenty-Fourth Air Force, and commander, Air Forces Cyber), on or about 16 January 2015; Cyber Advisory Group, subject: Read Ahead, 10 July 2014; CSAF, subject: Vector Check, late April 2014; Lt Gen James McLaughlin (deputy commander, US Cyber Command [USCC]), 3 March 2014; Hon. Newt Gingrich, 25 February 2014; Lt Gen Harry Raduege (USAF, retired), Mr. Frank DiGiovanni (director, Force Readiness and Training), and VAMD Michael Rogers (commander, USCC), 7 February 2014; and Lt Gen Burton Field (deputy chief of staff for operations, HAF/A3), Maj Gen Jeff Lofgren (deputy commander, US Air Forces Central Command), Lt Gen Jon Davis, USMC (deputy commander, USCYBERCOM), and Dr. Kamal Jabbour (Cyber Security Advanced Course in Engineering Boot Camp program founder), 12 September 2013.

2. In addition, the near prohibition of attending non-DOD conferences at this study's inception meant that researchers could not interview large numbers of cyber experts at professional gatherings where they are available. Having to knock on dozens of doors significantly slowed and complicated the research process.

3. George and Bennett, *Case Studies and Theory Development*, 18–20.

4. Cyberspace experts were the first set of authorities the research team interviewed. Experts from numerous backgrounds, career fields, and occupations were interviewed for this study.

5. The cutoff date for research data and analysis was 1 September 2014 although in some instances more current data is cited.

6. Creswell, *Qualitative Inquiry and Research Design*, 135; and Dalkey and Helmer, "Experimental Application of the Delphi Method," 458–67. Originally developed by the RAND Corporation in the early 1950s, the Delphi method is used to "obtain the most reliable consensus of opinion of a group of experts. It attempts to achieve this by a series of intensive questionnaires interspersed with controlled opinion feedback" (Dalkey and Helmer, "Experimental Application of the Delphi Method," 458).

Chapter 2

Connecting Technology and Policy

Cyberspace exists where the wave-particle duality of radiation, when modulated with bits, creates an information flow that moves across a man-made physical infrastructure. The laws of physics bound the movement of data across computer networks, the use of which is advanced technologically by man and often restricted by policy. The man-made portion of cyberspace is built on core protocols and standards developed and codified by standard-setting organizations. These organizational precepts dictate the extent, configuration, and makeup of the entirety of cyberspace. Other regulations defining the general rules of the road and technology capabilities for operating in cyberspace come from international standard-setting organizations and the DOD.

Domestically, policy not only regulates the acquisition of information technology, weapons platforms, and the IT integrated onto those platforms but also guides the use of technology at the tactical, operational, and strategic levels of warfare operations. Similarly, personnel policies affect the makeup of the cyberspace workforce. Government personnel are managed via Office of Personnel Management (OPM) policies and guidelines. Thus, not only the physical infrastructure but also the various policies established for cyberspace limit its boundaries and use. Figure 4 illustrates some of the technologies and policies that affect cyberspace and the cyberspace workforce. This chapter discusses the interplay between technology and select laws and policies.

Another focus is technological trends that Air Force planners should include when forming human capital strategies. The Air Force will misallocate human cyberspace capital if it recruits, educates, trains, and equips cyberspace operators for the technological realities of today without considering what the cyberspace landscape may look like in 2020. Admittedly, it is a fool's errand to try to predict technology trends in a domain that evolves rapidly. However, throughout the course of the study, we discovered that many interviewees focused on the cyberspace workforce within the paradigm of today's technology.

Because parts of the cyberspace environment change more rapidly than in other domains (e.g., Moore's law regarding the doubling of data density on integrated circuits about every 18 months), the Air Force and

DOD must prepare for the next generation of cyberspace conflict by evaluating how technological trends will affect cyberspace workforce requirements. For example, the Joint Information Environment (JIE) is introducing a cloud computing paradigm for providing applications and services to the DOD.[1] This evolution has the potential to reduce manpower requirements for traditional DOD information network operations due to its anticipated efficiencies.[2]

Figure 4. Technologies and policies affecting cyberspace operations

[a]Transmission-control protocol/Internet Protocol, file transfer protocol, hypertext transfer protocol, Internet Protocol version 6
[b]Domain Name System, generic top-level domain names
[c]National Security Strategy, National Military Strategy
[d]Internet Corporation for Assigned Names and Numbers, Internet Engineering Task Force, World Wide Web Consortium

Another example of the change in the cyberspace landscape is in broadband and mobile technologies. The importance of the electromagnetic spectrum for cyberspace operations will increase as these technologies continue to be exploited. Thus, cyberspace operators will face spectrum management challenges—something they have not historically considered since their traditional focus has been on the logical elements of cyberspace.

Since cyberspace workforce planners must consider how the future cyberspace landscape may look, the following discussion identifies potential game-changing technologies and policies that could affect cyberspace personnel requirements. The DHS National Initiative for Cybersecurity Education (NICE) Cyber Workforce Framework is an excellent tool to organize the knowledge, skills, and abilities (KSA) for the military and civilian workforce. This tool is helpful to Air Force and national cyberspace workforce planners and managers, but they must also be able to recognize technological and policy shifts that could influence training and education requirements. It is beyond the scope of this study to provide a comprehensive overview or forecast of technology trends and drivers. However, this information provides a basis to stimulate strategic discussions on issues pertaining to core curriculum design, training needs, workforce composition, and other areas related to the development of the future USAF cyberspace force.

Comparing Information Technology and Operational Technology

The implications of merging IT into platforms and using it to command and control military operations are the soft underbelly of all Air Force core missions. Airlift, for example, is not possible without cyberspace enabling such an operation—take Air Force One for example. The Air Force provides the air transport for the president of the United States on the Air Force One VC-25. Although all aircraft have computer networks embedded within them, Air Force One has "state of the art navigation, electronic and communications equipment . . . and the capability for in-flight refueling."[3] It is the responsibility of Twenty-Fourth Air Force to assure the mission of Air Force One by providing cybersecurity support to the president.[4] Thus, cyberspace is an enabler for the air operations of Air Force One.

Indeed, cyberspace is often viewed as an enabler for all air operations and the core missions, not just those of Air Force One. Such outlooks are perpetuated by academic discussions about whether cyberspace is a separate domain. For instance, one argument is that "understanding cyberspace as a warfighting domain is not helpful when it comes to understanding what can and should be done to defend and attack networked systems." Yet later Martin Libicki argues, "Such a stance suggests that the term be totally avoided, but since [I have] no intention of following such advice, the second-best alternative is to use the term carefully."[5] Two problems arise here. The first is that cyber operations are more than the defense of networks and networked systems. The second is that not identifying cyberspace as a domain prevents the vast military culture from giving cyberspace the attention it deserves in terms of organizing, training, and equipping for war—a point that Libicki concedes.

Not understanding cyberspace as a domain of warfare risks relegating it to a realm of desktop computers rather than mission-essential components in a non-cyber-educated commander's mind. Cyberspace is more than just a computer system that allows information to flow from one commander to another. Viewing it as a mere enabler also has a negative effect on the career field, which becomes synonymous with providing DODIN operations rather than a force providing operational effects. Failure to identify cyber as an operational domain of warfare also prevents commanders from utilizing existing joint doctrine. They cannot begin mapping their mission's dependence on cyberspace to defend key assets at the right time if they do not recognize the dependence of cyber on their mission. Neither can they maneuver in this space to provide strategic sovereign options to the president. Further, as confirmed in our interviews across the cyber career fields, these perceptions of cyber as an enabling rather than operational domain of warfare demoralize cyberspace operators and disincentivize computer and electrical engineers from entering the officer ranks as cyberspace officers (see chap. 7). Ultimately, such views limit the utilization of cyberspace operators when, in fact, they could provide a cost-effective way for the Air Force to project power. They also create conflict between cyberspace operators and the decision makers who may one day ask them to produce effects in, through, or by means of cyberspace.

Hence, operationalizing the domain—rather than relegating it to the status of an enabler for core functions—is essential to fully utilizing the promise of cyberspace operations. Interesting academic arguments about the "Platonic forms" of cyberspace aside, cyberspace will continue to serve as an enabler until embraced as a fully operational domain. At that time, commanders should understand mission dependencies on cyber, and decisions about priorities should be crafted around the potential availability and integrity of systems that can be put at risk.

The popular perception of cyberspace as only the network is a particularly troubling finding of our study. Just as in traditional kinetic warfare, the spectrum of operations in cyberspace is large and ranges from traditional intelligence activities to those that aim to damage and destroy physical property (fig. 5). Across this spectrum, different platforms are affected. Some activities by nefarious actors in cyberspace may not warrant a response by the US military. Others could prompt the use of force or a physical military attack. USCYBERCOM has defined actions that may require the use of force as those that misuse cyberspace and result in physical damage, destruction, injury, or death. Such activities entail the creation of malicious effects in cyber-physical systems or operational technology (OT). OT includes—but is not limited to—industrial control systems (ICS), building control systems (BCS), and embedded processors and controllers found in weapons platforms. We emphasize the distinction between these and ITs that exist to facilitate corporate processes and do not have an immediate operational impact.

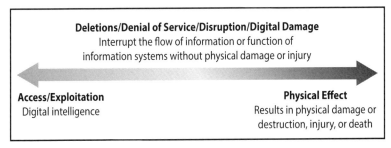

Figure 5. Spectrum of operations in cyberspace. (Courtesy of Judge Advocate, USCYBERCOM, Fort Meade, MD.)

The unique characteristics of OT do not allow for traditional IT paradigms of cybersecurity to prevent intrusions, detect malicious code, and conduct digital forensics after the event. Technologically these differences—in addition to challenges to conducting traditional

IT cybersecurity on remote sensors and programmable logic controllers (PLC)—make patch configuration/management, attack identification, and attribution difficult. Table 2 illustrates the differing operating paradigms of IT and OT systems (the latter using the example of ICSs).

> Given that risks to Air Force core missions from cyber dependencies are platform specific, we emphasize the importance of distinguishing between IT and OT.

Table 2. IT system and ICS comparison

Attribute	Information technology system	Industrial control system
Confidentiality	Data confidentiality and integrity are paramount.	Low
Integrity	Primary focus is protecting IT assets and the information stored on or transmitted via these assets. Central server may require more protection.	Primary goal is to protect edge clients (e.g., field devices such as process controllers). Protection of central server is also important.
Availability	Fault tolerance is less important—momentary downtime is not a major risk. Less critical emergency interaction	Fault tolerance is essential—even momentary downtime may not be acceptable. Response to human and other emergency interaction is critical.
Authentication	Tightly restricted access control can be implemented to the degree necessary for security.	Access to ICS should be strictly controlled but should not hamper or interfere with human-machine interaction.
Major risk impact	Delay of business operations	Regulatory noncompliance, environmental impacts, loss of life, equipment, or production
Component lifetime	3–5 years	15–20 years

Table 2 (*continued*)

Attribute	Information technology system	Industrial control system
Access to components	Components are usually local and easy to access.	Components can be isolated and remote, requiring extensive physical effort to gain access to them.
Operating systems	Designed for use with typical operating systems. Upgrades are straightforward with the availability of automated deployment tools.	Differing and possibly proprietary operating systems, often without security capabilities built in. Software changes must be carefully made, usually by software vendors, because of the specialized control algorithms and perhaps modified hardware and software involved.
Change management	Software changes are applied in a timely fashion in the presence of good security policy and procedures. The procedures are often automated.	Software changes must be thoroughly tested and deployed incrementally throughout a system to ensure that the integrity of the control system is maintained. ICS outages often must be planned and scheduled days/weeks in advance. ICS may use operating systems that are no longer supported.

Adapted from National Institute of Standards and Technology, Special Publication 800-82, *Guide to Industrial Control Systems (ICS) Security* (Gaithersburg, MD: NIST, June 2011), 3-3–3-4.

Because of OT's distinct attributes, cyberspace personnel who work with it require different skill sets than do those being recruited in the core cyberspace Air Force specialty codes (AFSC) (17 series, 1B4, and 3D). The engineering field (62E in particular) should be teamed with the cyberspace workforce to use its complementary knowledge sets to identify vulnerabilities and develop cybersecurity requirements. The Air Force Institute of Technology (AFIT) ICS test bed should be leveraged by an engineering/cybersecurity team to understand vulnerabilities, develop best practices, and help foster trusted partnerships. Without these relationships in place, US critical infrastructure will continue to be at risk due to incorrect operational paradigms being applied to the defense of OT.

Focusing on OT rather than IT emphasizes the distinction between the two communities rather than detracts from the network security and data integrity mission sets. The US homeland defense mission represents a specific area within the Air Force that demands data trustworthiness. Cyberspace operations are vital to this mission in at least two ways. First, the nation's early warning systems and their operators transmit information through cyberspace. That information is processed by data analysts for exploitation and dissemination. An early warning system compromised by a malicious cyber event or an unintended interaction between a system and user could leave the nation vulnerable to attack. At a time when nuclear and ballistic missile technologies are proliferating, a compromise of the early warning system is unacceptable. Second, command and control for air sovereignty depends on elements of cyberspace to disseminate critical information. An action that causes delay in the delivery or causes commanders to question the integrity of data in these networks at a specific time conducive to an adversarial operational objective could seriously degrade a core homeland defense function.[6] Consequently, the information assurance of homeland defense data must remain a priority for the United States, particularly as potential adversaries are developing their cyber-warfare arsenals.

Therefore, a key challenge in the field of cyber operations is that much of the debate has been focused on traditional information management and computer networking. These are traditional IT roles. However, our emphasis on developing a cyber workforce is on those with expertise in OTs—encompassing embedded controllers in weapons systems and platforms developed by the commercial sector and upon which national critical infrastructure and core Air Force missions rely. Poor system design of OT and its interface with physical processes has been responsible for several incidents involving destruction. One such example in the private sector is the Pacific Gas and Electric (PG&E) gas transmission pipeline explosion on 9 September 2010 in San Bruno, California. The blast was the result of pressure relieving and limiting devices controlled by a PLC that failed to protect against accidental overpressure in the pipeline. Sensors erroneously reported low pressure, causing the ICS to open valves automatically. This malfunction raised the pressure above safe levels and created an explosion, excavating a crater 72 feet long, 26 feet wide, and 28 feet deep (fig. 6).[7] To contain the ensuing fire, "more than 900 emergency responders from the city of San Bruno and surrounding jurisdictions executed a coordinated emergency response, which included defensive operations, search and evacuation, and medical operations. Once the flow of natural gas was interrupted, firefighting operations continued for 2 days."[8]

Figure 6. PG&E gas transmission pipeline explosion. Crater and ruptured pipeline (*top*) and aerial view of fire (*bottom*). (Reproduced from National Transportation Safety Board [NTSB], *Pacific Gas and Electric Company Natural Gas Transmission Pipeline Rupture and Fire, San Bruno, California, September 9, 2010*, Pipeline Accident Report NTSB/PAR-11/01 [Washington, DC: NTSB, 30 August 2011], 1–2, http://www.ntsb.gov/investigations/AccidentReports/Reports/PAR1101.pdf.)

From a manpower perspective, the skill sets to defend from potential attacks of this type or to create such effects by targeting platforms and processes are not taught in typical computer science (CS) curricula. Computer and electrical engineering are conducive to the national security–critical OT on which the Air Force must focus. Because OT specialists are usually computer engineers or electrical engineers, cyberspace human capital managers have a manpower challenge since these engineers are not generally the focus of DOD cyberspace recruiting in the 17-series career field. Most engineers tend to enter the 62E (engineering) career field. Most 17-series personnel are thus from the CS and computer networking fields. These professions typically concentrate on the technologies that enable data and information to flow and not on assuring the integrity and availability of information that may affect an Air Force mission and fulfill a commander's mission objective.

Irregular cyberspace warfare is a growing area of concern because nonstate actors are proving adept at waging cyberspace warfare from remote locations using less-sophisticated methods and equipment. The reported hacking of an American drone's video feeds by Iranian-backed insurgents is one of many examples.[9] Given the speed with which irregular adversaries can learn and adapt, the Air Force will undoubtedly face opposed network operations from nonstate actors in the years ahead. Establishing the right balance in cyberspace will prove a challenge that the Air Force must overcome against peer and irregular adversaries alike. Although it is unlikely that the Air Force will have exclusive responsibility for cyberspace, the service should expect to ensure its own ability to operate in the cyberspace domain. The first part of this capability is understanding the difference between IT and OT. The second part is distinguishing between core and peripheral technologies and then factoring in their evolution as we prepare to fight in the future.

There is clear evidence that China and Russia, potential adversaries in a peer competition, are investing heavily in cyberspace warfare capabilities.[10] This development poses a very real risk to civil and military networks. Not only can such capabilities slow or disrupt the flow of information but also a penetration of secured networks calls into question the validity of the very data upon which the Air Force relies. Given the United States' conventional advantage, cyberspace is an attractive target. In the view of some adversaries, the damage done by a successful cyber attack may be enough to preempt American involvement in a crisis, such as a Chinese attack on Taiwan.[11] As the Air Force moves toward further network integration of command and control, communications, and weapons platforms, an adversary with advanced cyberspace warfare capabilities will pose an increasing threat to mission objectives.[12] Understanding a mission's dependence on cyberspace will prove a strategic necessity over the coming generation.

The Air Force's dependence on OT to conduct missions is expected to grow. In the past year alone, threat actors deploying malware such as Sandworm and Black Energy have increasingly been targeting OT for information-gathering purposes. The Sandworm malware in particular contains modules targeting ICS supervisory control and data acquisition (SCADA) systems. One report states that "given the function of these systems, and historical precedents such as Stuxnet and destructive incidents in the [Persian] Gulf, we are still weighing the possibility that these intrusions could be reconnaissance-for-attack."[13] These cases demonstrate both the threat-actor intent and the fact that when OT fails, physical infrastructures and lives are put at risk. Had the pipeline explosion been a malicious act, this incident would have met USCYBERCOM's definition of an armed attack through cyberspace. Responding to such an attack would require cyberspace experts with specific knowledge of OTs. This expertise is typically found in the fields of computer engineering (CE) and electrical engineering (EE), occupational areas that are not traditionally associated with cyber operations in traditional DODIN or DCO specialties.

Cyberspace effects on physical platforms are not science fiction. ICSs, BCSs, and embedded microprocessors that control physical processes are all parts of cyberspace that extend beyond the conventional paradigm of cyberspace as being just the Internet. Devices that can be affected by a malicious cyber event can cause operational disruption resulting in mission failure, property damage or destruction, or loss of life.

Core and Peripheral Technologies

In addition to identifying the conceptual difference between IT and OT, this study distinguishes between *core* and *peripheral* technologies to address another common cyber myth: that cyberspace changes in rapid cycles. This is true in terms of computing and data flow speeds, but core technologies remain constant. This section provides a brief overview of core and peripheral technologies and how they are affected by policy.

Core cyberspace technologies include the underlying internationally standardized protocols such as file transfer protocol (FTP), Internet Protocol (IP), and 802.11x wireless communications protocols. Peripheral technologies are those that are built on core technologies. The standardization of these peripheral technologies permits global interoperability of networked devices. Take the case of the relationship between core Internet technologies and the applications developed there over time. The World Wide Web (WWW) exists only because computers interconnected via MAC and IP addresses, both core protocols, use hypertext transfer protocol (HTTP), another core element of cyberspace, to communicate data and information via the Domain Name System (DNS), yet another core technology. This core underlying infrastructure has remained more or less the same, with minimal version changes over the past two decades. What has changed, and continues to change rapidly, is the development of new applications utilizing the core Internet platforms. OTs are also made up of core technologies. ICSs have proprietary control protocols that allow data to transit from sensors to remote machines or operators. Peripheral applications are then built on top of the core ICS platforms, such as SCADA, that present machine data to users.

Most cyberspace users are familiar with peripheral technologies but have only fleeting knowledge of the underlying core technologies, such as the transmission-control protocol (TCP)/IP networking protocol, and the political processes by which they are established as international standards. The importance of the core of cyberspace cannot be overlooked. Since cyber is a man-made domain, understanding and shaping the core infrastructure is mission critical. Computer systems are able to send information that other computers can understand because of common, man-made standards that machines use to send and receive data. Cyberspace technologies are based on the work of computer scientists and engineers around the globe who establish the standards and rules according to which the Internet operates. Many of these standards began as US government programs under the Defense Advanced Research Projects Agency (DARPA), DISA, or other projects that the government privatized in the mid-1990s. However, current protocols and standards are reaching their limits as global cyberspace growth has exploded. For peripheral technology growth to continue, which in the past was a catalyst for innovation and prosperity globally, the underlying core technologies need to change. But other countries are becoming leaders in the development of the next-generation Internet.

China, for instance, is making great leaps forward in setting standards for the future of cyberspace. As reported in 2011 by the US-China Economic and Security Review Commission, "If current trends continue, China (combined with proxy interests) will effectively become the principal market driver in many sectors, including telecom, on the basis of consumption, production, and innovation."[14] Furthermore, participants in international standards-setting bodies have noted that, as a result of Chinese understanding of international standards-setting agreements, "China's international negotiators are becoming more adept than those in the United States. It is, therefore, no longer clear whether the US would prevail against Chinese efforts in cases of standards disputes at the international level."[15]

This lack of US government leadership in the future of Internet governance at the standards-setting bodies has implications for both national security and mission assurance. In the national security context, technical management of the protocols and standards matters because it may allow adversarial states to exert power and influence over the underlying cyber infrastructure. In the mission assurance context, creating unique protocols for military interoperability can minimize the common vulnerability landscape and thereby increase adversaries' costs to maintain a contested environment. One research discussion noted that the Air Force Research Laboratory (AFRL) could create a secure protocol for military applications in 40 lines of code. So developing and applying this capability to help the United States return to a strategic leadership role in future cyberspace development are not as cost intensive as the conventional wisdom suggests. However, they do require a significant investment in attracting or growing an educated cyberspace workforce.

A key finding of the research team is that potential competitor nations are shaping the standards-setting bodies that will determine the functioning of the foundation of cyberspace in the future. The cyberspace workforce must consist of people educated in the science and mathematics of cyberspace to substantively create mathematically secure core technologies as well as to contribute to standards-setting bodies. The DOD and USAF should document their roles and provide metrics on their participation and position with Internet governance bodies. Global norms and standards stem from the practices of nations and their operational forces. Further, due to the community dynamics of individuals within the bodies, nations must maintain constant contact with their peers within each standards-setting community, as the Air Force does.

Internet Protocol Version Six

Unbeknownst to many people, the fundamental structure of the Internet is changing for the first time in its history with the exhaustion of Internet Protocol version 4 (IPv4) and the adoption of Internet Protocol version 6 (IPv6). International calls for transitioning to IPv6 have been ongoing since 1996. These calls intensified in 2013 at the Ministerial Conference on the Information Society in Latin America and the Caribbean held in Montevideo, Uruguay. At this conference, the Internet Corporation for Assigned Names and Numbers (ICANN) issued a declaration stating that the "transition to IPv6 [must] remain a top priority globally" and that "in particular Internet content providers must serve content with both IPv4 and IPv6 services to be fully reachable on the global Internet."[16] The Air Force has a tremendous opportunity and responsibility to lead the DOD and nation in the transition to IPv6. This conversion will enable the Air Force to better accomplish its mission but will require the service to train its cyberspace operators to keep pace with technological change. As Gen Mark A. Welsh III, Air Force chief of staff, emphasized in his foreword to the latest Air Force strategy document, "The Air Force's ability to continue to adapt and respond faster than our potential adversaries is the greatest challenge we face over the next 30 years."[17] With China leading the world in operational deployment of IPv6-*only* networks, it is time for the DOD and nation to get serious about enabling IPv6 on hardware it already owns.[18] However, the United States faces issues, or myths, that are important to understand in transitioning to IPv6.

Myth 1: Global IPv4 depletion trends do not apply to the DOD and Air Force. The first myth is that IPv4 address depletion is not a problem for the DOD since a large allocation of worldwide IPv4 addresses was reserved for national security purposes.[19] Historically, the DOD has been a repository of technical expertise regarding the Internet—partly due to the Internet's initial development within DARPA. Since the birth of the Internet at DARPA, the DOD has been operating all ".mil" domains—a top-level domain for the DOD's exclusive use—and the DNS name servers to support them. Consequently, the DOD has had to employ the expertise necessary to maintain those systems. In the early 1990s, the DOD acquired a significant amount of the IPv4 space—12 blocks of /8 block space. Since each /8 block contains 16,777,214 IP addresses, the DOD has over 200 million addresses available in IPv4 space. Similarly, the DOD recently purchased a /13 block of IPv6 space—the equivalent of 42 decillion IP address spaces.[20]

Conventional wisdom across much of the Air Force is that the DOD and Air Force have no reason to worry about IP address depletion. Indeed, only a very small percentage of the Air Force network uses any IPs from those 12 allocations. Huge chunks of the Air Force network predate the assignment of those /8 networks, thus skewing DOD projections of estimated future use. Getting a more accurate estimate would require analyzing all IPv4 addresses that the Air Force uses—most of which were directly acquired before the DOD received its large allocations.[21] Calculations on the publicly available DOD Network Integration Center (DODNIC) "WHOIS" database reveal that the DOD has slightly more than 317 /16 networks currently listed as reserve networks (RNET) allocated for future assignment.[22] There is also a mixture of smaller allocations. Of the 317 /16 networks, one unused /8 network (29.0.0.0/8) is currently being held in reserve. This single unused /8 network is not adequate address space for future applications to support the entire DOD.

Internet Protocol address space is critical to delivering elements of power in all Air Force core missions, which require large amounts of such space per platform to support a robust and redundant communications infrastructure. These platforms must have multiple network switches to ensure both resilient command and control and mission objectives. One example that illustrates this point within the global mobility mission involves the new KC-46 tanker aircraft. By 2027, 179 new KC-46 aircraft are expected to be assembled, all of which need IP address space.[23]

Another example highlighting the need for increased IP address space is identified in the Air Force strategy document *America's Air Force: A Call to the Future*: "Expanding requirements and a growing threat to high cost air-breathing assets will also necessitate a shift from an architecture focused on dedicated ISR [intelligence, surveillance, and reconnaissance] platforms to one based on a diverse network of sensors arrayed across the air, space, and cyber domains, placing a premium on the ability to draw data from any and all US systems."[24] The flexible, global, and integrated ISR capability requires the expanded address space provided in IPv6 to network a massive number of sensors together. This vast address space would give sensors their own static IP addresses.

Myth 2: Current education and training in IPv6 is sufficient. The second myth about the transition to IPv6 has to do with the education and training of cyberspace operators. A significant portion of Air Force networking equipment is IPv6 capable; however, without properly trained cyberspace operators, IPv6 should not be enabled. Serious security vulnerabilities are associated with enabling IPv6 on Air Force networks. For example, many host-based defense and forensics tools cannot handle the multiple addresses of IPv6 because of the enormous size of the smallest IPv6 subnets, which are 4 billion times larger than the entire IPv4 range. An IPv6 scanner could take days or weeks to find all hosts on the Air Force network, let alone actually scan them for vulnerabilities.

Another problem is in the ability of IPv4 intrusion detection systems (IDS) to inspect the contents of an IPv6-tunneled packet and vice versa. Because IPv4 IDSs cannot inspect IPv6-tunneled packets, the enabling capability opens Air Force networks to potential security vulnerabilities. There is even a threat of exactly when the network is enabled to do the opposite and tunnel IPv4 over IPv6. Enabling IPv6 on Air Force networks without the appropriate network defense tools and without properly educated and trained operators could leave those networks susceptible.

Without experienced operators, the United States could face exposure to threat actors who have years of experience and understanding. The Air Force's cyber schoolhouses presently offer an insufficient two hours of instruction on the general background of IPv6 in their curricula. Detailed, specific IPv6 training should be required, but within the DOD, some individuals view such training as unnecessary because it does not represent the current operational reality.[25]

Instead, the preference is to reserve that type of training for future cyber follow-on training units (FTU). These FTUs will train cyberspace operators in the latest capability advancements as they move between assignments. Thinking that cyberspace operators can simply be trained after the capability becomes operational is flawed. Instead, they need hands-on experience before technology is made operational—the Air Force's procedure with other weapon systems.

One National Institute of Standards and Technology (NIST) report notes that "prevention of unauthorized access to IPv6 networks will likely be more difficult in the early years of IPv6 deployments."[26] If the defense of Air Force and DOD networks is going to become more difficult with the implementation of IPv6, then cyberspace operators should have even more time to become familiar with IPv6. They must have time to become highly proficient experts, just as it takes time for pilots to become experts in their airframes. The Air Force should begin a robust IPv6 educating and training program now so that cyber warriors will be ready when IPv6 is enabled on Air Force networks.

Critics might argue that there are not enough hours in the cyberspace curriculum for both IPv4 and IPv6. However, given the interrelationship between the protocols, teaching IPv6 also effectively teaches principles of IPv4. At a minimum, the Air Force must also ensure that Airmen already in cyber career fields get more exposure to IPv6. One short-term solution is for cyberspace operators to complete courses through the Federal Virtual Training Environment (FedVTE) as more long-term training solutions are developed.[27]

Myth 3: Conversion is too expensive in a time of austerity. Another myth about the transition to IPv6 is the cost. According to critics, the right time to conduct the transition is not in a budget-constrained environment with competing priorities—an assertion that is partly true. The cost of conversion does not lie in purchasing IPv6-capable equipment but in training and educating cyberspace warriors.

Currently, the DOD network architecture is already capable of supporting the conversion to IPv6. The Air Force Networking Integration Center (AFNIC) has been an advocate for IPv6 since 2002, and several federal requirements have been issued since then mandating IPv6-capable equipment. In 2003 the DOD issued a memorandum requiring the purchase of IPv6-capable equipment to replace old items during the normal tech refresh.[28] Section 221 of the 2006 National Defense Authorization Act (Public Law 109-163) has an IPv6 inspection requirement for the Air Force chief information officer (CIO) to use as a metric for individual acquisition programs; any program that fails the inspection requirement could see its funding delayed.[29] The purchase of IPv6-capable equipment became a federal regulation in December 2009 when the Civilian Agency Acquisition Council and the Defense Acquisition Regulations Council issued a ruling amending the Federal Acquisition Regulations.[30] Consequently, converting the physical DOD network architecture to IPv6 incurs no additional cost.[31]

The expense associated with converting to IPv6 lies in educating and training Air Force and DOD cyberspace operators. If current cyberspace warriors are not trained on IPv6 immediately, the Air Force and DOD, at a minimum, will be required to double their cyberspace manpower during the transition to IPv6. The transition would require two staffs of network administrators and support personnel: one trained in IPv4 and the other trained in IPv6. In 2005 the NIST-estimated cost of training one IPv6 expert was about $2,000.[32] Although that cost has probably increased, training cyberspace operators on IPv6 now would still be less expensive in the long run. Doing so would result in a cyber workforce of IPv6 experts by the time a transition is mandated versus maintaining two distinct staffs required to ensure network integrity during the transition. Starting now to prepare for a potential best case 2029 depletion date will save the Air Force and DOD money they will inevitably have to spend.

Myth 4: Foreign actors are sitting idly by. The fourth and final myth exposed by this study deals with foreign competitors. As discussed in the policy chapter, the domination of IPv6 by foreign actors poses a tremendous challenge to assuring mission success. Our Chinese competitors, among others, are gaining experience in operating IPv6 networks while the DOD and Air Force seem to be ignoring the problem. Current DOD CIO strategies outline a phased approach to transitioning DOD networks to full IPv6.[33] This phased approach requires IPv4/IPv6 dual stacking—that is, running the two networks in parallel. Dual stacking introduces both well-documented and unknown security vulnerabilities that will take time for our cyber operators to understand. During this transition, the United States can expect potential adversaries to exploit those vulnerabilities and leverage their inherent advantages of IPv6 domination.

Linguistic Challenges in Cyber Operations

English has been the predominant language for the Internet because of the preponderance of US-based hosting of the foundation of networks and services, but its continued status as the lingua franca is uncertain. This incertitude is especially true with the increased frequency of calls to "limit the storage, movement, and/or processing of digital data to specific geographies, jurisdictions, and companies" around the world to include non-English-speaking countries.[34] Air Force cyberspace operators will have the most difficulty operating in environments where nation-states develop and deploy their own telecommunications networks or alternate DNS systems for domestic use. Indeed, countries such as China, Iran, and Russia have already developed and deployed such communications systems.[35] Doing so allows a nation-state to use sophisticated communications routes that require an educated cadre not only of engineers but also of linguists specializing in the languages in which these networks will function.

This capability differs from simply controlling Internet access points. These country-level intranets may or may not be connected to the global Internet, and the trend to maintain separation is growing.[36] Evidence of this trend is the Russian development of a Federal Information and Telecommunications System (SFITS). The Russian Federal Agency for Government Communications and Information (FAPSI) developed SFITS on a foundation of Russian-developed hardware and software completely disconnected from the Internet.[37] With this system, Russia considers itself the "only country which is capable of providing one-hundred percent security for consumers at the very first stage of the mass introduction of SFITS in daily life."[38]

Along with the rise of the altnerative Domain Name System (altDNS), an increasing trend is the use of non-Latin characters in URLs and generic top-level domain names (gTLD). ICANN has limited TLD extensions such as .com or .org. However, in 2011 ICANN allowed applicants to create their own domain name extensions, such as ".culture." If organizations run their own TLDs, they may operate them as they wish, thus making the gTLD either as open or closed to the public as the organization wishes.

In addition to new gTLDs, the use of non-Latin script in domain names is increasing. In the past, Latin-based characters from A to Z were used to resolve URLs, but ICANN recently launched an effort to use non-Latin scripts in URLs. When characters from Greek, Persian, Cyrillic, and Chinese languages are used as URLs, more users will have access to the Internet in their native language.[39] The Internet will be open to masses of new users who may not have accessed it previously because of the English language barrier. Such an influx presents a significant human capital dilemma because the cultural and linguistic challenges facing the cyberspace profession today will only intensify.

Broadband Mobility

The use of broadband mobile devices is another significant change in the cyberspace landscape. The increase in broadband mobility presents both opportunities and risks for US military operations. In the developing world, countries tend to skip over the plain old telephone system (POTS) and install wireless communications infrastructures, including broadband Internet and cellular communications. Much of the technology used to develop those infrastructures comes from China. Chinese entities such as Huawei are on the leading edge of developing the standards of next-generation mobile 4G long-term evolution (LTE) networks.[40] Low-priced Chinese-made computer hardware makes such networks cost effective for the developing world.[41]

Beyond just the broadband network infrastructure, different challenges for the US military come from the shift in interpersonal communication brought about by mobile broadband. Mobile broadband users no longer have to wait for the media to share the news of the day—it is instantly available as users share it on various messaging and social media services. This change means that national security planners and cyberspace operators must take into account how specific actions will be communicated across broadband devices on such networks.

Because of this shift in interpersonal communications, the military must understand the importance of exploiting the mind to achieve effects in the real world. Cyberspace operators also have to mitigate potential adversary operations that seek to exploit the human mind. Such efforts extend well beyond terrorist efforts to radicalize and recruit individuals to their cause and have broader implications for US operations.

Take, for example, the events that transpired in India in August 2012. After short message service (SMS) (i.e., text messages) and social media messages falsely warned of impending Muslim attacks against migrants across northeastern India, including major cities such as Bangalore, mass panic and exodus of targeted populations ensued. Indian prime minister Manmohan Singh warned, "What is at stake is the unity and integrity of our country."[42]

From this example, it is clear that information distributed over broadband mobile networks can have a very real impact on a large number of people's perceptions of the world around them. Those views could lead them to actions with consequences for national security.

Areas where cyberspace and neuroscience overlap must therefore be considered in developing the cyberspace workforce structure. Broadband mobile is changing the cyberspace landscape; the United States must identify opportunities to counter and deter adversarial actions in the domain and articulate the military's role.

Peripheral Technologies That Will Benefit from Core Technology Trends

Having a keen understanding of existing and emergent core technologies such as IPv6 is one part of the cyber problem. The other is assuring that rapidly changing peripheral technologies are also understood by cyber operators and career field managers so that the workforce tackling the problems of today is also being shaped to take into account tomorrow's technologies. The examination below is by no means an exhaustive assessment of technologies that will affect the mission. However, these key technologies will shape the cyber environment and may require both skilled operators and material in the training curriculum.

Cloud Computing and Big Data

The NIST defines *cloud computing* as a model for "enabling ubiquitous, convenient, on-demand network access to a shared pool of configurable computing resources (e.g., networks, servers, storage, applications, and services) that can be rapidly provisioned and released with minimal management effort or service provider interaction."[43] An increasing trend today within the commercial sector is locating many independent services on one physical host. This paradigm, from an operational perspective, allows for a greater tolerance to operate resiliently in a contested environment. Cloud computing permits secure computer architectures to transparently continue operations in the face of multiple faults that would otherwise cause a system to fail. Highly resilient systems that restart quickly and restore data contribute to such operability. In a virtual environment, sensors detect virtualized machine failures and conduct a replacement of the virtual machine with a duplicate backup based on the snapshot of a trusted virtualized environment. Even though any data that had not been backed up would be lost, system functionality would be restored.

Virtualization is one technology proposed as a solution to create more resilient systems for the US military.[44] In brief, virtualization makes it easier for one cyberspace authority to install and manage instances of a specific operating system configuration. This capability lends itself to automating the installation of the same operating system across several virtual machines. Such massive deployments create software monocultures that can spread malicious software. However, such a uniform ecosystem also makes deploying patches to vulnerabilities more efficient and effective. The major risk of centralized management of virtual assets is a single point of failure, but the upside is that virtualized environments enable the protected deployment of security services. Although this benefit enhances mitigation efforts against rootkits and social engineering attacks, other risks—such as problems with anomalous activity detection—still exist. Nonetheless, the efficiencies of cloud computing have engendered its increasing use, changing the future cyberspace landscape. However, we often overlook the fact that virtualization demands intense software coding. The adoption of cloud architectures such as the JIE may create operational efficiencies and free some DODIN operators for retraining into other mission fields, but it is essential that our operators also have a more solid knowledge of computer languages and coding best principles.

Ubiquitous Computing

Ubiquitous computing, also known as the Internet of things, is based on the idea that all devices everywhere are connected through the Internet or another TCP/IP network. Although this concept is not yet reality, more devices are adding Internet connectivity to their capabilities and can communicate with other devices over the Internet. This expanded connectivity is expected to drastically alter the way societies function. It represents a paradigm shift away from networked laptops and desktops toward networked objects sensing their environments and communicating what they sense among themselves.

Ubiquitous computing does not change core Internet topology. Rather, it is a shift in the next generation of Web applications. The world is on the cusp of entering Web 3.0—the semantic Web. Web 1.0 was the static Web: people read information without interacting with the media. Web 2.0 is the interactive and social web. The trend toward Web 2.0 started circa 2000 but did not fully take off until later in the first decade of the century with the popularization of services such as YouTube and Facebook. Web 3.0, the next evolution of the Web, began at the start of the second decade and is expected to intensify into the third decade of this century.

The semantic Web involves ubiquitous computing—machines connecting data not previously linked.[45] Machines will be able to understand data in a way that a human can via the metadata.[46] This capacity is more than an extension of the Internet to mobile and other devices; it includes independent systems that operate on their own infrastructure and rely only partially on the Internet. These objects—from books to cars, from electrical appliances to food—create the Internet of things. Some objects may have their own IPv6 addresses while others will be embedded in complex systems and use sensors to obtain information from their environments (such as food products that record the temperature along the supply chain).

Internet Protocol Television and Software-Defined Radio

The rise of on-demand video and audio online services has prompted a shift from traditional television and radio to Internet Protocol television (IPTV) and software-defined radio. These technologies allow for the broadcasting of audio and video material over a packet-switch IP network. However, IPv4 networks limit the transmission to a unicast model. That is, in terms of user experience, if someone wants to change a program, pressing the "next channel" button will require the device to establish a new connection, creating a lag in load time of the next channel or program being requested. IPv6 solves this channel load delay because it allows for multicasting.

Standards for platforms capable of running IPTV services are just now emerging. American companies such as AT&T support the International Telecommunication Union's (ITU) G.hn standard, which allows IPTV services to evolve into a format resembling the seamlessness of television today.[47] The result will be similar to the change that occurred when cable and satellite broadcast transformed the television landscape. As such, IPTV will present new opportunities for the United States to broadcast messages worldwide with the capability to target specific devices or send generic messages to large groups of devices. While these opportunities will exist on the open Internet, extremist entities could use IPTV in conjunction with devices embedded into closed networks to maintain a grip on the minds of their followers within self-referential environments.

Air Force Acquisition and the Cyber Workforce

Perhaps the more critical policy decisions affecting technology are those guiding our acquisition of defense cyber systems. Considerations in this area include the need to standardize systems and IT configurations across the Air Force and to create a small cadre of officers dual qualified as cyber operators and acquisition professionals. Further, transitioning to IPv6 is essential.

The Air Force's computing systems and associated software can best be described as a "patchwork quilt" of confusion, creating serious systemic vulnerabilities. First, not every major command (MAJCOM) uses the same hardware or software. The result is a hodgepodge of systems and differing standards that affects not only supporting and defending these disparate systems but also training in the cyber career fields (i.e., How should AETC or MAJCOMs train against a nonstandard piece of equipment?). Second, the life-cycle management of our systems often appears to be an afterthought in that the Air Force does not contract for life-cycle support. With myriad systems, the life-cycle support costs are significantly increased. To make matters worse, the personnel responsible for protecting Air Force systems are geographically dispersed. These issues present a problem because the innumerable variants of operating systems and practices make it more difficult for IT professionals to protect vital systems and create unanticipated weaknesses and vulnerabilities in system interfaces. This study recommends that the Air Force CIO establish and develop enforcement mechanisms to ensure standard Air Force–wide IT configurations, allowing better network integration and fewer base-specific failures with security/network defense tools. Another helpful step would be to bring together a core group of programmers who can disseminate best practices throughout the Air Force.

Along with establishing standard IT systems and hardware, the acquisition community also needs to assure a baseline level of quality in the implemented software. Toward that end, the Air Force should devote sufficient resources to this important task since it is certainly preferable to the hacking of weapon systems data that has clearly occurred in the recent past.[48] Efforts to ensure software security are expensive, but the Air Force can take steps to mitigate the cost. This study recommends that the Air Force increasingly rely on its enlisted programmers to supply the talent to perform many software assurance activities. Although civilians and officers can perform these functions admirably, they are often considerably more expensive to obtain and retain. Second, efforts are under way to take advantage of a change in regulations that allows the Air Force to hold vendors financially liable for inept software designs and/or coding that leaves systems vulnerable.[49] Any revenue arising from these efforts should be directed toward addressing the specific problem the vendor created and then enhancing software assurance so that it does not happen again. Finally, since fixing poor programming can be more difficult and costly than writing it properly in the first place, the DOD and Air Force should provide adequate incentives for secure programming that far exceeds the level necessary to avoid liability.[50]

The final aspect of the acquisition problem is the lack of cyber-qualified acquisition program managers and the reluctance of existing program managers to grant cyber specialists decision authority over programmatic decisions.[51] Observers of the debacle of the Expeditionary Combat Support System (ECSS) attribute parts of this program's failure to the lack of integration of cyber experts into the early stages of program design.[52] Procurement programs in the DOD cannot and will not keep up with cyber development cycles. To stay ahead of cyber, the Air Force needs to have connections with industry—being disconnected from Silicon Valley guarantees obsolescence, hampers education, and limits training. Although industry drives innovation, cyber-educated acquisitions personnel are important because they can supply industry with set specifications for mathematically provable secure hardware/software. Every Air Force mission requires networked connectivity to some degree or another. Additionally, every weapon system depends on data and signals—both internally to accomplish its own mission and externally to connect and work with the rest of the forces. To establish a secure software/hardware environment as industry builds our platforms, the Air Force needs 62Es, systems engineers, and other acquisition personnel who understand the intricacies of a platform's reliance on cyber. To assure mission success, they need to acquire and design security into key cyber components of the cyber terrain on which a platform relies. Conceptualizing, requiring these specifications to be built into the hardware/software, and holding industry responsible will increase the cost of successfully exploiting Air Force systems to the adversary.

Despite the addition of cyberspace as the third domain in which the Air Force conducts operations, the grooming of a cyber-qualified acquisition corps has largely been neglected. Engineering, science, and technology management tracks explicitly call for a relevant degree and have a much more elaborate development plan, but the same is not true of the cyber track.[53] Although an IT certification track is offered through Defense Acquisition University, the curriculum has no specialized cyber content. In fact, only one course dealing specifically with IT acquisition is required at each certification level. Furthermore, a technical baccalaureate degree is merely mentioned as preferred, and a bachelor's degree in business administration qualifies as a "preferred" degree.[54] A technical cyber track should be developed to allow for cultivation of highly trained acquisition civilians and officers. Such a program could be roughly modeled after the engineering track, which offers substantial training and marries professionals' technical backgrounds with the practicalities of the defense acquisition system.

Within cyber acquisitions are the 2210 series of IT professionals and the 1101 series of acquisition/program management (PM) professionals. Both series require courses in basic systems acquisition, information systems, and software acquisition management—accounting for 118 hours of instruction—but then the courses diverge. The 2210s receive training on technical reviews and software measurement and dive deeply into information systems acquisition and software acquisition management, for 281 hours of total instruction time. The program managers receive training in systems planning, engineering, logistics, financial management, cost analysis, earned value management, contracts, and research and development (R&D) before taking four in-depth courses dealing with program management tools. Instructional time for the program management track totals 470 hours.

Although one could argue that the program manager is more qualified to manage the program, finding cyber-qualified 1101s is problematic. The 2210s have a distinct advantage in specific IT-related instruction.[55] However, a ceiling apparently exists in IT/software-dominant program executive officers and organizations and missed opportunities for a sustainable career path for the field. Additionally, the top nonsupervisory 2210-series professional standard core personnel document is for a GS-13 while other functional areas may include up to a GS-15. Extending the structure to a GS-15 opens the door to additional training such as Cyber 400, ensures that 2210s can compete for advancement, and demonstrates once again a commitment to a viable career path in IT program management.[56] Various options can improve IT/software acquisition, including utilization of 2210s as the PM with support from an 1101. Based upon what they may be called upon to do, it makes sense for PMs to take some additional courses in information systems and software management. The 2210s could take the role of advising and assisting the acquisition team, as do engineers (discussed above).

National Initiative for Cybersecurity Education

Both the "Comprehensive National Cybersecurity Initiative" and the complementary *Department of Defense Cyberspace Workforce Strategy* identify significant cybersecurity workforce development gaps in the nation's manpower and offer pathways to resolve some workforce challenges.[57] Specifically, education and awareness are identified as key national gaps. The DHS became the lead organization to develop strategies for workforce planning, professionalization, recruitment, and retention for the cybersecurity field.[58] These strategies are being developed across the nation via the department's Workforce Development Initiative within its Science and Technology Directorate, Office of University Programs.[59] Major activities under this initiative include the following:[60]

- Cybersecurity Workforce Planning Diagnostic: gives organizations an interactive tool to help them make informed decisions about cybersecurity workforce planning.[61]
- National Recruitment and Retention Strategy: focuses on tactics and strategies to acquire cybersecurity professionals from such groups as (1) women and minorities, (2) veterans, and (3) two-year college graduates.
- National Cybersecurity Workforce Framework ("the Framework"): identifies gaps and deficiencies in both the size and capability of the cybersecurity workforce.[62]

NICE and Air Force Cyberspace Operators

A key finding of this study is that management of human capital for Air Force cyberspace—including recruitment, training, and development—was hampered by the question about who constitutes a cyberspace operator. When the Air Force's communications career field (personnel with the 33S AFSC) was transitioned into the 17D AFSC (now 17 series), the assumption was that any Airman who touched a computer was automatically a cyberspace warrior. However, the DOD has three broad categories of cyberspace operations—offensive, defensive, and information networks (see fig. 1, chap. 1)—each requiring individuals with different KSAs. Transitioning a group of Airmen from a single AFSC into a new cyberspace AFSC will not meet the DOD's needs on the operational cyberspace floor; that group of Airmen simply does not have enough diversity in KSAs to carry out all varying cyberspace operations.

Identifying cyberspace operators is a problem not only within military ranks but also among the federal civilian workforce. The lack of a harmonized cybersecurity civilian workforce was unanimously voiced during research interviews. The research team discovered a trend involving the conversion of positions that were traditionally engineering to interdisciplinary positions. Previously these positions were open only to individuals in the 0854 (CE) or 0855 (EE) fields who met specific qualification standards required for all professional engineering positions.[63] Prior to the conversion from engineering billets to interdisciplinary billets, personnel were required to have a degree in professional engineering (i.e., bachelor of science in CE, EE, etc.) to fill one of these positions. However, one interviewee noted that because certain cyberspace billets were converted to interdisciplinary ones, he was able to fill the position without an engineering degree. The individual was in the cybersecurity position because the 1550 career field (CS) was now eligible to fill what had previously been limited to the 0854 and 0855 career fields.[64]

Because federal civilian cyberspace billets are in transition, confusion exists about who cyberspace operators are. Currently, many federal civilian personnel who are actually cyberspace operators have occupational series codes not considered cyber while other civilians who are not really cyberspace operators have the 2210 (IT management) code. Researchers found that the AFPC could not reliably identify which civilians were working cyberspace operations and which were not, even when the operations were clearly defined.

Applying the NICE Framework to the Workforce

To help resolve the confusion about who makes up the cyberspace workforce, the NICE framework provides a codified structure that identifies specialty areas of cybersecurity professionals (fig. 7). It establishes a common taxonomy and lexicon that organizes cybersecurity work into categories and specialty areas, along with the KSAs that cybersecurity professionals must demonstrate for different positions within the specialty areas.[65] The framework was developed and validated by teams of psychologists and subject matter experts (SME)—many of whom were former Air Force employees—from government, private industry, critical infrastructure, academic, and nonprofit organizations. Thirty-one functional work specialties within the cybersecurity field are outlined.

Securely Provision	Secure Acquisition	Secure Software Engineering	Systems Security Architecture	Technology Research and Development	Systems Requirements Planning	Test and Evaluation	Systems Development
Oversee and Govern	Legal Advice and Advocacy	Strategic Planning and Policy	Education and Training	Info Systems Security Operations (ISSO)	Security Program Management	Risk Management	Knowledge Management
Operate and Maintain	Data Administration	Customer Service and Tech Support	Network Services	System Administration	Systems Security Analysis		
Protect and Defend	Enterprise Network Defense (END) Analysis	Incident Response	END Infrastructure Support	Vulnerability Assessment and Management			
Analyze	All-Source Intelligence	Exploitation Analysis	Targets	Threat Analysis			
Collect and Operate	Collection Operations	Cyber Operations	Cyber Operational Planning				
Investigate	Investigation	Digital Forensics					

Figure 7. NICE framework. (Adapted from NICE, "National Cybersecurity Workforce Framework," March 2013, http://csrc.nist.gov/nice/framework.)

OPM is scheduled to mandate NICE for the civilian workforce by 2017. The Air Staff Cyber Career Field Management Office is in the process of mapping military cyberspace positions within the DOD to the NICE framework, which supports the broader objectives of the DOD *Cyberspace Workforce Strategy*. Since the NICE framework is currently in electronic form, an opportunity exists for the

Office of the Deputy Chief of Staff for Personnel (HAF/A1) to create an electronic personnel tracking mechanism mapped to NICE. Such a mechanism could create efficiencies by establishing special experience identifiers (SEI) to classify cyberspace personnel with unique capabilities.

An additional benefit of the NICE framework is that it seeks to categorize and track cyber personnel in leadership, management, training, and education. This tool will provide direction and advocacy so that individuals and organizations may effectively conduct cybersecurity work in the technical fields.[66] It is our determination that the legal, strategic, and policy development aspects of cyber operations are a largely overlooked segment of the cyber workforce. However, the oversight and governance of cyber operations are integral to operationalizing the domain; this process is managed by personnel including legal advisors and strategic planners as well as educators and trainers. Currently, the bench is not deep with individuals who truly understand both technology and policy. As one senior leader at US-CYBERCOM informed the research team, this scarcity results in a lack of trust to operationalize the cyber domain. The role of individuals in the oversight and governance functions of the NICE framework is to craft national and DOD policies and interpret OCO and DCO in ways that will enhance the utilization of cyberspace as an aspect of American national power. Below is a selection of US, DOD, and Air Force policies that shape the utilization of cyber power.

National Policies

Numerous documents articulate US national and cybersecurity policies:

- The *National Security Strategy* (*NSS*) articulates the US president's vision for cybersecurity, stating that the nation should "defend [itself], consistent with U.S. and international law, against cyber attacks and impose costs on malicious cyber actors, including through prosecution of illegal cyber activity."[67]
- The *National Strategy to Secure Cyberspace* (*NSSC*) is the main strategy document regarding the US government's priorities and response framework for cyberspace threats. It codifies earlier presidential directives and laws into a coherent national strategy.[68]

- The "Comprehensive National Cybersecurity Initiative" was first created in January 2008 when President George W. Bush signed classified joint Presidential Directive 54 / Homeland Security Presidential Directive 23.[69]
- The *International Strategy for Cyberspace* describes how the United States should coordinate its efforts to promote the ideals of openness, security, and prosperity on the Internet.[70]
- The *Administration Strategy for Mitigating the Theft of U.S. Trade Secrets* includes US government responses to intellectual property theft in the commercial sector.[71]
- The *Cyberspace Policy Review* was directed by President Barack Obama to evaluate US cybersecurity structures and policies.[72]
- Executive Order (EO) 13636, Improving Critical Infrastructure Cybersecurity, was "designed to increase the level of core capabilities for our critical infrastructure to manage cyber risk . . . by focusing on three key areas: (1) information sharing, (2) privacy, and (3) the adoption of cybersecurity practices."[73]

DOD and Air Force Policies

Specific policies also guide cyberspace operations within the DOD:

- *National Military Strategy for Cyberspace Operations (NMS-CO)*[74]
- *Department of Defense Strategy for Operating in Cyberspace*[75]
- JP 3-12 (R), *Cyberspace Operations*, 5 February 2013
- Curtis E. LeMay Center for Doctrine Development and Education, *Annex 3-12, Cyberspace Operations*, 30 November 2011, https://doctrine.af.mil/download.jsp?filename=3-12-Annex-CYBERSPACE-OPS.pdf
- Air Force Policy Directive 10-17, *Cyberspace Operations*, 31 July 2012

In addition to such policies, existing international legal frameworks clarify how law and policy should treat specific instances of the use of force and cyber attacks in warfare. The *Tallinn Manual on the International Law Applicable to Cyber Warfare*—perhaps the most comprehensive work on the issue to date—defines *cyber attack* as a "cyber operation, whether offensive or defensive, that is reasonably expected to cause injury or death to persons or damage or destruction to objects." Further, "a cyber operation constitutes a use of force when its scale and effects are comparable to non-cyber operations rising to the level of a use of force."[76] These definitions are parsimonious and allow for a clearer interpretation of actions in cyberspace. Furthermore, the only systems they apply to are ICSs and other OTs as described above.

However, US law has broader definitions for cyberspace operations that apply to a much larger range of systems. Different sections of the *US Code* necessitate distinct responses to acts of cyber espionage, cybercrime, and cyber attack. Clear definitions for these various acts of cyber aggression are therefore required. Additionally, the intended targets and potential effects of such acts must also be understood. Such acts of cyberspace aggression include not only individuals doing something illegal and crime syndicates carrying out a more sophisticated attack but also nation-states spying on or actually carrying out offensive cyberspace operations against other nations. To distinguish between organized crime and armed attacks in cyberspace, the research team adopted the following definitions of *cyber espionage*, *cybercrime*, *cyber disruption*, and *cyber attack*:

- *Cyber espionage*: The act of securing information of a military or political nature that a competing nation holds secret.[77]
- *Cybercrime*: Any interference with the functioning of a computer system, with the fraudulent or dishonest intent of procuring, without right, an economic benefit for oneself or another person.[78]
- *Cyber disruption*: The serious hindering, without right, of the functioning of a computer system by inputting, transmitting, damaging, deleting, deteriorating, altering, or suppressing computer data.[79]
- *Cyber attack*: "[A] cyber operation, whether offensive or defensive, that is reasonably expected to cause injury or death to persons or damage or destruction to objects."[80]

The paradigms required to address cybercrime and cyber espionage are not the same as those needed to succeed in cyberspace warfare. Understanding the distinctions among the various types of malicious cyberspace activity helps policy makers decide whether to adopt existing international law or develop global norms. Such decisions—critical to ensuring stability in cyberspace—cannot be judiciously made without a workforce possessing the technical aptitude to apply knowledge of priorities or appropriately provide legally sound advice. Currently, this situation is not the case. For example, the persistent confusion between IT and OT results in the misperception that all OCOs can result in effects and unintended consequences if the target is on an open network or on closed critical infrastructure networks. Centralization of specific attacks against certain targets might be necessary in these sorts of missions.

However, even if prescribed concepts of operations are authorized for use, the dynamic environment of cyberspace and current command and control structures do not allow for flexible responses to changing network topologies. A cyber warrior carrying out a mission set authorized by USCYBERCOM might have to stop the attack without completing the objective because the adversary has updated his computer system with the latest vulnerability patch, thereby not allowing the cyber operator to continue with the preapproved route. Having to go back up the chain of command to receive authorization to continue with a new attack vector could have negative effects on kinetic missions that rely on exploitation of the adversary's information system. Cyber judge advocate generals (JAG) and strategic policy makers with a keen sense for the technology could craft guidance allowing for a cyber operator's flexible response to actively engage with changing network topologies and achieve the desired effect without losing operational advantage. Thus, we recommend mapping the KSAs of cyber JAGs and strategic planners to the NICE framework and using SEIs. Doing so will begin to establish a workforce of social and behavioral scientists who have demonstrated a technical aptitude beyond that reflected in introductory courses. Such a cadre would have more of the requisite skills to exercise strategic policy and provide legal guidance about cyber operations.

Summary

General Welsh states that "the Air Force provides critical capabilities that enhance the military's capacity to navigate accurately, observe clearly, communicate securely, and strike precisely."[81] Cyberspace is no less important than physical assets in fighting a potential peer competitor. America's technologically advanced systems in command and control, communications, targeting, and battlespace awareness provide an unrivalled advantage that depends heavily on cyberspace and cyberspace assets in space. Past and present reliance on cyberspace capabilities during operational conflicts leaves little doubt about its growing importance. To protect America's vital interests in cyberspace during the coming decades, the Air Force must begin thinking through the impact of cyber to the mission within the technology and policy contexts outlined in this chapter.

We make the following recommendations based on the preceding discussion:

Recommendations Summary

- Manpower planners must account for the JIE and other systemic technological paradigm shifts as they assess their 5-to-10-year workforce requirements.
- The DOD and USAF should document their roles and provide metrics on their participation and position with Internet governance bodies.
- The USAF CIO should develop and establish enforcement mechanisms to ensure standard Air Force–wide IT configurations, allowing better network integration and fewer base-specific failures with security/network defense tools.
- The USAF should embed the life-cycle-management process as part of its cyber decision making.
- The USAF should increasingly rely on its enlisted programmers to supply the talent to perform many software assurance activities. Although civilians and officers can perform these functions admirably, they are often considerably more expensive to obtain and retain.
- The DOD and Air Force should provide adequate incentives for secure programming that far exceeds the level necessary to avoid liability.
- The USAF should examine holding vendors financially liable for inept software design and/or coding that leaves systems vulnerable.
- Incorporate the DHS's NICE framework across cyberspace career fields.
- Create electronic professional development tracking mechanisms (such as SEIs) mapped to NICE.
- Recognize cyberspace as a domain with language and social science requirements, and catalog personnel.
- Mandate a firm transition date to IPv6 utilizing DOD acquisition policies and the JIE.
- The USAF needs to ensure that adequate training exists on cyberspace ranges within IPv6 environments for cyberspace operators. All current operators need to be proficient in IPv6 now.

> **RECOMMENDATIONS SUMMARY** (*continued*)
>
> - The DOD, particularly the USAF, should take a more active role in the development of the cyberspace infrastructure and the standards and norms of Internet governance mirroring its actions in the domain of space at ITU-Radiocommunications.
> - The USAF should develop and implement proprietary protocols designed to be mathematically secure.
> - Broadband mobility provides opportunities to engage with target audiences; social scientists and linguists will be critical to do so effectively. The USAF needs to ensure that it has an adequate number of linguists and social scientists educated / trained / experienced in cyberspace operations.
> - Develop formal partnerships between the engineering communities, which understand operational IT, and the cybersecurity communities, which understand network IT, to mitigate vulnerabilities and manage risk to critical infrastructure.
> - Bring together a core group of programmers who can disseminate best practices throughout the Air Force.
> - Ensure that a baseline level of quality is achieved in the implemented software. Toward that end, the Air Force should devote sufficient resources to this important task since doing so is certainly preferable to continuation of the recent hacking of weapon systems data.
> - Big-data analytics will require greater emphasis in the future, and the USAF and DOD will need to be able to recruit, train, and track analysts capable of manipulating big-data sets. Examine the need for big-data analysts, establish formal requirements to address these needs, and work to establish a mechanism to identify and track expertise.
> - Cultivate a culture of understanding the differences between IT and OT to serve as a foundation for discussion of the cyber dependencies of core Air Force missions.

Notes

1. Joint Chiefs of Staff, *Joint Information Environment*, 3.
2. Ibid., 3–7.
3. "VC-25—Air Force One," USAF fact sheet.
4. Vautrinot, briefing, subject: AFCYBER (Air Forces Cyber).
5. Libicki, "Cyberspace Is Not a Warfighting Domain," 322, 335.
6. [Yannakogeorgos], "Command and Control of Cyber Operations," 96–108.
7. National Transportation Safety Board, *Pacific Gas and Electric Company*, x, 5–6.
8. Ibid., x.
9. McCullagh, "US Was Warned of Predator Drone Hacking"; and Gorman, Dreazen, and Cole, "Insurgents Hack U.S. Drones."
10. Fritz, "How China Will Use Cyber Warfare," 28–80; Hart, "Longtime Battle Lines," D01; and Markoff, "Georgia Takes a Beating."

11. Fritz, "How China Will Use Cyber Warfare," 55–80; and Pilkington, "China Winning Cyber War."
12. Dowd, "World War 2.0," 34–37.
13. Hultquist, "Update on Sandworm Team."
14. US-China Economic and Security Review Commission, "National Security Implication of Investments and Products," 7.
15. Breznitz and Murphree, "Rise of China," 7.
16. ICANN, "Montevideo Statement."
17. Headquarters US Air Force, *America's Air Force*, 8.
18. Peng, "Research on IPv6 Environment," 345; and Coleman, "Next Generation Internet Policy," 497–512.
19. Air Force senior leaders and officer, enlisted, and civilian cyber operators, unattributed interviews by the authors, 2013–14.
20. "Ghost Route Hunter." Note that 1 decillion is 1 x 1,033 or 1 followed by 33 zeroes.
21. The author is grateful to the Air Force Systems Networking (AFSN) office members for their comments and collaboration in producing this section.
22. To do the calculations, one may visit the DODNIC website at https://www.nic.mil/cgi-bin/whoisweb and search for "DNIC-RNET." Doing so will bring up all the networks that the DODNIC considers "returned networks." (The NIC uses "RNET" to annotate networks returned to IP managers.) This information changes daily, depending on what gets issued on any day, but the number of RNETs is nearly always decreasing.
23. Boeing, "KC-46A Pegasus Customer."
24. Headquarters US Air Force, *America's Air Force*, 15.
25. E-mail exchange with HAF A3/6.
26. Frankel et al., *Secure Deployment of IPv6*, 2-6.
27. "Federal Virtual Training Environment (FedVTE)."
28. Stenbit to secretaries of military departments et al., memorandum.
29. The research team is grateful to AFNIC/NES for these observations. See House, National Defense Authorization Act for Fiscal Year 2006, Public Law 109-163, sec. 221.
30. "*Federal Acquisition Regulation*; FAR Case 2005–041, Internet Protocol Version 6 (IPv6)."
31. In actuality, the conversion to IPv6 could save the DOD money on the physical infrastructure. Communications devices with their own static IP addresses running solely IPv6 would consume less energy, providing longer lasting battery life in mobile devices on which command and control of many military operations depend. Lawson, "IPv6 Can Boost Mobile Performance."
32. Gallaher and Rowe, *IPv6 Economic Impact Assessment*, 4-19–4-20.
33. Strategy and Planning Committee, Federal Chief Information Officers Council, "Roadmap toward IPv6 Adoption."
34. Chander and Le, "Data Nationalism."
35. Ungerleider, "Iran Cracking Down"; and Rhoads and Fassihi, "Iran Vows to Unplug Internet."
36. This premise differs from that of Chris C. Demchak and Peter Dombrowski in "Rise of a Cybered Westphalian Age," 32–61, in which the sovereignty of the Inter-

net involves accessing points of Tier 1 ISP connections coming into the country and maintaining government control of them.

37. Thomas, "Russian View on Information Based Warfare," 28.
38. Ibid.
39. ICANN, "Internationalized Domain Names."
40. Mansfield, "LTE Category 4 Trial."
41. Anand, "Threats to India's Information Environment," 56–62.
42. Yardley, "Panic Seizes India," A1.
43. Mell and Grance, *NIST Definition of Cloud Computing*, 2.
44. USAF Chief Scientist, *Cyberspace Science and Technology Vision*, 54.
45. Berners-Lee, "Linked Data."
46. Shadbolt, Hall, and Berners-Lee, "Semantic Web Revisited," 100.
47. Buckley, "G.hn Home Networking Standards."
48. Nakishima, "Confidential Report."
49. House, National Defense Authorization Act for Fiscal Year 2013, sec. 933.
50. Dacus and and Yannakogeorgos, "Designing Cybersecurity into Defense Systems."
51. Col Kjall Gopaul (AFLCMC/HIZ20, Gunter Annex, Maxwell AFB, AL), interview by AFRI research team, March 2014.
52. Others have attributed the problem to a failure of the Air Force to engage in business-process reengineering; this finding is not incompatible with the findings by the research team. Engineering a process as complex as ECSS is partially a cyber endeavor, and cyber-qualified acquisition personnel would have been helpful in engineering this project. Whether cyber specialists would have saved the program is unknowable. For more on the failure, see Kreft, "Senate Report: Air Force 'Systematically Failed.' " See also Senate, "Expeditionary Combat Support System." The Senate's ECSS report notes that resistance to cultural change and a failure to get buy-in from the organizations affected by the technological change caused the program's failure (see especially pp. 16–18).
53. Defense Acquisition University, *2014 Course Catalog*, 74–86.
54. Ibid., 92–95.
55. Gopaul, "IT vs. PM [Program Management] Track."
56. Gopaul, interview.
57. White House, "Comprehensive National Cybersecurity Initiative"; and DOD, *Cyberspace Workforce Strategy*.
58. See Homeyer, Maxon, and Mills, "Cybersecurity Workforce Framework."
59. DHS, "Workforce Development Initiatives."
60. The process is being refined and updated as it unfolds. See the National Initiative for Cybersecurity Careers and Studies website, http://niccs.us-cert.gov.
61. "Cybersecurity Workforce Planning Diagnostic."
62. For details about the framework, see NICE, "National Cybersecurity Workforce Framework." For recent guidance on the framework, see NIST, "Update on the Cybersecurity Framework." The research team is indebted to the DHS/NICE for supporting this section of the study and appreciates the comments and feedback provided at the AFRI Cyber Advisory Group, Maxwell AFB, AL, July 2014.
63. OPM standards for the 0800 (all professional engineering positions), 0854, and 0855 occupational series are searchable at the OPM website, http://www.opm

.gov/policy-data-oversight/classification-qualifications/general-schedule-qualification-standards.

64. For OPM standards for the 1550 occupational series, see ibid.

65. KSAs within the NICE framework include specific degrees, training, and certifications as required by each specialty.

66. NICE, "National Cybersecurity Workforce Framework," 128.

67. White House, *National Security Strategy*, 13.

68. DHS, *National Strategy to Secure Cyberspace*.

69. White House, "Comprehensive National Cybersecurity Initiative."

70. National Security Council, *International Strategy for Cyberspace*.

71. Executive Office of the President, *Administration Strategy*.

72. Executive Office of the President, *Cyberspace Policy Review*.

73. White House, "Cybersecurity—Executive Order 13636."

74. Office of the Chairman of the Joint Chiefs of Staff, *Strategy for Cyberspace Operations*.

75. DOD, *Strategy for Operating in Cyberspace*.

76. Schmitt, *Tallinn Manual*, 45, 106.

77. Council of Europe, Convention on Cybercrime.

78. Ibid., title 2, art. 8b.

79. Ibid.

80. Schmitt, *Tallinn Manual*, 106.

81. Welsh, "Global Vigilance," 6.

Chapter 3

Recruit, Retain, Regain

How the Air Force recruits and selects individuals for cyber education and training is a key challenge to developing a cyber workforce that operationalizes the domain. One of the questions this study sought to answer was, What makes a good hacker? Do you start with a rocket scientist, a computer expert, or a Sherlock Holmes type of person? We discovered that identifying the attributes of a top-notch cyber operator is part of the problem. IT proficiency does not necessarily translate into having an aptitude or a proclivity for being an offensive or a defensive cyber operator. Thus, to operationalize the domain with personnel ready to defend Air Force missions and to serve on the Cyber Mission Force (CMF) and cyber protection teams (CPT), the USAF should focus on recruiting individuals who can operate in the OCO/DCO mission space and have DODIN experience versus those with solely DODIN experience.

Broadly, cyber operators are thought of as those who touch any aspect of any network. Such generalities have created misperceptions in the "what's in/out of cyberspace" discussion. More rigorous personnel requirements are useful. To an extent, this need has been resolved by creating the distinction between the DODIN and OCO/DCO. DODIN operators perform the critical functions of maintaining and sustaining the network provided to war fighters—often equated with hacking but in actuality involving building and sustaining networks. The Air Force information network function lies within A6, which has experience in and a tradition of attracting and developing this breed of cyber operator. OCO and DCO require skill sets from the intelligence, operations, and communications career fields to operationalize cyberspace and thus create effects that will protect and defend US national security interests, giving the president sovereign options to project US power.

Recruiting talent and retaining our investment in cyber operators in the OCO/DCO communities are key issues examined next. We also discuss the potential for regaining individuals who separated from service to practice cyber operations in the private sector but who may want to return to government service to apply lessons learned in industry to USAF missions.

Recruit

The key to force structure is to find educated people with a proclivity toward hacking. The recruitment pool is not as bleak as many portray it. A National Society of High School Scholars study on *The Emerging Workforce: Generational Trends* states that the Air Force places 18th out of 200 nationwide places to work.[2] It also notes that among millennials, the top career interests "are STEM [science, technology, engineering, and mathematics] fields, particularly medical, business and government. As for what they hope to find in the workplace, they ranked fair treatment, corporate social responsibility, and benefits the highest."[3]

However, the fact that individuals are interested in STEM does not mean that they will be good cyber operators. As the USAF's *Cyber Vision 2025* notes, "Some individuals have proven cyber aptitude without a technical degree, but these are the exception. . . . The Air Force needs an aptitude test to assess and admit only those non-cyber educated individuals who demonstrate both interest and aptitude."[4] Understanding what makes a great DCO/OCO operator is thus part of the challenge that the Air Force is currently working to resolve.

Individuals selected to protect US national security in the cyber arena must share some common traits. Expert interviews indicated that good hackers are autodidactic, able to work well on teams to solve problems in novel ways, and have critical thinking skills. Further, besides having technical aptitude, cyber recruits must be a good fit for the Air Force culture of integrity, service, and excellence. Willingness to work as part of a team versus maintaining a self-focused orientation—another important criterion—is generally not a problem for the Air Force since all levels of its education and training emphasize teamwork.

Equating technical aptitude as a measure of cyber operations potential in a recruit is problematic. As this study found, a perception exists that using a computer equates to knowing how it works. This view stems from generational differences resulting from the evolution of personal computing and networking from the 1980s to the present. While Generation Xers and early millennials grew up in the nascent days of computer networks—an era when experimentation and exploration on desktop/laptop computing platforms and networks were encouraged—today things are different. The convergence of broadband and mobile technologies has created push-button "app" ecosystems such as the iPhone Operating System (iOS) that do not leave a user much interface to interact with underlying hardware and software. As a result, although millennials in the latter half of their generational spectrum who have grown up with this technology paradigm may not understand how their platforms function, they demonstrate to previous generations that they are technologically savvy because of their aptitude for using applications.[5] Cyber career field managers anecdotally noted that some recruits had poor keyboard skills due to their use of mobile technology rather than desktop computers.[6] Thus, much like operating a car, the ability to use a computing device does not necessarily denote an understanding of how it works or having the skill to repair it or improve its performance.

Placing too much value on educational background could create a barrier to entry in the cyber operations field that will exclude those with latent aptitude, thereby depleting the recruitment pool from which operators are drawn. Put another way, individuals who have the potential to be talented cyber operators might possess neither a formal education nor the requisite industry-standard certificates. Discovering bright candidates who underachieved in high school/college is important. Some (not all) operators' backgrounds are not standard. They may come from the hacker communities or lack the financial or time resources to invest in a cyber certification program. Since the field is undermanned, entirely eliminating these people from the pool is counterproductive from an overall manning standpoint. Testing for cyberspace operations aptitude is one method that could assist in identifying such individuals during the recruitment process.

Measuring a prospective recruit's knowledge of basic computer and networking concepts is a good starting point to identify those with a potential aptitude for cyber operations. The 711th Human Performance Wing developed and the Air Force has instituted such a tool to test for these indicators of success. As awareness of the need for high-quality offensive and defensive cyber capabilities has grown, the Air Force, Navy, and Army have all looked for a way to augment the Armed Services Vocational Aptitude Battery (ASVAB) test for classifying new enlisted personnel in these military occupations. This "cyber test" emphasizes four content areas: (1) networking and communications, (2) computer operations, (3) security compliance, and (4) software programming and Web development. In 2007 development efforts resulted in a test for cyber classification. The cyber test has now been launched and is currently in operational use (fiscal year

[FY] 2014). Because of the continuously changing nature of the field, the test will need regular updating by a dedicated staff.

Analyses of test performance results indicated that the cyber test scores can increase the size of the qualified applicant pool without increasing school attrition.[7] An optimal percentile cut score of 60 was established for the target cyber and intelligence Air Force specialties. For example, enlisted applicants may be classified into AFSC 3D0X1, Knowledge Operations Management, with an ASVAB general composite score of 64 or one between 54 and 63 together with a cyber test score of 60.[8] This particular classification strategy increases the number of qualified individuals in the applicant pool while maintaining the same level of school performance; moreover, it can increase diversity numbers. Therefore, the cyber test can identify qualified applicants among those marginally below the current ASVAB electronic and general classification composite cut scores in Air Force cyber and intelligence specialties.

Other strategies could decrease the size of the qualified applicant pool while increasing school performance and graduation rates (and presumably field performance and retention)—for example, maintaining minimum cut scores on electronic/general composites and rank-ordering qualified applicants by cyber scores. Ideally, the entry-level cyber classification test will become part of the ASVAB (not just a special test), and optimum composites can be developed by the team at AFPC. Currently, all USAF applicants take the cyber test at the Military Entrance Processing Station, partly for research data on experimental items seeded within the current test, so the move from "special test" status to ASVAB subtest will have minimal impact on testing time.

The cyber test will go a long way toward identifying personnel with a knowledge base in computer sciences, but it does not measure a specific aptitude for OCO/DCO. The Air Force is currently participating in a joint effort with the Army to develop just such a test—one that contains 50 questions (25 on skills and 25 on aptitude). It was field-tested for seven months, concluding in January 2015. Once the testing data is collected, it will be compared with the Air Force Officer Qualifying Test (AFOQT) and ASVAB scores to see what, if any, correlations can be used as potential indicators of an aptitude for OCO/DCO. If the results are predictable, the cyber test will be evaluated for addition to the AFOQT and ASVAB.[9]

In addition to screening potential recruits, this study also determined that latent cyber operators may be found in other Air Force career fields. The USAF should therefore examine ways to give opportunities to Airmen in these other fields to transfer into the cyberspace warfare and network operations officer (17 series, or 17S), enlisted cyberspace defensive operations (1B4 series), cyberspace support (3D series), or cyber-related civilian career fields (see chap. 5, "Force Development," for detailed information on these fields). The cyber test could be one way to allow Airmen from other AFSCs who have an interest in cyber or have CS, CE, or EE degrees to demonstrate their aptitude to be cyber warriors.

Proper accessions will require more targeted recruiting and training. Models that predict cyber success are useful in selecting people for cyber training and potentially reducing washout rates.

Quantity of Recruits versus Quality of Education

Throughout the course of the study, research team members debated about the percentage of STEM versus non-STEM personnel needed within the Air Force. Although Air Staff cyber career development managers have mandated the requirements, discussion continued on the right balance among education, experience, and aptitude.

Part of the reason for the existence of the training versus education debate stems from persistent myths that the cost of entry into cyber operations is low. Some people have the perception that relatively unsophisticated nonstate actors (such as the proverbial teenager in his or her parents' basement) could cause incidents of national significance in the cyber arena. It is true that novices might successfully conduct criminal activity and disruptive denial-of-service attacks.[10] However, this concept is a myth when one considers the defense of national security missions against nation-state adversaries that the Air Force would care about. Industrial control systems, embedded processors and controllers, and other IT integrated into platforms require a different skill set than that of a proficient network hacker.[11] Those with master's and doctorate degrees are generally much better at conducting cyber warfare due to the theoretical and practical focus of education. Formal education shapes the minds of individuals with technical aptitude in a way that allows them to apply their knowledge of cyberspace to research, design, develop, test, and evaluate hardware, software, and firmware for the purpose of exploiting, defending, and attacking cyber and cyber physical systems. We need not look far to find a historical model for the cyber workforce that mandated advanced technical knowledge as a part of a certain career path. Initially, becoming a pilot in the Air Force required an engineering and science background. Eventually, we were able to move away from this requirement as we got the "science" right over years of learning. If we really are at the "Wright Flyer" stage of cyber, then the Air Force should utilize commissioning sources to shape the makeup of the cyber operations career field.

A sticking point was the benefits of formal education versus training. Essentially, if the best tools are available but the individuals using them have knowledge based on rote memorization to pass industry-standard certification, they may only be able to follow a checklist. Thus, advanced tools might not be used to their potential. Alternatively, if individuals are educated in the science and theory of cyber operations, then even with average tools they can make exceptional things happen. As some experts observe, "Training without education proved insufficient to assure mathematically complex, information centric systems. In a world where our peers educate their cyber operators first on the science of information assurance, then train them in the art of cyber warfare, our cyber workforce development continues to shun specialized education in favor of generalized training—a too-little-too late process with an established record of inadequacy for national security missions."[12] The research team agrees that education is key and thus strongly recommends that the USAF recruit cyber-educated Airmen from the 1B4, 1NX, and 3D career fields. Further, in lean years for tuition assistance, Airmen in these career fields should be prioritized to receive financial assistance toward their education in STEM fields.

Another potential option for obtaining the desired educated accessions candidates is through payment of bonuses to those with the requisite background and education. Title 37, section 324, of the *US Code* outlines the authority for the secretary of the Air Force (SECAF) to pay an accession bonus. The SECAF is authorized to pay individual recruits up to $60K (although the bonus is usually lower), which can be paid in a lump sum but is typically paid in four annual installments. For the 13N (nuclear and missile operations) career field, for instance, the USAF proposed an accession bonus of $24K paid in three annual installments of $8K. With the SECAF currently in favor of an accession bonus for 13Ns, there is the possibility of using an accession bonus in the 17S career field as well.[13] Although the research team did see the possibilities of this option, it found that recruiting candidates by means of this method was more difficult than through the Reserve Officer Training Corps (ROTC).[14]

Cyber Criminality and the Security Clearance Challenge

Moral attributes also contribute to identifying the right people to protect US national security. The Air Force culture is often seen as the antithesis of the hacker culture in which innovative potential cyber operators thrive. The specialized nature of cyber operations for national security purposes requires the recruitment of individuals who live according to the Air Force's core values and can obtain and maintain a Top Secret (TS)/sensitive compartmented information (SCI) security clearance. According to the Curtis E. LeMay Center for Doctrine Development and Education, core values "are a statement of those institutional values and principles of conduct that provide the moral framework within which military activities take place. The professional Air Force ethic consists of three fundamental and enduring values of integrity, service, and excellence."[15] As the Air Force seeks to boost the numbers in its cyber workforce, both military and civilian, this study urges caution in recruitment. Appropriate screening practices can help eliminate persons who might have a skewed moral compass and thus mitigate severe insider threats posed by individuals such as Chelsea (née Bradley) Manning or Edward Snowden.[16]

The Air Force should not be expected to forgo its core values to bring in the "best and brightest" hacker stereotypes. However, the age cohort from which we are recruiting the next Air Force cyber operators is being diluted due to cyber-criminal activity. Throughout our research, anecdotal stories persisted of some talented youths being unrecruitable due to crimes they committed under the Computer Fraud and Abuse Act and US Patriot Act or because they could not pass a polygraph test and NSA security screening required to operate on CMF teams. As depicted in figure 8, the correlation of four studies on cyber-criminal prosecutions indicates that the percentage of the populace indicted for criminal activity in cyberspace is highest in those ages that the USAF targets for recruitment. One could argue that by ignoring those with a criminal record, the Air Force would limit itself to a talent pool already sought after by corporations, organized criminal networks, and ad hoc hacker collectives competing for the hearts and minds of talented youth. This notion, however, relies on past paradigms of what it took to be a hacker.

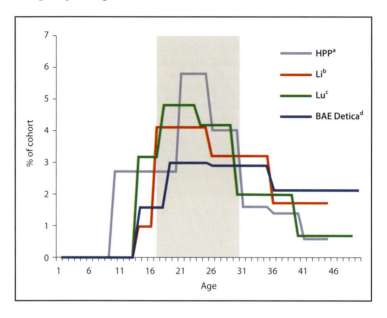

Figure 8. Age groups of cybercrime perpetrators. (Reproduced from United Nations Office on Drugs and Crime [UNODC], "Comprehensive Study on Cybercrime," draft, New York: United Nations, February 2013, 41.)

[a]Raoul Chiesa, Stefania Ducci, and Silvio Ciappi, *Profiling Hackers: The Science of Criminal Profiling as Applied to the World of Hacking* (Boca Raton, FL: CRC Press), 2009.
[b]Xingan Li, "The Criminal Phenomenon on the Internet: Hallmarks of Criminals and Victims Revisited through Typical Cases Prosecuted," *University of Ottawa Law and Technology Journal* 5, nos. 1–2 (2008): 125–40.
[c]ChiChao Lu, WenYuan Jen, Weiping Chang, and Shihchieh Chou, "Cybercrime and Cybercriminals," *Journal of Computers* 1, no. 6 (September 2006): 11–18.
[d]Michael R. McGuire, John Grieve Centre for Policing and Security, London Metropolitan University, *Organised Crime in the Digital Age* (London: BAE Systems Detica), March 2012.

Discussions with the hacker community revealed that two hacker types exist: inquisitive and destructive. Inquisitive hackers knowingly or unknowingly commit computer crimes because they are curious but have no malicious intent. Destructive hackers commit crimes because of their criminal tendencies. Over the past 30 years, inquisitive hackers had no cost-effective way to explore cyberspace other than to hack external systems, thus breaking the law and resulting in prosecution if they were caught. The dominant paradigm of how "harmless computer trespass" crimes are distinguished from computer felonies is obscure and may have resulted in overprosecution.[17]

Today, technology makes this dilemma a null point. One hacker we interviewed noted that—unlike in the past 30 years—inquisitive hackers can develop their own isolated virtual machine infrastructures on a non-network-connected personal computer to tinker with tactics, techniques, and procedures (TTP) without breaking the law. The computing power and random access memory (RAM) required to do so was not available at low cost in the 1980s and 1990s. Now someone can create this infrastructure for the cost of a typical desktop or laptop computer configuration (see inset). Inquisitive hackers with access to malware could set up their own "cyber range" on a single computer by running a virtual machine network allowing them to set up botmaster, victim, and bot propagator computers. This strategy would allow them to understand how to hack in a way that does not break the law. Malware researchers use this technique to reverse-engineer and understand malicious software without affecting the open Internet.[18] The argument that one was being "inquisitive" when conducting an act of cybercrime is no longer as valid as it was in the past. Further, despite media portrayals of government agencies such as the FBI discussing whether or not to loosen restrictions on hiring criminal hackers or drug users if they have special hacking skills, this option is not the wave of the future.[19]

> **The Inquisitive Hacker Requirements to Set Up a Legal Hacking Lab in the Comfort of Your Home**
>
> *Cyber Skills*
> - Sufficient knowledge of Linux to use Kali as the attacking platform; ability to navigate through directories, execute scripts and tools, and write basic bash scripts; a solid understanding of TCP/IP and various network services (DNS, DHCP, etc.)
> - Knowledge of Web programming language (HTML, CSS, etc.)
> - Knowledge of scripting language (Perl, Python, Ruby)
> - Understanding of information security verbiage and concepts
> - Patience and a desire to learn
>
> *Technology*
> - VMware workstation/Fusion installed
> - At least 60 gigabytes free on hard drive
> - Wired network support
> - Universal Serial Bus (USB) 2 or higher support
> - A reasonably sized display

A key finding of this study is that Air Force and government leaders have bought into the stereotype that the kind of people who are good at OCO/DCO are potentially overweight, socially awkward drug users. This perception clashes with the realities of individuals within the hacker community, many of whom are insulted by these stereotypes. We discovered that as senior leaders make statements that include such derogatory stereotypes and thus perpetuate them, talented, fit, and morally upstanding individuals with hacking talent are not motivated to enter the ranks of public service. Although core values are important, one discussant mentioned the noteworthy point that cyber operators are often those who view mission accomplishment as the highest goal. These operators are willing to hack a system to get a job done, believing that doing so—even to their own system—will incur a smaller penalty than failing to complete a project on time. This mind-set, however, flies in the face of current DOD policies. Indeed, anecdotal evidence surfaced during the study that although a cyber operator might have TS/SCI clearances from the Air Force or DOD, these may not transfer to the NSA because of violations of IT policy that amount to office pranks—take for example an Airman who decides to hack into his boss's computer to put a "best boss in the world" logo on his startup screen. This action runs afoul of Air Force policies of unauthorized access and would prevent the Airman from gaining clearance to operate at USCYBERCOM.

One model akin to the DOD in placing strict compliance standards on its IT staff is found in the financial industry, where the costs of inadvertent hacking are high. In that sector, operators are bound to follow security rules because of Securities and Exchange Commission (SEC) and Financial Industry Regulatory Authority regulations and the Gramm-Leach-Bliley Act, among other guidelines. According to SEC commissioner Luis A. Aguilar, such regulations create a climate in which the boards are accountable for cybersecurity and thus must "ensure that management has implemented effective risk management protocols." He adds that "boards of directors are already responsible for overseeing the management of all types of risk, including credit risk, liquidity risk, and operational risk—and there can be little doubt that cyber-risk also must be considered as part of board's overall risk oversight."[20] Therefore, it is essential that cyber operators in the USAF and across government are aware of the zero tolerance of "cyber pranks" and the potential negative effect on their career progression and acceptance to the CMF.

Overall, this study finds that the Air Force should not hire—under any circumstances—anyone who does not adhere to the service's core values. It should not amend its requirements to find suitable candidates for cyber operator roles. Moreover, the Air Force should not put national security missions at risk by actively recruiting from the destructive hacker pool. Instead, it should leverage games and competitions to serve as an outlet for those with inquisitive hacking skills and instill our core values into individuals who aspire to join the ranks of the "good guys" defending the nation in the role or capacity they choose.

Games and Competitions as Recruitment Tools

Games and competitions are another legal outlet that the Air Force and DOD can leverage to attract talent into the workforce. The Air Force Association's (AFA) CyberPatriot—a yearlong national contest that pits the six-member teams against 26 other high schools and 2 middle schools—is one starting point. It is not designed to be an Air Force recruitment tool but an AFA effort to increase awareness of cyberspace. Its goal is to attract students in middle and high school to the cyber domain so that they enroll in STEM degree programs in college. However, as currently structured, CyberPatriot does not fit the bill for providing a legal outlet for hacking skills that OCO/DCO recruits could bring to the cyber fight. One of its operating principles—cyber citizenship—states, "The CyberPatriot competition teaches Internet ethics and safety and defensive activity only. It is not a hacking competition nor does it teach or tolerate hacking or any activity related to the unauthorized entry, use, or modification of a computer, system, or network by a person, persons, or tools."[21] As confirmed in interviews with AFA personnel, this parameter is a result of risk aversion on the part of AFA leadership to avoid the perception of the association sponsoring a hacking competition. Consequently, talented potential recruits for cyber operations may be more attracted to the DEFCON, Black Hat, and CanSecWest hacking conferences where "black hat" and "white hat" hackers converge to share true hacking techniques, not the latest patch-management delivery methods.

Hence, due to the focus on CyberPatriot, the USAF may be missing an entire talent pool that has no incentive to show off its innovative hacking techniques but is inclined to enter the cyber fracas provided by other hacking competitions. This study concludes that the USAF can take one of two actions. One is to encourage the AFA to redirect CyberPatriot's mission to encourage offensive-type activity in the competition. The other is for the USAF to create its own hacking competition modeled after cyber games held at DEFCON or Black Hat and similar competitions that the National Initiative for Cybersecurity Careers and Studies tracks in its Cyber Competition Project.[22]

Another issue with CyberPatriot is that it instills a "defend everything, don't let anything get through" mentality in students. Doing so might be good in a game situation, but it does not accurately reflect a cyber warfare environment. Rather, CyberPatriot should emphasize a mission assurance paradigm in which students understand the importance of key cyber aspects of the specific mission being defended; recognize which functions are essential to assure mission success; prioritize the defense of these cyber-enabled, mission-essential functions; and then perform the appropriate level of defense that the mission requires. If the USAF were informing the competition, points could be awarded for innovative methods in achieving offensive and defensive goals if and only if the behavior occurred within the competition network or the confines of the controlled competition environment. The research team concludes that CyberPatriot and other cyber competitions would be enhanced if this mission assurance instead of a patch-management paradigm were more deeply embedded in the cyber competition scenarios.

Growing the Civilian Workforce

The success of scholarship/internship programs as civilian recruitment tools within the DOD and other government agencies is a useful model for recruiting talented students into the Air Force's civilian workforce, attracting new students and renewing the workforce as people retire. Internships allow for the controlled funding and management of accessions and have been advantageously used in the USAF to gain skilled people.[23] The Pathways Program provides eligible students with paid opportunities to work in and explore federal careers while they are still in school. Another initiative that specifically aims to bolster civilians with STEM degrees is the Science, Mathematics, and Research for Transformation (SMART) scholarship program, part of the National Defense Education Program. SMART participation is limited to US citizens who can obtain and maintain a security clearance; are pursuing undergraduate, master's, and doctoral degrees; and have demonstrated ability and special aptitude for excelling in STEM fields. Upon acceptance into the program, students receive full tuition and education-related fees, a stipend, a health insurance allowance, summer research internships, and other benefits.[24] Upon completion of their studies, graduates are assigned to a DOD laboratory for a period of postgraduation employment service as a DOD civilian, based on how many academic years they received funding from the SMART program.[25] However, although the program concentrates on STEM, it does not stress cyber-specific STEM (fig. 9).

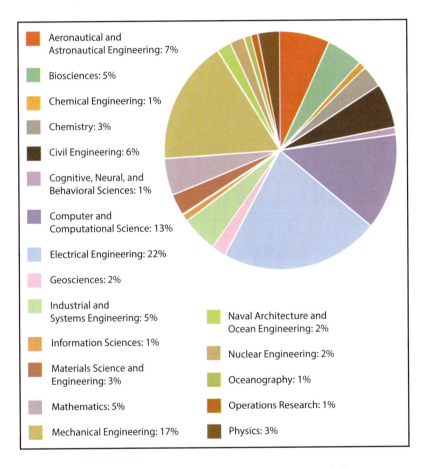

Figure 9. Percentage of SMART funds awarded by discipline. (Reproduced from "SMART Program Stats, 2014 Award Statistics," SMART, http://smart.asee.org/program_stats/2014_award_data.)

Another potential civilian cyber force multiplier is the Cyber ACE (Advanced Course in Engineering) Information Assurance Internship Program, which runs for three months in the summer at the Air

Force Research Laboratory in Rome, New York. As of this writing, however, the program has received no Air Force funding. The program's mission is to develop the next generation of cyber leaders with the attributes of technical excellence, leadership ability, and communication skills.[26] To be eligible for the internship, candidates must be enrolled in an undergraduate course of study, have US citizenship, qualify for a DOD Secret clearance, and have a cumulative grade point average of 3.5 or higher in their academic program. Once accepted, students are given a full-time paid research internship that allows them to hone their technical skills while they work on cutting-edge research. ACE also seeks to develop future cyber leaders for the USAF who understand technology, leadership, and principles of risk management. The program's graduates are shining examples of cyber leaders across the DOD. For instance, the Air Force's 2013 Computer Network Operations Development Program consisted entirely of ACE graduates. The program has also seen its first squadron detachment commander (315th Network Warfare Squadron/Detachment 2) and can claim distinguished graduates in the USAF's Remotely Piloted Aircraft course and the 3d Combat Communications Group / Combat Readiness School. Moreover, huge contingents at Twenty-Fourth Air Force and NSA/USCYBERCOM are ACE graduates. The program could use a million dollars per year of Air Force program objective memorandum (POM) dollars to keep graduating 30–40 students each year—or only $25K–$30K per student (see chap. 7 for more detail on ACE).[27]

One model to ramp up the production of civilians for the cyber workforce is the DHS's CyberCorps Scholarship for Service. The OPM states that this is a "unique program designed to increase and strengthen the cadre of federal information assurance professionals" by offering scholarships that may fund the entire cost of attending a participating university. In addition, the program provides yearly stipends ranging from $20K to $30K for undergraduate through doctoral students. The scholarships are funded through grants awarded by the National Science Foundation.[28]

Although CyberPatriot's goal is to steer students with a STEM background into careers in cybersecurity, it does not foster locating people who have an aptitude for thinking outside the box in cyber operations. This dilemma exists not only in the Air Force but also throughout the government. The USAF needs to collaborate across interagencies on talent pipeline management. The success of scholarship/internship programs as civilian recruitment tools at other agencies/departments portends a useful model for the USAF's civilian workforce.

Retain

Retention of personnel depends on a variety of factors, such as pay, currency training, furloughs, and the ability to attend professional non-DOD conferences. Due to existing budgetary constraints, the Air Force cannot compete with the compensation offered by the commercial and private sectors.[29] However, it does provide individuals with opportunities that are unmatched outside the military. The fact that most individuals in the cyber workforce opt to stay in the military produces a low attrition rate. However, this result cannot be taken as a good-news story since the quality of personnel leaving the service was not quantifiable. Anecdotal evidence indicates that the best and brightest tend to leave the active force. This study also found that retention dynamics are associated with the job satisfaction derived from performing key tasks related to national defense. As long as these operators are not transferred to positions away from national missions, high retention will likely persist. However, because the needs of the Air Force outweigh individual preference, it cannot guarantee cyber operators that they will not be transferred to other positions. When such transfers occur, other incentives should exist to retain these highly skilled operators.

The USAF must be able to manage its personnel. This study found several cases in which contractors had recruited operators directly from the operations floor. Because of Privacy Act restrictions, the research team could not question them personally. However, it learned that these senior noncommissioned officers (NCO) left the Air Force less than 24 months from retirement as a result of being reassigned off the USCYBERCOM ops floor. Consequently, they remained in cyber operations in contractor status, at a higher salary, without having to relocate. Therefore, we recommend that the USAF explore the legalities of including noncompete clauses in contractor agreements so that contractors are prohibited from recruiting or hiring Air Force members more than one year from retirement.

The service needs to provide a career path for cyber operators that offers both the discipline and agility to align their talents for the Air Force's cyber mission. The best retention of cyber operators (17S,

1B4, 3D, and 14N) occurs in operational units while the highest losses come when these personnel are assigned to duties outside an operational unit and must depart the "cyber cockpit." Multiple back-to-back assignments to such units appear likely to reduce attrition. Therefore, there may be a need to manage this group of people like a very specialized corps.

One could argue that cyber operators wanting to specialize sounds exactly like what pilots want to do: fly. However, in cyberspace, this analogy is flawed. Combat-qualified pilots are limited by biology to how many years they can fly with the same efficiency and effectiveness. Flying in high or low g-force environments during training or military operations places the human body under stress that wears down a pilot's ability to fly over time.[30] Even if pilots want to focus on flying for their entire Air Force career, biologically they would not be able to remain mission qualified due to physiological and psychological stressors on the body. In cyberspace, the exact opposite is true because of the interplay among human cognition, digital technology, and the complex sociotechnical interactions required in cyber operations.[31] Experience and hands-on console time increase combat effectiveness in all fields of cyber operations. For example, to recognize anomalous patterns, cyber operators must understand a normal one; that ability can be developed only over time and with more experience. If cyber operators cannot recognize anomalies, their ability to operate effectively will be limited. Hence, developing these individuals with specialized experience in DODIN, DCO, or OCO roles breeds expertise and allows for more real-world efficiency over time.

Stress exists in the human-technology interface of every military mission set. In cyberspace the complex interactions of humans and technology increase cerebral stress on an operator above that experienced in typical military and intelligence applications.[32] Cyberspace is a highly dynamic domain, and decisions must be made on incomplete or deceptive information. Massive data may indicate that an attack is under way or that it may just be an anomaly. By itself, the sheer volume of data overwhelms the limited data-processing capability of the human brain as it tries to sift through both the technical data dumps that may indicate either false positives or complex, multistage attacks.[33] In DCO, intrusion detection systems aid operators in identifying threats by presenting them with data sources such as firewall logs and vulnerability reports. Granted, this complexity has motivated the development of a variety of automated tools to assist operators in identifying cyber threats and vulnerabilities.[18] However, researchers at the AFRL's 711th Human Performance Wing have determined that suspicion of the data may degrade human performance because of the "simultaneous state of cognitive activity, uncertainty, and perceived malintent about underlying information that is being electronically generated, collated, sent, analyzed, or implemented by an external agent."[19] Hence, it is up to an individual operator to trust, suspect, or mistrust the data to provide some response. The ability to make the right decisions in an accurate and timely manner depends on situational awareness derived from experience and mental agility.[36]

As of this writing, Vint Cerf, one of the founding fathers of the TCP/IP protocol that is the backbone of the current Internet is 71 years old. However, with a hands-on keyboard and an agile mind, he continues to contribute to furthering the technical theory and practice in the domain.[37] A pilot simply would not be able to make this contribution by strapping into the cockpit at the age of 71 to demonstrate a new TTP.

Better retention may reduce training demand signal / accessions requirements. However, more data is needed to attempt to quantify this impact.

Regain

Perhaps no task in the cyber realm is as daunting for the USAF as recruiting and retaining the "right people" and ensuring they stay competitive with their peers in other career fields. Over time, the corporate USAF is realizing that maintaining a skilled and technically current cyber workforce in the face of rapidly shifting technology from one paradigm to the next is increasingly difficult. Perhaps a unique aspect of emerging technologies in the cyber realm is that even the poorest adversaries can stay current on the developments because of the ease with which the technology proliferates. This phenomenon could drive a need for the USAF to find a way to allow talented members of the cyber workforce to gain knowledge in ways that it simply can't match.

According to *Federal Computer Week*, USCYBERCOM will look to recruit, and undoubtedly retain, approximately 5,000 new cyber professionals in the near future.[38] Where and how AFPC and core cyber AFSC representatives vector these new personnel for successful career and expertise progression will be a critical piece of the puzzle. Exclusive to the cyber realm is the ever-evolving nature of the technology that actually drives the cyber "battlefield." As such, consideration should be given to allowing officers and enlisted personnel a path to explore the civilian sector so they can gain valuable expertise and human networking links that can be garnered only from the civilian sector. The "off-ramp" from military service may take several forms, each permitting the military to retain personnel while diversifying their experience and expertise. This study focuses on the less traditional ideas for allowing a member to depart and return to service.

One method of achieving this goal would be for the USAF to consider various types of "on- and off-ramps" that give select individuals an opportunity to separate from uniformed service, enter the private sector, and then return at a later date as a uniformed member either via active duty, the Guard, or the Reserve. A similar program announced in May 2014, the Career Intermission Pilot Program (CIPP), will allow members to take a period of time outside the Air Force to pursue personal goals and return at a later date with no adverse effect on their careers.[39] The CIPP could be adapted and expanded to allow cyber warriors to exit the Air Force and obtain degrees or work in the civilian sector, gaining potentially vital experience they can then bring back with them to the service. Presenting skilled individuals with such an accommodation can help solidify the cutting-edge human knowledge that the future cyber force will require to remain relevant as a war-fighting capability.

An added benefit to an adapted CIPP for cyber would be the potential relationships and partnerships that the USAF could gain in the civilian sector. As discovered in interviews with private-sector businesses, some amount of friction has been generated between the military and the civilian cyber sector due to events precipitated by people such as Edward Snowden. An adapted CIPP could help to eliminate such strains and create/rebuild strong ties within the various military and civilian-sector organizations that benefit from this program. Another point to consider is that such a program might also recommend that some of these cyber intermission program participants be pointed in the direction of venture capitalists/startup companies. Many of today's newest technologies existed only in someone's garage 10 years ago.

At face value, the suggestion of on-/off-ramps seems innocuous and a common-sense approach to cyber force management; however, the task of developing and maintaining these programs may not be as simple. The mere suggestion of voluntarily separating and later reacquiring cyber-savvy officers and enlisted personnel is not without difficulty since several pieces of the personnel puzzle will require further inquiry. This brief investigation simply scratches the surface of a potential tool for keeping the right people and, equally important, growing them in the right way. Such an undertaking can be as simple as assuring those individuals who separate that they may return within three years in a seamless way to other, more selective programs. This study also acknowledges a few of the challenges the personnel system will have to overcome. If this path is undertaken, the book may need to be rewritten with regard to what USAF leadership looks at when considering individuals for selection to these special programs and for promotion.

Another such ramp could be similar to Palace Chase and would be contingent on successful employment with cyber companies. Individuals would owe a commitment to the Air Force Reserve (AFR) or Air National Guard (ANG) in the field of cyber and be subject to a nondisclosure agreement with the employing cyber company. One appropriate path involves attaching those members to a predetermined unit based on the location of their civilian employment. Each individual's prescribed service commitment would be designed as the best balance between the interest and goals of the individual and the needs and requirements of the Air Force. As a result, a one-size-fits-all commitment would not be appropriate.

An additional possibility would be something similar to the Air Force Fellows program. In this instance, however, the parameters would differ in that it would essentially put a service member on sabbatical—effectively separated from military—and free to pursue a career with a select company recognized in the cyber industry. At the end of a given period, that individual would be contractually obligated to return to active duty and serve out a minimum, predetermined active duty service commitment (ADSC). Such a program would again require a process to select the appropriate rank and career for individuals to separate and remain competitive when they return. This program would be similar to the CIPP, which allows Airmen to separate and return to active duty with an ADSC but in a different year-group for promotion.[40] Although a basic framework exists for programs such as this one, overcoming internal and external challenges will require some work.

Implementing these ideas will necessitate a change in the general view of a break in service as a negative career move. The message needs to be loud and clear that these members serve a purpose and that the break allows them to return to the force as warriors sharpened by a heightened awareness of the latest cyber trends, technology, and threats. Additionally, the general cyber force needs to understand that these programs are competitive in nature and that selection for such a program highlights the member's future potential in the USAF. Similar to selection for intermediate or senior developmental education in-residence, being chosen for one of these opportunities would highlight an individual for future leadership and advisory roles in the USAF. Subject matter experts must come together to consider these challenges and set a clearly defined way ahead to mitigate and address them.

Offering USAF members the ability to off-ramp from the service and then later on-ramp is a crucial part of maintaining a healthy, relevant cyber force leadership pool. Affording our cyber warriors the chance to become experts—not only through DOD/USAF training but also through direct interaction with industry leaders in cyber and cyber security—would build a robust structure within the crew force and ensure that the USAF stays at the cutting edge of trends and technology. Making these programs work, from the simple (e.g., allowing seamless transitions for voluntary separations and return to active duty) to the more complex (such as a Palace Chase–type or adapted CIPP program), will require thinking outside the box, revisiting old ideas, and inventing new ones.

The Air Force Warrant Officer and Cyber Technology: A Good Fit?

In response to questions regarding force structure, the research team examined whether alternative personnel constructs—including reestablishment of the warrant officer (WO) corps—would enhance cyberspace force recruitment, development, and retention. For reasons described here, the team concluded that these options would not add value within the cyber enterprise.

The genesis of the question of alternative personnel management constructs lies in the need for long-term commitments, the focus to maintain cyber proficiency, and the disruptive effect on this focus that can be generated by the normal Air Force assignment process. As stated above, the study concluded that once cyber proficiency and experience are obtained, skilled practitioners should remain in the field and rise through the ranks into supervision. Over time, this practice will generate a cadre of cyber professionals consisting of midgrade enlisted personnel and junior officers. One proposed solution to the technical expertise / longevity-in-the-job conundrum is reinstatement of the Air Force WO program. Members of both the cyber officer and enlisted corps suggested early in the study that the use of WOs would provide stability in the cyber arena, offer needed continuity of effort/expertise, and bridge the gap between officers and enlisted personnel.

WOs are authorized by 10 *US Code*, section 571, and have two rank tiers.[41] The respective service secretaries may appoint the grade of regular warrant officer, W-1, either by warrant or commission.[42] Any promotions or appointments to the subsequent chief warrant officer grades (W-2 through W-5), called the regular officer grades, must be made by presidential commission.

Historically, the Air Force Warrant Officer Program was a legacy from the Army Air Corps, a holdover rank structure that came with the creation of the Air Force in 1947. Earlier, the Army Warrant Officer Program had an up-and-down existence in the interwar years and was primarily used to reward NCOs for superior performance and as a career advancement tool for those Soldiers too old to be commissioned as lieutenants.[43] The use of WOs grew during World War II as the need for technicians increased exponentially during the conflict. Following the creation of a separate Air Force, they continued to fill jobs in numerous technical fields for the next decade. However, WOs fell into a rank/social/supervisory category in the new Air Force that one author described as being "neither fish nor fowl."[44] With the advent of the "supergrades" of E-8 and E-9 by the Military Pay Act of 1958, 21,000 new enlisted authorizations were added to Air Force rolls—authorizations originally slated for more WOs a few years earlier.[45] In 1959 the Air Force vice-chief of staff, Gen Curtis LeMay, approved a plan to sharply reduce WO ranks but—tellingly— not to completely eliminate them, reasoning that they might be needed in the future.[46] Nevertheless, planners decided that there was no need to retain the WO program, in part because WOs counted against officer end strength and might jeopardize the growth of company grade officer authorizations within the service.[47] In 1980 the last Air Force WO retired from active duty.[48] Even today the Air Force WO program has not been completely eliminated; the CSAF can revive it with the stroke of a pen.

Several practical problems are associated with such a revival. The first concerns economies of scale. Reviving an entire rank structure for just one career field—in this case, those AFSCs related to cyber—would produce a requirement for only a few hundred WOs, given current manning projections for Air Force cyber units. The result would be a "boutique" rank structure that would not attain the respect or understanding that it carried when the warrant system was widely used, as in World War II. Second, the use of WOs actually reduces the compensation the Air Force can pay its personnel. WOs in the grades of W-2 through W-5 are commissioned officers and, in accordance with Title 10, are counted against commissioned officer end strength. The pay for O-1s through O-5s is superior to that for W-1s through W-5s, thus reducing the compensation for Air Force commissioned billets.

Reintroduction of a separate rank structure between enlisted members and officers would entail the creation of accession and promotion boards and an administrative overhead to manage them. Initial training costs, including a WO course similar to the Army's at Fort Rucker, Alabama, would add expense. These expenses would also raise multiple questions concerning WO recruiting, personnel management, and the potential for "green-to-blue" (or vice versa) interservice transfer programs.

The research team found a need for continuity in cyber warfare positions and believes that certain specialized career fields will require a strong emphasis on continuing training/education to maintain currency, but it does not advocate the reestablishment of WOs as the method to achieve these ends. HAF/A2, in conjunction with A1, has already designated the 1N4X1A AFSC to provide for sustained cyber intelligence expertise, and the 1B4 and 17-series career fields can attain the same ends in the cyberspace community. Ensuring that successful careers can be built by cyber operators while they stay in their specialty for a longer time than may be optimum for other fields is crucial. Rather than the reintroduction of WOs to the Air Force, bonuses and other incentives that do not impinge upon either long-term retirement commitments or congressionally mandated commissioned officer end strength seem preferable to addressing retention.

Summary

The rapid pace of technological change is a major concern in training and certifying generic cybersecurity personnel. Air Force requirements for types and numbers of cyber personnel will reflect developments in cyber technology. We recommend that the Air Force continue to use and update cyber tests to screen recruits for their understanding of cyber technology. Further, the service should develop measures to identify people—in and outside the service—with a proclivity toward hacking. For the OCO/DCO mission sets, it is critical to discover individuals who identify with Air Force core values and are innovative, autodidactic team players who can operate outside the bounds of a TTP checklist.

Models that predict cyber success are useful in selecting people for cyber training and could reduce washback/washout rates at the cyber schoolhouse. We strongly recommend that the USAF recruit cyber-educated Airmen. Further, it should offer tuition assistance—especially in CE or EE—to Airmen in the 1B4, 1NX, and 3D specialties to enhance their education in cyber fields. As we argue throughout this study, these fields pertain to the national security mission sets more so than a traditional CS degree.

In our interviews, cyber professionals indicated a strong bias toward the best cyber warrior possessing both a bachelor of science degree in CE or EE and a master of science. Although cyberspace operations are as a trade "technologically heavy," this study determined that it is not enough to have a workforce focused only on the STEM fields. The current nationwide push to increase STEM education is appropriate given the poor ranking of US students in these fields compared to that of their global peers. However, a STEM background is not necessarily indicative of a good cyber operator. Indeed, interviews with several government and nongovernment leaders, as well as discussions with hacker communities, indicate that creative thinking skills differentiate the best from the rest in cyber operations. Therefore, we recommend that a portion of cyber operators continue to be produced from the arts, humanities, and social sciences to assure that cyber professions include a cadre of creative thinkers from what is referred to as STEAM (science, technology, engineering, arts, and mathematics) fields. The cyber field also requires a cadre of lawyers and strategic plans and policy makers with a cyber aptitude to craft and interpret laws and policy. Identifying people from STEAM fields with a proclivity for ethical hacking is a challenge. However, the newly created cyber test being administered to determine the technological aptitude of potential recruits is part of the solution.

To attract the best and brightest cyber talent, senior US Air Force and government leaders should refrain from propagating traditional hacker stereotypes. These portrayals not only clash with the realities of hacker community characteristics but also disincentivize talented individuals from entering public service. In terms of retention, offering duty assignments with interesting challenges is one way to reduce the numbers of people who leave the Air Force for more lucrative careers in the private sector. One policy mechanism that could facilitate a healthy, relevant cyber force and leadership pool involves giving USAF members the ability to off-ramp from the service to go to the private sector and then later on-ramp. This practice could help to build a robust structure in the cyber career fields and ensure that the USAF stays at the cutting edge of technology trends.

Recommendations Summary

- Examine ways to give opportunities to Airmen in other career fields to transfer into 17X/1B4/3D or cyber-related civilian career fields.
- The cyber test could be one way to allow Airmen from other AFSCs who have an interest in cyber or have CS, CE, or EE degrees to demonstrate their aptitude to be cyber warriors.
- The USAF should not put national security missions at risk by actively seeking to recruit from the destructive hacker pool. Instead, it should leverage games and competitions to serve as an outlet for people with inquisitive hacking skills and instill our core values into those who aspire to join the ranks of the "good guys" defending the nation in the role or capacity they choose.
- The USAF should explore the legalities of including noncompete clauses within contractor agreements so contractors are prohibited from recruiting or hiring current USAF employees who are not retiring within one year.
- Recruit cyber-educated Airmen from the 1B4, 1NX, and 3D career fields.
- Offer tuition assistance—especially in CE or EE—to Airmen in the 1B4, 1NX, and 3D specialties to enhance their education in cyber fields.
- Continue to produce a portion of cyber operators from the arts, humanities, and social sciences to assure that cyber professions include a cadre of creative thinkers.

Notes

1. Paulsen et al., "NICE," 0076–79.
2. Thurman, *2013 Millennial Career Survey*, 8.
3. Ibid.
4. USAF Chief Scientist, *Cyber Vision 2025*, 70.
5. Brown and Czerniewicz, "Debunking the 'Digital Native,'" 357–69.
6. AC3/A6C career field managers (Pentagon, Washington, DC), interviews with Panayotis Yannakogeorgos, 7 July 2013.
7. Gregory Manley, "Air Force Cyber Test Development," Cyber Test Working Group (CTWG) Telecon, 9 July 2013.
8. Trippe et al., "Cyber/Information Technology Knowledge Test," 195.
9. Sanders to Geis, e-mail.
10. Broadhurst and Chantler, "Cybercrime Update," 21–56.
11. Stouffer, Falco, and Scarfone, "Industrial Control Systems (ICS) Security," 800–882.
12. Jabbour and Muccio, "On Mission Assurance," 109.
13. McGarry, "New Bonuses."
14. For sources and a more detailed discussion, see chap. 7, "Educating and Training Cyber Forces."
15. Curtis E. LeMay Center, *Volume II, Leadership*, 16.
16. Nurse et al., "Understanding Insider Threat," 214–28.
17. Skibell, "Cybercrime and Misdemeanors," 909.
18. Binsalleeh et al., "Zeus Botnet Crimeware Toolkit," 31–38.
19. Calabresi and Miller, "Up in Smoke."
20. Aguilar, "Boards of Directors."
21. Air Force Association, *CyberPatriot VII: National Youth Cyber Defense Competition Rules and Procedures*, vii. The following rules from the AFA's CyberPatriot rules book are associated with identifying talented patch managers / systems administrators but not cyber operators:

5008. OFFENSIVE ACTIVITY AND TAMPERING PROHIBITED. Participants shall not conduct offensive activity or tampering against other teams, Competitors, the competition system, or non-participants to gain a competitive advantage. Offensive activity includes:

1. Hacking.
2. Interference with another team's ability to compete.
3. Social engineering or posting of false information to platforms including the CyberPatriot Facebook page, Twitter, text, chat, email, etc.
4. Tampering with, copying, or modifying components of competition images, the competition scoring system, or other competition software or hardware.
5. Changing or tampering with system, client, or host timekeeping devices (e.g., clocks).
6. Tampering with or modifying documents belonging to other participants or the CyberPatriot Program Office.

7. Any other activity aimed at manipulating or deceiving other Competitors or the CyberPatriot Program Office, or competition staff (ibid., 38).

22. National Initiative for Cybersecurity Careers and Studies, "Cyber Competitions."

23. Air Staff Civilian Cyber Workforce Development Office members, interview by AFRI research team, Pentagon, Washington, DC, June 2013.

24. "Benefits Summary."

25. "Post-Graduation Employment Placement."

26. Air Force Research Laboratory, *ACE Information Assurance*, pamphlet.

27. Dr. Kamal Jabbour (CYBER ACE program founder), interview by Pano Yannakogeorgos, July 2014.

28. "CyberCorps: Scholarship for Service."

29. In interviews with some private-sector companies, researchers found that salary offers to talented cyber operators were between one and two orders of magnitude higher than the salary structure allowed in DOD regulations.

30. Lurie et al., "Bruxism in Military Pilots," 137–39; Kikukawa, Tachibana, and Yagura, "G-Related Musculoskeletal Spine Symptoms," 269–72; Vanderbeek, "Period Prevalence of Acute Neck Injury," 1176–80; and Hoogerheide, Rempt, and Hoogenboom, "Acquired Myopia in Young Pilots," 209–15.

31. Knott et al., "Human Factors in Cyber Warfare," 399–403.

32. McNeese et al., "Perspectives on the Role of Cognition," 268–71.

33. Biros and Eppich, "Human Element Key to Intrusion Detection."

34. Zhong et al., "Experience in Cyber Analysis," 263–65.

35. Bobko, Barelka, and Hirshfield, "State-Level Suspicion," 500.

36. Dutt, Ahn, and Gonzalez, "Modeling the Security Analyst," 280–92; and Dutt, Ahn, and Gonzalez, "Modeling Detection," 605–18.

37. Burleigh et al., "Delay-Tolerant Networking," 128–36.

38. Corrin, "Is There a Cybersecurity Workforce Crisis?"

39. Svan, "Air Force to Test Sabbatical Program."

40. Losey, "Air Force to Offer 3 Years Off."

41. "Warrant Officers: Grades," 10 *US Code*, sec. 571; see also the Warrant Officer Act of 1954, Public Law 379, H. R. 6374.

42. See "Warrant Officers: Grades," 10 *US Code*, sec. 571, para. (b).

43. For a lively, detailed account of the history of the Air Force WO program, see Grandstaff, "Neither Fish nor Fowl," 40–51. See also Callander, "In-Betweeners."

44. Grandstaff, "Neither Fish nor Fowl." The quotation (and subsequent title of the article) comes from the author's PhD dissertation at the University of Wisconsin–Madison, "A Great Way of Life: Personnel Policy, Professionalism, and the Creation of a Career Enlisted Corps in the United States Air Force," 1992.

45. See the Military Pay Act of 1958, Public Law 85-422, par. (3), amended 37 *USC*, sec. 232 (c), to cap the number of E-8s and E-9s at 2 percent and 1 percent, respectively, of the enlisted force.

46. Grandstaff, *Foundation of the Force*, 41.

47. Ibid., 49.

48. James H. Long was the last active duty WO to retire. See Callander, "In-Betweeners." The last ANG CWO-4, Bobby Barrow, retired and was promoted at retirement to CWO-5 in 1992. West, "Last Known Warrant (Officer) Retires," 16.

Chapter 4

Understanding the Impact of Millennials on the Cyber Workforce

For some readers, suggesting that millennials (Americans born roughly between 1981 and 2000) differ from members of previous generations in ways certain to affect the USAF's ability to recruit, train, educate, and retain Airmen may appear a bold claim.[1] The reality, however, is that a wealth of evidence drawn from more than a decade of interviews, surveys, and other methods of analysis clearly suggests that millennials vary in ways that will require the Air Force to modify how it looks at its human capital.

To gain a perspective of generational influences, we review distinguishing millennial attributes and then discuss the relationship between maturation and generational issues and variances among traditionalists (1925–45), boomers (1946–64), Xers (1965–80), and millennials. Next, we examine how the Air Force can effectively adapt to variations in generational characteristics.[2] Given the distinct challenges the service faces in recruiting high-quality STEAM talent, simply ignoring how the current generation of young Airmen thinks and acts is not an option for the Air Force.[3]

These challenges are not insignificant. For example, in a 2013 survey sponsored by Raytheon, working as a "cybersecurity professional" ranked 12th in popularity among millennial respondents, behind such choices as entertainer, entrepreneur, doctor, journalist, and nurse.[4] Given the limited appeal of the cyber field to the current generation and the pool of qualified 18-to-24-year-old Americans from which the Air Force can draw (estimated at 25 percent of this age group), failing to modify the service's approach to recruiting, training, educating, and retaining young Airmen may jeopardize elements of the Air Force mission.

The news is not all bad. A 2013 survey of more than 9,000 millennials 18–27 years old ranked the Air Force 18th out of the 210 most desirable places to work.[5] When we consider that the four most important "workforce incentives" valued by millennials are interesting work, promotion opportunities, competitive pay, and medical insurance, the Air Force is well positioned to compete effectively in a tight marketplace for cyber talent. However, contrary to popular belief, service leaders should not be willing to adapt and change Air Force values and to attune their hiring to the misperceptions of the characteristics of the current generation.

Who Are the Millennials?

Born between 1981 and 2000, millennials, or "Gen Y" as they are also known, are the first digital natives.[6] While previous generations experienced the fundamental changes brought about by major technological developments, millennials have never known a time without computers and many of the other modern technologies we now take for granted. Together with changing societal norms, demographics, parenting styles, and culture, these advances have influenced millennials in profound ways. In short, their values, beliefs, and expectations are very different from those of previous generations.

Studies of millennial traits use descriptors such as *entitled, optimistic, civic minded, close parental involvement, work-life balance, impatient, multitasking,* and *team oriented*.[7] Of specific importance to the Air Force is that millennials tend to view themselves as citizens of the world to a greater extent than do members of previous generations.[8] The ubiquity and global connectivity of technology have enabled them to build relationships, often through social media, with people having similar interests from around the world. As a result of this dramatic expansion in communication, millennials often think of themselves in global rather than national terms. Since patriotism is one prime motivator in attracting Airmen, this stance may cause concern when it comes to questions of preference of foreign countries on security clearance adjudications required to enter cyber operator career fields.

What may also prove a challenge for the Air Force is the strong aversion of millennials to the notion of "paying dues."[9] Rather, they are acculturated to expect rapid promotion if they have the requisite skills. Given the unwillingness of "helicopter parents" to let their children fail, exercise independence, or suffer from low self-esteem, the character traits described here are not surprising. Thus, when it comes to the workplace, as Bruce Tulgan observes, millennials expect "performance-based compensation, flexible schedules, flexible location, marketable skills, access to decision makers, personal credit for results, a clear area of responsibility, and the chance for creative expression."[10]

The distinctive traits attributed to millennials are not restricted to values and beliefs. An increasing number of scientific studies are examining the impact of technology usage (gaming, Internet, etc.) on the brain and finding that millennials—particularly those frequently engaged with technology—have altered brain wiring and chemistry.[11] Thus, to dismiss the notion that millennials are different is to discard a wealth of social scientific and neurological evidence that suggests otherwise.

Maturational Theory versus Generational Theory

For those who remain skeptical of suggestions that millennials are fundamentally dissimilar to members of previous generations, a brief overview of maturation and generational theories may be useful. In examining the two, we can distinguish between what can be expected of individuals as they move through the natural stages of life (childhood, adolescence, adulthood, marriage, family, etc.) and what is unique from one generation to the next.

Maturational theory examines how individuals change, mature, and develop their values, attitudes, and preferences as a function of age.[12] Examples of such maturational issues are numerous. Young adults, for instance, tend to be more politically liberal than senior citizens.[13] Studies suggest that as Americans age, they tend to become more conservative in their outlook.[14] This shift in political views illustrates a maturational issue. In the workplace, maturational issues play an important role in shaping the behavior of employees. For example, as individuals marry, have children, and purchase a house, they tend to be more interested in workplace stability and are therefore less likely to change employers.[15] These maturational issues are juxtaposed against generational issues.

Just as maturational theory seeks to explain how the values and beliefs of individuals develop during a lifetime, so does generational theory—first developed by German sociologist Karl Manheim—seek to explain how external events and circumstances shape attitudes and values.[16] Defined as a group that shares birth years and significant life events, a generation (age cohort) often has a common set of attitudes or beliefs distinctly different from that of previous or later generations.[17] Shared influential economic, political, social, and technological events—such as the Great Depression, World War II, the Civil Rights

Movement, and the prevalent use of the cell phone—shape generational beliefs and attitudes. Experiencing such events at a formative age (usually as preteens/teens and young adults) particularly affects a cohort's worldview and approach to living within society (cohort effects). As *Managing the Millennials* indicates, "Each age cohort tends to develop its own characteristic patterns of attitudes and expectations about what is and is not possible to achieve in life, about what is good and what is bad, and about whom to trust and what to fear."[18]

Thus, as people grow up and grow old together, all while the surrounding sociological structure around them is changing, interplay occurs between these events and the attitudes and values of those experiencing them.[19] In short, suggesting that as millennials age they will share the same values as their boomer and Xer bosses is only partially correct. Although they will share some characteristics as they build families and careers, millennials will also have values and beliefs distinctly different from those of their predecessors.

Traditionalists, Boomers, and Xers

Before recommendations to effectively recruit, train, retain, and manage millennial Airmen are suggested, the following briefly describes three generations that preceded the millennials. Some of the issues that distinguish one generation from another thus become apparent.

Traditionalists (1900–45)

Born between 1900 and 1945, traditionalists were most influenced by defining events such as the Great Depression, the New Deal, World War II, and the Korean War. Aphorisms like "save for a rainy day" and "waste not want not" aptly apply to this generation. If one characteristic best captures this group's view toward work, it would be loyalty. God-fearing, hard-working, patriotic, conformist, socially and financially conservative, and rigid, traditionalists expected to spend an entire career with the same company, from which they would one day retire and draw a pension.[20]

Baby Boomers (1946–64)

With close to 80 million baby boomers—twice the number of traditionalists—this generation is quite large. Heavily influenced by the Vietnam War; Civil Rights Movement; assassinations of John F. Kennedy, Martin Luther King, and Robert Kennedy; and Watergate, baby boomers grew to be workaholic, idealistic, materialistic, self-focused, and competitive. They, too, sought to spend a career in a single company. However, they were not content to have a secure position but strived to make their way to the top of the corporate ladder.[21] The baby boomer generation dominates the top ranks of politics and business, but this hierarchy will soon change as boomers retire and Xers take their place.

Xers (1965–80)

The smallest group of the four generations, Xers grew to adulthood on the cusp of the greatest technological revolutions (computing, communications, the Internet) in history. Although the millennials have never known a time without cell phones, the Internet, laptops, social media, and Skype, the Xers were still young enough to be comfortable with these technological developments and were often early adopters. Often called the "latchkey kids," Xers have values and beliefs shaped by events such as the AIDS epidemic, *Challenger* space shuttle disaster, fall of the Berlin Wall, Oklahoma City bombing, and Bill Clinton–Monica Lewinsky scandal. This generation is often described as skeptical, self-reliant, cynical, distrustful of authority, resourceful, and entrepreneurial. Unlike millennials, Xers prefer working independently rather than in teams. As Ron Alsop notes, "Xers don't trust institutions and don't expect job security."[22] They were the first generation to watch their parents devote their lives to a company, spending long days away from their families only to get laid off before that dedication reaped a clear reward. Influenced by such experiences, this generation was the first that, on a large scale, desired to create a "work-life balance" wherein total commitment to the job often came second to family concerns.[23]

This deviation from a long-standing cultural norm (devotion to work) is even more deeply ingrained in millennials, who are increasingly seeking ways to make work fit their lifestyle rather than the other way around. For the Air Force, this preference for flexibility and the ability to switch jobs frequently may prove problematic when recruiting, training, retaining, and managing millennials. However, the following strategies can improve the service's success in these areas.

Adapting to Millennials

The weight of evidence suggests that the millennial generation varies from preceding generations in ways that are proving challenging to their boomer and Xer bosses. However, the Air Force has the opportunity to utilize its natural advantages, while also undertaking modest changes in approach, to maximize its use of limited human resources. With that objective in mind, we offer the following recommendations.

Recruiting

According to a KEYGroup survey, health benefits, work-life balance, and promotion opportunities are the top three motivators for millennials when they choose an employer. Surprisingly, salary came in 21st in importance.[24] This news is very good for the Air Force. Although health care has long been a draw for Americans interested in joining the military, its rising cost and recent legislation have significantly increased the desire for medical insurance. With its no-cost and low-cost health care, the Air Force has the opportunity to appeal to a primary desire of millennials when it seeks to recruit them. Given the Air Force's structure, the service also has the opportunity to appeal to millennials' desire for promotion. For the average enlisted member, the chances of being promoted in rank seven or eight times (master sergeant or senior master sergeant) are good. For an officer, an average career may bring four to six promotions in rank. Increased status and responsibility may also accompany higher rank. In short, for millennials, who are impatient for advancement, the chances for promotion in the Air Force are often greater than those in the private sector.[25] The Air Force should highlight both points as it attempts to recruit from a smaller pool of qualified 18-to-24-year-old millennials.

More than any previous generation, millennials view themselves as citizens of the world rather than strictly as Americans. Although this outlook may naturally seem to diminish the sense of patriotism that is a hallmark of recruiting, the quality and number of recruits joining the US military in the post-9/11 era are better than ever.[26] The Air Force can improve its millennial recruiting by appealing to the desire of young Americans to promote peace and security more broadly and to their role in performing that function as an Air Force member. The service should not change its maxims to appeal to millennials, but emphasizing its larger global role will attract a more worldly generation.

Successfully recruiting the best and brightest millennials will depend not only on the Air Force's provision of health care and promotion opportunities but also, to a large extent, on its ability to convince millennials that they will gain useful skills in the service.[27] With millennials coming of age during a decade that saw a recession after 9/11 and the "Great Recession," young people are particularly concerned about finding a job and developing in-demand skills. Given its technical focus, the USAF is particularly well positioned to appeal to this desire. In many respects, the highly skilled jobs that are the hallmark of the Air Force are one of its greatest recruiting tools. This natural advantage is more important now than perhaps at any point in the past. Taken together, the USAF's inherent characteristics give it a significant edge in successfully recruiting millennials. The main challenge will come in effectively crafting its message to highlight those attributes most desirable to this generation. Thus, the unique DOD mission set (Title 10) is attractive to millennials and should be leveraged in recruitment campaigns.

Training

The term "helicopter parent" was created to describe the overinvolved, overprotective parents of millennials. One real result of this parenting style is the raising of *the* generation least experienced with failure. In many respects, the desire to protect millennial children from the realities and disappointments of life has left them ill prepared for adulthood.[28] For the Air Force, this conditioning presents a particular challenge when training Airmen unaccustomed to being told they are wrong or have failed. Whereas previous generations were more likely to accept negative feedback, learn from their mistakes, and adjust their actions to attain success, millennials are much more likely to respond poorly to such feedback, become despondent, and attempt to quit.

Minimizing washout rates and maximizing training throughput will require an adjustment to training techniques from basic military training all the way through advanced skills training. Throughout the literature, several techniques are suggested for improving the quality of training:

- Develop an effective coaching system.
- Give constant feedback.

- Frame discussions of performance to focus on building the required behavior or skill.[29]

This approach may seem antithetical to the demanding and rigorous approach preferred by many Airmen. However, if the objective is to train an operationally effective force, these techniques are useful in accomplishing these objectives.

Retaining

In many respects, the organizational characteristics that lead to success in retention are not significantly different from those for recruiting. Just as the Air Force's opportunity for regular promotion is certain to appeal to impatient millennials as they contemplate joining, so is it certain to be a key factor in their retention.[30] Thus, maximizing the opportunity not only for promotion in rank but also for responsibility and authority is central to creating an environment where millennials see their trajectory as upward.

Perhaps most important to retention is the Air Force's ability to communicate how the work Airmen perform is vital to the larger national security mission. Conveying this message is important because millennials have repeatedly identified the creation of "social capital" as the single most important aspect of work when it comes to determining their preferred employer. In other words, they have a need to feel that their work is more than just a paycheck; it must contribute to the "greater good."[31] Because no previous generation has placed as much importance on this variable, the Air Force may need to emphasize its contribution to the greater good. As an example of this sentiment in action, the current retention rate of Air Force offensive cyber operators (17 series) remains above 95 percent despite private industry's willingness to pay these Airmen two or three times their current salaries.[32] This retention rate is the result of a high sense of mission importance.

Creating and expanding collaborative work environments—a natural strength of the military as a whole—will also aid in improving retention of millennial Airmen. More than any previous generation, millennials have grown to adulthood in an environment where they work collaboratively, both in person and remotely. Fostering a culture of teamwork will appeal to their natural preferences and bind them to fellow Airmen, both of which will help improve retention.[33]

Managing

Effective strategies for managing millennials is a final area that deserves discussion. Indeed, managers from the boomer and Xer generations can become most frustrated with their millennial subordinates. Three recommendations may be particularly helpful.

Given their familial and social experiences growing up, millennials respond best to managers who employ a transformational leadership style.[34] These managers are charismatic, inspirational, and intellectually stimulating, showing individual consideration for their subordinates. This style is opposed to transactional leadership whereby a manager identifies requirements of a subordinate and, in return for accomplishing specified tasks, rewards him or her upon their completion. Although transactional leaders are more acceptable to and preferred by previous generations, such is not the case with millennials. Thus, developing Airmen leaders with the skills to employ a transformational style of leadership will aid the service in maximizing the effective management of Airmen.

Managers will also be called upon to provide much more frequent feedback to millennial Airmen than is currently the norm. Millennials have grown up in an environment where they received constant encouragement and mentoring from their parents and teachers. Consequently, the contents of the annual officer/enlisted performance report is inadequate feedback.[35] Even the standard midterm counseling will be viewed as too little, too late. Rather, feedback through informal means should occur as millennials take on new tasks or complete projects. The combination of regular feedback and mentoring will ensure that millennials understand whether they are meeting expectations and what they can do to improve their performance.

Finally, the impatience of millennials—discussed previously—places an added requirement on managers. Millennials have a strong expectation that they will be provided a clear path to success and promotion.[36] Although many managers may see such assumptions as unreasonable, giving millennials requisites for career advancement and professional success promotes not only the effective management of subordinates but also retention through higher job satisfaction. For the Air Force, both of these outcomes are increasingly important as fiscal constraints place additional responsibilities on every Airman.

Summary

While the above recommendations pertain to more than just the millennial generation, they have been identified as particularly important to a generation that varies significantly from those that came before it. For the Air Force, much of what has been outlined here is designed to aid leaders in the effective recruiting, training, retaining, and managing of millennials. Carrying out these actions is no small task. The need to address issues that arise as one generation interacts with another is nothing new. Effectively adjusting to the beliefs and values of the incoming generation is always important to an organization's success. The same is true of the Air Force as it attempts to build a cyber force unparalleled in its ability to fight and win the nation's wars in cyberspace.

In recruiting and retaining millennials, the Air Force can capitalize on several dynamics. Gaining social capital is important to millennials. The idea that they are doing something for the greater good is a key factor for them in terms of job satisfaction.[37] The mission of the Air Force is ideal for such a mind-set and can be leveraged into its recruitment campaigns. The Air Force must also educate the upwardly mobile-minded about their promotion potential and grow these individuals through mentoring and developmental opportunities. Combined with benefits like comprehensive medical care, the integration of millennial values into leadership and recruitment practices will enhance the Air Force's ability to gain and retain the talent it needs from this cohort and continue to dominate its chosen domains.

RECOMMENDATIONS SUMMARY

- The USAF should highlight its health-care benefits and high promotion potential as it attempts to recruit from a smaller pool of qualified 18-to-24-year-old millennials.
- The USAF can improve its millennial recruiting by appealing to the desire of young Americans to promote peace and security more broadly and their role in performing that function as a USAF member. Given its technical focus, the USAF is particularly well positioned to appeal to this desire.
- In many respects, the highly skilled jobs that are the hallmark of the USAF are one of its greatest recruiting tools. The unique DOD mission set (Title 10) is attractive and should be leveraged in recruitment campaigns.

Notes

1. Lancaster and Stillman, *When Generations Collide*, 13.
2. Ibid.
3. Shulenberger and Olsonbaker, *Solving the Shortage of STEM Personnel*, 9–14. See also Barbie, "Air Force Facing Shortage of Researchers."
4. Raytheon, *Preparing Millennials to Lead in Cyberspace*, 3.
5. Thurman, *Emerging Workforce*, 4.
6. Spiegel, *Gen Y Handbook*, 1.
7. Alsop, *Trophy Kids Grow Up*, 5; and Tapscott, *Grown Up Digital*, 9–38.
8. Spiegel, *Gen Y Handbook*, 1.
9. Borges et al., "Differences in Motives," 570–76.
10. Tulgan, *Not Everyone Gets a Trophy*, 30–32.
11. Green and Bavelier, "Action Video Games Modify Visual Attention," 534–37; Richtel, "Digital Devices Deprive Brain"; and Stafford, "Does the Internet Rewire Your Brain?" See also Doidge, *Brain That Changes Itself*.
12. Espinoza, Ukleja, and Rusch, *Managing the Millennials*, 14–17.
13. Halpin and Agne, *Political Ideology of the Millennial Generation*.
14. "Millennials in Adulthood."
15. Clark, *Life Course Events*, 10–14.
16. Espinoza, Ukleja, and Rusch, *Managing the Millennials*, 15.
17. Codrington, *Generation Theory*, 1–16.
18. Espinoza, Ukleja, and Rusch, *Managing the Millennials*, 17–18.
19. Riley, "Significance of Age in Sociology," 1–14.
20. Lancaster and Stillman, *When Generations Collide*, 18–20.
21. Alsop, *Trophy Kids Grow Up*, 5.
22. Ibid., 6.
23. Lancaster and Stillman, *When Generations Collide*, 24–26.
24. Sujansky and Ferri-Reed, *Keeping the Millennials*, 51.
25. Espinoza, Ukleja, and Rusch, *Managing the Millennials*, 31–46.
26. Lowther, "Post-9/11 American Serviceman," 76–84.
27. Alsop, *Trophy Kids Grow Up*, 33–35.
28. Ibid., 46–73.
29. Sujansky and Ferri-Reed, *Keeping the Millennials*, 103–5.
30. Lancaster and Stillman, *M-Factor*, 164–66.
31. Ibid., 86–87.
32. Air Force Personnel Center analyst, interview by research team, November 2013.
33. Lancaster and Stillman, *M-Factor*, 228.
34. Summers, "Leadership Style Preferences," 34–38.
35. Sujansky and Ferri-Reed, *Keeping the Millennials*, 104–5.
36. Lancaster and Stillman, *M-Factor*, 147–48.
37. Ibid., 86–87.

Chapter 5

Force Development

Distinct from education and training, the development of cyber forces is defined in this study as the assignments and processes by which Airmen in a cyber or cyber-related AFSC career improve their skills over time. The goal of force development, for both officer and enlisted personnel, is to create Airmen who can lead within cyber teams and at the squadron, group, wing, and eventually numbered air force (NAF) or MAJCOM level. This goal is consistent with the CSAF's original tasking of ensuring that our force-development constructs span an Airman's career.[1]

The concept of cyberspace touches a wide variety of career fields, but this study primarily focused on development of the five AFSCs most clearly associated with cyber systems: the officer career fields of 14N, 17D, and 17S and the enlisted career fields of 1N4 and 1B4. The authors acknowledge that these career fields comprise approximately 5 percent of the broader cyber enterprise.[2] We begin by addressing a couple of overall issues that hamper analysis of the cyber force in general. Next we explore force development of the above five AFSCs. We then briefly examine the 3D-series career field and other issues associated with force development.

This study found three key overall challenges in attempting to formalize cyber force development. The first is the issue of cyber hygiene. Although our new accessions were born and raised in the digital age, they do not intrinsically understand how to recognize malware, phishing, or other forms of attacks that can turn into insider threats. Since insider threats are the cause of most breaches of network security, it is imperative that new recruits and accessions be educated to the analysis level of Bloom's taxonomy in the recognition and response to cyber threats.[3] Every Airman must be a cyber defender, able to recognize and respond to cyber threats and to understand the vulnerabilities of cyber.[4] Instruction in cyber hygiene via computer may be fine for annual refresher training but is insufficient for initial security training for Air Force personnel—the opportunities for, and cost of, carelessness are substantial. Awareness of how our evolving cyber requirements fit into each member's day-to-day military life and how the various domains interact will become increasingly important in the coming years. This training requirement applies to Air Force senior leadership as well. As TTPs evolve rapidly in this domain, leaders must stay abreast of these changes to ensure that the Air Force provides its best cyber effects to defend the nation.[5] The avenue of choice, however, for staying current as a leader in this field is growing up in or immersion in it.[6] This study recommends that a short course in cyber hygiene that achieves analysis-level learning objectives in cyber information assurance operations be included as part of all accessions programs (Basic Military Training [BMT], Officer Training School [OTS], US Air Force Academy [USAFA], and Reserve Officer Training Corps [ROTC]) (Office of Primary Responsibility [OPR]: AETC, USAFA, Air Force CIO).

Second, the Air Force has continuous difficulty with both defining the cyber enterprise and determining who is and is not in cyber. Follow-on studies should look closely at the cyber intelligence collection field (1N2) and dive more deeply into the enlisted 3DXX career field set. For reasons described next, much work also needs to be done with regard to developing cyber civilians.

The third major current challenge in cyber force development is that the USAF cannot track its civilians who are part of the cyber domain. This study found that many civilians working national-level cyber problems do not have a cyberspace civilian occupational specialty (COS) identifier.[7] Some civilians were transplanted to cyber units but retained their initial COS, resulting in the AFPC's analysis division being unable to identify civilians presently in cyberspace billets.[8] Further, in tracking civilian cyber operators, virtually all cyberspace duties are placed in a single occupational series (2210) basket, making it currently impossible to parse, analyze, or categorize specific civilian specialties within the Air Force structure.[9]

The DHS is leading a whole-of-government effort to address the categorization problem, but OPM is not scheduled to complete reclassification of the cyber civilian workforce until at least 2018.[10] The eventual goal is to put civilians into seven groups of cyberspace-related duty codes standardized across all government agencies in accordance with the National Initiative for Cybersecurity Education. When fielded, this framework will form the basis for civilian force development.[11] Until then, however, laying out a force development structure for the 2200-series civilian career field would likely be overcome by events prior to its completion. Thus, this study recommends that while the USAF continues to work with the DHS in implementing the NICE framework, it should not undertake wholesale changes to the 2210 COS until the framework is finalized (OPR: HAF/A6S [Cyberspace Strategy and Policy]).

14N Intelligence Officer

The four Air Force AFSCs for the officer intelligence career field are variants of the basic 14N designation. A 14N1 is an entry-level officer not yet considered a subject matter expert in any of the six intelligence disciplines (geospatial intelligence [GEOINT], human intelligence [HUMINT], measurement and signature intelligence [MASINT], open source intelligence [OSINT], signals intelligence [SIGINT], or technical intelligence [TECHINT].[12] However, there is no cyber intelligence officer discipline and no differentiation among these disciplines in the AFSC designation.[13] The remaining three AFSCs include a 14N2, which represents an individual with an "intermediate" level of qualification in at least one of the above six disciplines; a 14N3, a highly qualified individual in at least one of the six disciplines; and a 14N4, the AFSC awarded to those who serve on a MAJCOM or equivalent staff and oversee one or more of these subspecialties.[14] Again, the AFSC does not distinguish among the disciplines that an Airman has mastered.

This study was initially concerned with the lack of tracking of expertise within these six disciplines of the intelligence career field and the inability to deliberately use or develop an Airman's expertise. To address this issue, in 2014 HAF/A2 (Intelligence) used a career path management tool to manually complete the coding of the duty history records of approximately 30,000 Airmen. This tool uses a six-digit identifier that includes in its coding the organizational level, discipline, and duties that the individual performed during each separate work assignment. It can be used for tracking these disciplines as well as several other aspects of an Airman's career. However, at present this study finds that the AFPC is not using this tool and its associated coding in the assignment of Airmen in the intelligence career field.

The research team encountered many members unable to find Air Force–level guidance regarding management of this career field. The AFPC-hosted web page for the 14N career field has the headline "This page is your primary link to personnel actions affecting your career, future opportunities and your personal development within your specialty." Yet this "home" for all personnel management of all four components of the 14N career field is nearly devoid of content.[15] The 14XX Intelligence Officer Assignment Team does maintain a separate website outside the myPers portal (on the Air Force portal) that contains the career-management guide, information on force-management actions, and guidance for intelligence officers in planning their career progression. Anecdotally, however, the research team found that many officers' lack of awareness of the existence of this other site resulted in significant confusion among some 14N officers regarding how their career is being managed. This study concludes that the USAF has failed to properly communicate to the members of the 14N career field the plan for their management. This study recommends building a robust 14XX website for the 14N career field maintained by Headquarters (HQ) AFPC and clearly communicating that website's location to the field (OPR: HAF/A2 and AFPC).[16]

In attempting to clarify how 14N officers are developed, the research team met with AFSPC leadership; the Air Force Intelligence, Surveillance, and Reconnaissance Agency (AFISRA); HAF/A2; HAF/A3 (Operations); and HAF/A6 (Communications). We found career management guidance dispersed across this set of agencies. AFSPC maintains a cyber career-management road map but does not own the cyberspace 14N officer corps. That corps is owned by Twenty-Fifth Air Force (formerly known as AFISRA), which resides with Air Combat Command (ACC).[17] The road map states that this is only "the AFSPC plan for development of intelligence professionals within the Cyberspace domain" and that implementation of this plan "will require close coordination between AFSPC, HAF/A2, AFISRA and Air Combat Command."[18] Before becoming Twenty-Fifth Air Force, AFISRA also compiled products that discuss various aspects of recruiting, retaining, educating, training, and developing our intelligence forces.[19] The totality of these documents suggests that the management of our 14N community, and perhaps the 1N4 cyberspace community, has not been conducted on a corporate basis but at lower levels. The decision to move AFISRA as Twenty-Fifth Air Force under ACC seems to make this management model more complex and provides further justification for moving management of the 14N cyberspace intelligence officers to the USAF corporate level. Although acknowledging that this process is under way, this study recommends that the functional manager for the 14XX career field consolidate all documents and management of the career field at the corporate

USAF level and work with AFPC to publish the appropriate Air Force–level guidance (OPR: HAF/A2, AFPC).

For 14N career fields, current recruiting is for personnel with a STEM background.[20] Nevertheless, only 2.9 percent of 14N officers have a scientific degree relating to cyberspace, and roughly two-thirds have degrees outside the hard sciences.[21]

Initial Air Force training of the 14N career field occurs through the Intelligence Officer Course taught by the 17th Training Wing (TW) at Goodfellow AFB, Texas.[22] The course is a broad overview of the intelligence career field and includes separate blocks that touch on each of the intelligence disciplines and functional competencies. At the expense of this breadth, the syllabus is not particularly deep on any one topic. The cyberspace segment of the course seems remarkably shallow and lasts less than two days.[23] To put this situation in perspective, the 14N training course is taught over a six-month period, for a total of 1,049.5 hours of instruction.[24] By comparison, the air block course of instruction—Air Forces, Surface-to-Air Forces, and Integrated Air Defense Systems (IADS)—lasts four weeks (174 hours of instruction) during the same six-month training program.[25] This study recognizes the need for the Intelligence Officer Course to span the intelligence field and those missions in which the majority of 14Ns will serve, but the limited duration of the cyberspace segment was surprising. Therefore, the team recommends that the intelligence community, including Twenty-Fifth Air Force, reexamine the intelligence training course to determine if recent events in cyberspace warrant adjustment of its content and reallocation of time across the various intelligence disciplines and competencies (OPR: 17th TW, AETC/A3 (Operations), Twenty-Fifth Air Force, HAF/A2).

Each class includes approximately 19 officers, with several classes conducted at one time, and fills only a few cyber positions. Further, no concrete criteria for cyber assignments come out of Goodfellow. The training wing has an assignment-selection process; however, since cyber-related instruction lasts only two days, it is difficult to make an accurate assessment for a cyber assignment in a broad overview course. The process includes test scores, STEM concentrations in undergraduate school, student wishes, and instructor inputs to help determine a student's aptitude for a follow-on cyber assignment.[26]

It might prove useful to work toward training coordination / synchronization from initial school to end assignment. Although many courses are zero-sum options (something goes in / something comes out), given the intelligence community's dependence on cyber, additional cyber instruction time and content should be added to the course. Strengthening cyber instruction for 14Ns calls for more hands-on training, and cyber should play a more significant role in class exercises.

Follow-on training for 14Ns, if any, is determined by their gaining unit or command. It is more likely they will receive on-the-job training (OJT) for their role at that particular unit. If selected for duty in support of USCYBERCOM, officers receive over a year's worth of training before being able to conduct ISR in the cyber domain.[27] For personnel on a national mission team (NMT), both OJT and training last nearly three years before the member is fully mission qualified.[28] At some point later in their careers, 14N officers may attend the Cyber 200 or 300 courses, which have a hacking bent.[29] Since the demand for hacking-capable intelligence analysts is relatively small, only 10 to 20 attend each year.

As stated above, despite HAF/A2 having coded its Airmen using the career-path management tool, neither the MAJOMs nor AFPC yet use it to manage assignments. The 14N officers who spend this extensive period in training do not necessarily receive a special experience identifier and thus may not have their specialized expertise tracked by the corporate USAF process.[30] A subset of these individuals eventually has a personnel record annotation for specialized cyberspace training, and these are the officers selected for the Computer Network Operations Development Program (CNODP). These officers incur a three-year active duty service commitment, but much of this time is spent in training—including a System and Network Interdisciplinary Program, Global Network Exploitation and Vulnerability Analyst Development Program, and Computer Network Exploitation program—followed by OJT.[31] Depending on the student, this program can take between 12 and 18 months to complete, and while training records are annotated with program completion, no special experience identifier is awarded for CNODP completion.[32] Cyber-skilled officers are manually tracked at both Twenty-Fourth and Twenty-Fifth Air Forces. However, the lack of SEIs, combined with a general preference to broaden officers in the 14N career field as they are groomed for future leadership positions, can and does lead to AFPC selecting some officers for only one tour in cyberspace prior to moving them to other intelligence specialties.[33] This assignment process creates a training demand signal of up to two man-years to replace their expertise.[34]

The lengthy training pipeline to acquire specialized cyber skills leads this study to conclude that highly experienced cyberspace 14N officers should be specially managed as a resource. The value of doing so is already mentioned in the AFSPC road map.[35] Acknowledging that changes in this direction are already under way, this study recommends that cyberspace 14Ns be assigned a minimum of two—preferably three—back-to-back cyberspace tours before career broadening into other areas to reduce the training demand and create more highly experienced cyberspace intelligence officers.

The research team acknowledges that HAF/A2 will be tracking these 14Ns via the career path tool, but it finds that AFPC would be the better place for career tracking to occur. That these officers' skill sets are special is already reflected in the fact that a tracking mechanism exists at the NAF and AFSPC levels. However, because the career path tool is not currently in active use at AFPC, this study recommends that these officers be given an SEI that tracks this specialized expertise and makes it easier for the assignment system to manage them as the specialized resource they are (OPR: HAF/A2, Twenty-Fifth Air Force, and AFPC).[36]

Advancement to higher-level 14N AFSCs requires additional education, experience, and training. To receive the intermediate AFSC of 14N2, entry-level officers must complete initial and mission qualification training for at least one ISR functional competency, complete the distributed-learning Intermediate ISR Skills Course (ISR 200), serve for a minimum of 12 months performing intelligence functions, and be recommended by their supervisor. Advancement to the fully qualified AFSC 14N3 requires advanced skills training in their original specialty or qualification in a second ISR specialty, completion of ISR 300, six years of commissioned experience in the intelligence career field, and a recommendation by their supervisor.[37]

Building on existing 14N career field documents, this study proposes formalizing a construct for 14N development for those officers who eventually develop a specialization within the domain of cyberspace, perhaps along the lines of the diagram in figure 10. All such officers would enter the intelligence career field via intelligence officer school. Officers may begin in any of the intelligence specialties after completing their initial training. At some point early in their career—ideally not later than their second assignment—officers receive their first posting to a cyber unit. If this unit is at the national level, then extensive USCYBERCOM qualification training will be necessary; successful completion of that training and the Cyber Intelligence Follow-on Training Unit (CIFTU) course by these officers will earn them the cyberspace SEI. Completion of the CNODP would be highly desired at this time. Due to the rapid evolution of the cyberspace domain, combined with the training requirements to operate in this domain, career management should default to a minimum of two—ideally three—back-to-back tours in cyber-related duty.[38] Officers who eventually serve more than two tours in cyberspace-related operations may command at the team or squadron level since nearly half of the commanders for operations in this domain are expected to come from the intelligence community. Developmental and broadening assignment opportunities for field grade officers will exist with joint force cyber component commanders or on the staffs at the NAF, MAJCOM, joint, HAF, or NSA levels. As was first pointed out in the AFSPC road map, a cyber-centric path to senior command is now possible, with officers potentially commanding at team, squadron, group, and wing levels without the traditional broadening across the field of "INTs" (intelligence) that has historically been the norm within the 14N community.[39] It is important to note that the number of such officers will likely be limited by the few groups and wings available for cyber-centric commanders. Officers who began in cyber and have completed broadening assignments, taken the requisite professional military education (PME) courses, and shown a range of skills may also be asked to serve in senior positions of command or in senior staff positions as colonels.

17 Series—Cyberspace Warfare and Network Operations Officers

The 17-series career field is in flux. As this study began, cyberspace operations officers were classified as 17DXAs and 17DXBs. On 1 November 2014, these two specialties were redesignated as 17S (cyber warfare operations officer) and 17D (network operations officer), respectively.[40]

Personnel holding the 17D AFSC are involved in establishing cyberspace systems, providing information assurance, and defending our fielded infrastructure and mission platforms.[41] The 17D designation is usually reserved for individuals assigned to Air Force wings, groups, or squadrons and are the cyber forces that ensure our operational units' ability to operate both in garrison and in the field. Officers with the 17S AFSC work in cyberspace defense and are active in planning and performing active network defense operations in support of joint, national, and Air Force objectives.⁴² The 17S cyber warfare operations officers support Air Force operations at the network level and are more often based at network or headquarters operations facilities not collocated with our operational flying units.

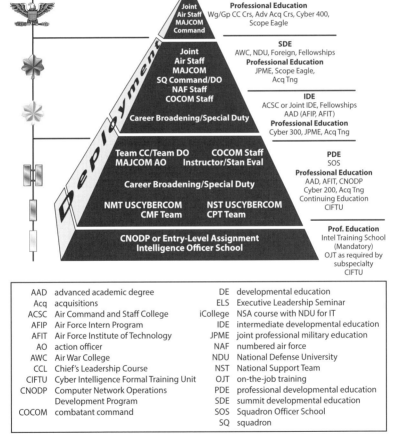

Figure 10. Notional 14N (cyber) career development pyramid

As of 31 March 2014, the 17-series career fields had 2,459 authorizations, of which approximately 2,291 were filled (fig. 11).⁴³ Slightly more than one-fourth of the assignments were in joint positions, with AFSPC and AFISRA accounting for 30 percent of those billets/numbers. The rest of the career field was split proportionally across the MAJCOMs. As of this writing, the designation of AFISRA as Twenty-Fifth Air Force will result in the ACC slice of the pie increasing to approximately 20 percent, leaving AFSPC with just over 20 percent.

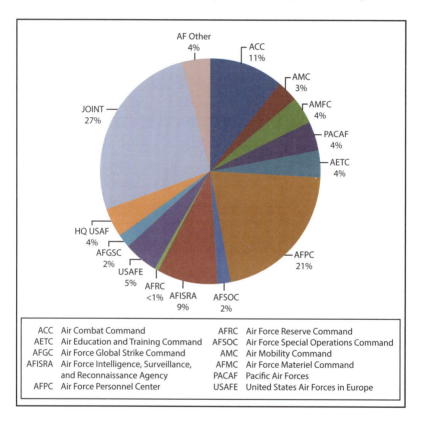

Figure 11. Breakdown of the 17D community as of 31 March 2014. (Reproduced from 17D Officer Assignment Team, Cyberspace Operations "Spread the Word" briefing, 9–11 April 2014, Lt Col Ross Morrell, 17D assignments chief, HAF Personnel Center, to Dr. John P. Geis II, AFRI, e-mail, 22 April 2014.)

USCYBERCOM's current demand signal will require the 17-series career fields to grow by about another 500 personnel before all of the proposed expansion of the national mission sets is complete.[44] The planned final demand calls for 2,943 17-series career officers, requiring an estimated accession of 219 per year to sustain the field at current attrition rates.[45] Yet A3C/A6C (Cyberspace Operations and Warfighting Integration) data suggests that the USAF plans to access only 195 per year, and AFPC's data shows a major shortfall due to a failure to access the proper number of 17Ds from 2010 to 2014 (fig. 12).[46] The result would appear to be the creation of a shortfall that will hit the Air Force in a few years' time. This deficit may be exacerbated by the separation of 136 computer operations professionals under the Enhanced Selective Early Retirement Board process that concluded in late 2014, further reducing our existing force structure.[47]

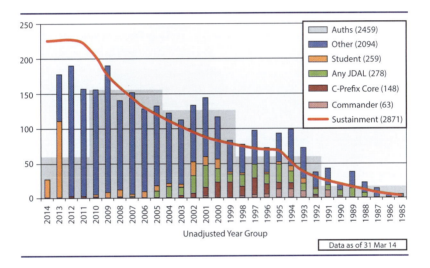

Figure 12. Inventory and sustainment of 17D career field as of 31 March 2014. (Adapted from Stephen Losey, "A Leaner Force: Key Changes Emerge after Tough Year of Airman Cuts," *Air Force Times*, 24 November 2014, http://www.airforcetimes.com/story/military/careers/2014/11/17/air-force-cuts-rank-afsc/19161847.)

This shortfall could come concomitantly with an economic expansion that would increase Air Force attrition. Recent news reports suggest that the corporate sector, both domestically and abroad, is beginning to have faith in the ongoing economic recovery and will soon resume hiring on a large scale.[48] This study finds risk that an improving economy may result in simultaneous increases in attrition and difficulty in accessing officers, particularly through OTS.[49] Combined with the need to grow our force, an economic upswing could create an extended period of personnel shortages in the 17-series career fields. This study recommends that these trends be monitored closely and that the personnel community stand ready on short notice to implement retention and accessions incentives should these trends appear and/or heighten (OPR: A1 with Offices of Collateral Responsibility [OCR] of A3C/A6C, AFSPC, and Twenty-Fourth Air Force).

For officer students, many of whom are fresh from their commissioning source, cyber training for the 17S career field is a lengthy process. Officers in this field establish cyber systems, conduct information assurance, and defend cyber infrastructures and platforms at the operational level.[50] Their training begins with 115 days of instruction (920 academic hours or approximately 24 weeks) at Keesler AFB, Mississippi, in the Undergraduate Cyber Training course. Designed to meet the needs of the Air Force, this two-part course also has a joint bent: the instruction is approximately 40 percent Air Force specific and 60 percent general or joint training. The curriculum teaches the basics of what a cyber force member needs to know; however, more time may be needed to address matters beyond the rudimentary level, especially given the rapid rate of increasing threats to the nation's networks.

Cyber has both art and science aspects. As with other Air Force specialties, the range of aptitudes for cyber-related skills is broad. Some personnel enter the field with little cyber experience, others have taken numerous courses in college, and fewer may have attended cyber camps. Those with education in certain areas—such as EE, CE, and CS—appear to do quite well in their training. The art may come through continual exposure to and practice in the discipline or through some inborn ability or aptitude to navigate the diverse tasks required.

Officers who attended cyber camps or completed multiple cyber-related courses in college have arguably learned the science of cyber. In fact, cyber-camp training relegates much of the basic course training to an elementary level. As is noted in the chapter on cyber education and training, officers who attended programs such as the Advanced Course in Engineering or Cyber Security Boot Camp—a two-month summer program for junior or senior ROTC cadets designed to develop future cybersecurity officers—generally excelled in the Undergraduate Cyber Training (UCT) program.[51] To continue this trend, we recommend fully funding the AFIT/AFRL distinct

ACE programs to produce more of these highly capable cyber officers (see chap. 7). We also recommend that a "cyber College Level Examination Program (CLEP)" exam for UCT be developed for individuals with deeper cyber education or experience. Doing so would create additional on-ramps for individuals to enter the program and potentially help avoid repeated training for officers with technical degrees, such as those in CS, CE, and EE. Those time savings could shorten the pipeline for some individuals, leaving the UCT course for others without the requisite education or experience.

The UCT Phase 1 course provides training to personnel in the 17D/S AFSC (table 3). They are trained under the provisions of the Air Force Security Assistance Program in the knowledge and skills necessary to perform duties across the spectrum of the cyberspace domain. This course presents an introduction to cyberspace domain fundamentals and operations; doctrine and guidance; organizations, roles, and responsibilities; network fundamentals/management; and deployed communications systems.[52]

Table 3. UCT Phase 1

Introduction to cyber operations	Deployed operations
Orientation	Planning military operations
Career forces	Deploying organizations
Cyber organizations and missions	Developing expeditionary concepts for posturing and deploying Air Force capabilities
Domain operations	
Mission assurance	Mobilizing air forces
Continuity of operations	Deploying cyber systems
Enterprise networks	
Transmission systems and frequency spectrum	
Convergent technologies	
Plans and programs	
Information technology systems	
DOD cyber fundamentals	

Table 3 (*continued*)

Network fundamentals	DoD 8570.01M (Information Assurance Workforce Improvement Program) Boot Camp and Certification
Network fundamentals	Security concepts Cryptography and applications Infrastructure security Security in transmission Operational security Certification testing Course graduation and critique

Adapted from 81st TW Plan of Instruction (POI), Undergraduate Cyber Training (Phase 1), E3OQR17D1 0A1A, 22 October 2012.

UCT Phase 2 develops the foundation from Phase 1, building a strong framework of specifics necessary to protect and defend a computer network (table 4). At the end of each block, as with the 1B4X1 training, students have an opportunity to demonstrate what they learned by taking a written test.

Table 4. UCT Phase 2

Cyber surety	Laws and ethics
Sensitive compartmented information facility (SCIF) orientation Information assurance and cyber surety Certification and accreditation Security tools employment Confidentiality, integrity, and authentication Standardization and evaluation	Federal laws governing network monitoring International and operations law Ethics, regulations, and obligations Internet regulatory agencies and coordination
Attacking and exploiting cyber networks	**USAF enterprise operations**
Attacking and exploiting cyber networks	Network defense operations
Telephony networking	**Industrial control systems**
Telephony networks	Industrial control networks
Space and satellite networks	**Battlefield networks**
Satellite and space communications	Integrated air defense networks Combat support (command and control / tactical data link (TDL) networks

Table 4 (continued)

Cyber network threats and defense	Fighting through a cyber attack (capstone)
Cyber network threats and defense	Fight through a cyber attack Course graduation and critique

Adapted from 81st TW POI, Undergraduate Cyber Training (Phase 2), E3OBR17D1 0A1A, 2 October 2012.

Upon graduation from UCT, officers—like 1B4X1s—attend the Intermediate Network Warfare Training (INWT) course at the 39th Information Operations Squadron (IOS) for eight weeks to expand on the basic skills learned at Keesler. In addition, the 39 IOS cyber FTU offers weapons-system-specific initial qualification training (IQT) for two to four weeks, depending on the system training needed. Officer training then continues with mission qualification training at the gaining unit. The entire process for a 17S to become fully mission qualified takes at least 66 weeks.[53]

Some officers with a stronger inclination toward or aptitude for the requisite skills will be directed to the (soon to be) 17S AFSC for cyberspace defense. Those assigned to NMTs complete another 44 weeks of coursework and OJT administered by USCYBERCOM before "flying solo" in their missions.[54]

The research team analyzed accessions of cyberspace officers through OTS during periods of economic growth. In the most robust years, just prior to the recession of 2007, OTS failed to recruit any officers in the highly specialized cyberspace degree programs.[55] The team also found statistically significant and substantively strong negative correlations between OTS recruiting in the cyber-relevant degree fields and economic growth. Due to the need for stable accessions of technically savvy officers in the cyber domain and the stability that ROTC and the USAFA confer in officer accessions, we further recommend that the Air Force plan to access its cyberspace officers entirely through the USAFA and ROTC (OPR: HAF/A1D, AU, USAFA, SAF/FM, AETC).

Cyberspace operations officers cannot be created overnight. Newly accessed second lieutenants begin with UCT, a six-month course in basic cyberspace skills. These officers then proceed to the 39 IOS, where they top off their skills in the INWT course. From there, they enter mission qualification training at their final gaining unit. The 17Ds don't achieve full mission qualification in fewer than 66 weeks from the day they entered the service, and most of them will take longer.[56] Clearly, the lag time is considerable from the moment of recruitment or accessions to full development of a mission-ready cyberspace operator.

For those officers assigned to national cyber mission teams (CMT) (17S), this path is longer still. Added to all the courses above is an extensive in-house training course administered by USCYBERCOM. This course, which has an OJT component, lasts a minimum of 44 weeks and can involve as much as 6 months of additional OJT for operators who are slower to achieve the needed level of proficiency.[57] For these operators, this timeline can stretch to well over two years (fig. 13).[58]

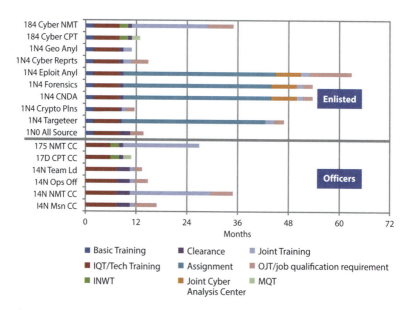

Figure 13. Developmental timeline for some cyberspace specialties. (Provided by Maj Rosaiah D. Manigault, chief of cyberspace ISR operations, AFISRA/A3C, to Dr. John P. Geis II, AFRI, e-mail, 7 March 2014.)

Like their rated flying counterparts, cyberspace operators face serious challenges in remaining operationally current. Cyberspace tools, vulnerabilities, and some of the underlying technologies change rapidly—sometimes at an exponential rate. Cyber operators in the field are then forced to be in training on a recurring basis, sometimes as often as every 90 days.[59] These field units, however, have no manning or budget to conduct this in-house training activity.

Although training frequency varies by unit and mission, the essential point is that—much like flying—cyberspace operations is a field that someone can step away from for only a short period. An operator must continually undergo some level of requalification training to be at the proficiency level needed to work in or supervise a cyberspace operations center.

In terms of force management, this precept is highly analogous to the way pilots, computer systems officers, and other rated operations personnel are managed. If placed in a staff position or taken out of a cockpit for more than about a year, these operators must reenter their field via a transition course that updates them on the weapon system and enables them to regain proficiency in a safe environment where operational missions are not at risk. In essence, it retrains them to the point where they are current and proficient in the weapon system. This study finds that for cyberspace operators who have been away from the mission for staff tours or other duties, a similar retraining concept is required. The team recommends that a formal transition course be established for operators on the national mission or support teams and on the cyber mission, support, or protection teams. This course should be required—similar to the rated force—for those who spend more than 12 but fewer than 48 months away from the operations floor. Beyond a 48-month absence, this study recommends full mission requalification.

From a force development standpoint, a career pyramid highly analogous to the rated career field appears appropriate for the cyberspace operations career field (fig. 14). Eleven percent of this field is currently designated as 17S AFSC positions.[60] These personnel are involved in the NMTs, national support teams, CMTs, cyber support teams, and CPTs. The remaining 89 percent of the officers in the cyberspace operations career field are designated as 17Ds. They maintain day-to-day operations for the squadrons, groups, wings, and higher-level organizations in the Air Force.

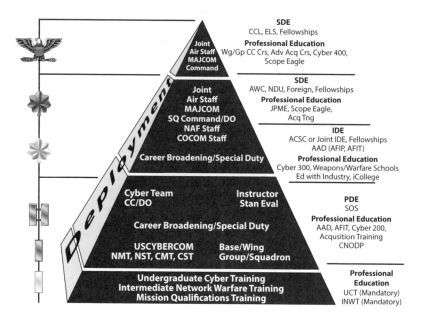

Figure 14. 17D career pyramid

1B4 Enlisted Cyberspace Defensive Operations

The enlisted 1B4X1 career field is the enlisted counterpart to the 17S officer career field. Enlisted cyberspace defensive operators are major components of our cyberspace mission forces, national mission forces, and cyberspace protection teams being built by USCYBERCOM. As such, this career field is critical to the success of USAF cyberspace operations. It is also one in which manning is currently very tight.

At present, the career field is poorly manned. Of the 483 authorizations, only 298 are filled—a rate of 61.7 percent.[61] For this reason, the 1B4 career field is among a small number of enlisted AFSCs that currently receive selective reenlistment bonuses. As of 1 January 2015, the bonus multiplier was 2.0 for zone A, 4.0 for zone B, and 3.0 for zone C, making these bonuses among the most generous in the Air Force.[62]

Retention in the career field is satisfactory. Interviews with commanders suggest a mean retention rate of around 97 percent for enlisted personnel working in the NMTs or at USCYBERCOM. Airmen at these locations and in these missions have a high level of job satisfaction, believe their day-to-day duties are crucial to national security, and appear to have good morale.[63] Headquarters Air Force tracking indicates that overall retention rates for the field range from a high of 93 percent for those in zone E (more than 18 years of service) to a low of 71 percent for those in zone B (6–10 years of service).[64] Retention issues appear to arise at the point where an individual assigned to the national mission receives an assignment either to a support or to an educational institution. At this juncture, anecdotal information suggests that a retention problem may exist. For example, three senior enlisted NCOs with over 18 years of service—less than two years from retirement—gave up their prospective retirement benefits and separated in the past year rather than accept assignment away from the national mission to become instructors at Keesler's cyberspace training unit. A contract firm hired these cyber operators, allowing them to remain in the national capital region.[65]

The career field is undermanned largely due to the rapid growth of its manpower requirements. Significant investment is under way to improve the capacity of the 81 TW to handle additional student throughput.[66] AFSPC committed $800,000 in the FY 2014 budget to build four new facilities for student instruction at the classified level. It allocated an additional $1.5 million for cyberspace range facilities to expand the wing's ability to graduate new cyberspace students, both officer and enlisted, at an accelerated rate.

While these investments will help increase throughput and quality of training, this study revealed that the cyber-range facilities at Keesler and elsewhere in our Air Force are operated and funded on an ad hoc basis, unlike range facilities in the other operational domains. This study recommends that all cyberspace training ranges—including those at Keesler AFB and Hurlburt Field, Florida—be made formal programs embedded within the POM process in the same manner as the training ranges in the air domain. The POM process should be used for maintenance, operations, and upgrade of facilities on a planned rather than an ad hoc basis (OPR: AETC, AFSPC, SAF/Financial Management [FM]).

The development of enlisted cyberspace operators begins after their first assignment. Designation of this field as "retrain only" means that prospective cyberspace defense operators must complete an introductory assignment and then apply for the necessary retraining into the 1B4 career field. Those being retrained often come from one of the 3D (cyberspace systems) career fields, discussed later.[67]

The 1B4X1 students are all retraining NCOs, many of whom come from the 3D cyberspace career fields. As shown in table 5, these 11 diverse cyber support specialties form the core for enlisted cyber support. However, they are in a state of transition.

Table 5. Enlisted cyber support AFSCs

AFSC	Career field description
3D0X1	Knowledge operations*
3D0X2	Cyber systems operations
3D0X3	Cyber surety
3D0X4	Computer systems programs
3D1X1	Client systems
3D1X2	Cyber transport
3D1X3	Radio frequency transport
3D1X4	Spectrum operations
3D1X5	Radar*
3D1X6	Airfield operations*
3D1X7	Cable and antenna systems

Adapted from 81st TW POI, *Undergraduate Cyber Training (Phase 2)*, E3OBR17D1 0A1A, 2 October 2012.
*Source material is in a state of transition at the time of this writing.

As stated, many 3DX Airmen are retraining to fill the 1B4X1 void created by increased emphasis on cyber defense. Currently, the 1B4X1 career field does not admit new recruits—only Airmen transitioning to their second assignment. This practice presents certain advantages, especially considering the duration of the training. These (re)trainees have completed at least one assignment, are familiar with the normal Air Force / military lifestyle, have a basic knowledge gained in BMT, and already understand the basic customs and courtesies. In other words, they have a level of military experience and maturity desired in this career field.

At the time of this writing, the 1B4 course throughput is problematic. The current schedule of four classes yearly with 12 students each is insufficient to meet the Air Force's cyber force requirements, especially as the demand for 1B4s increases for the national mission at USCYBERCOM. Students enter their initial phase of training to become cyber defense operators at Keesler, where they learn the fundamentals and foundations for their cyber mission. This course provides 1B4X1 training for performing their duties to develop, sustain, and enhance network capabilities to defend national interests from attack and to create effects in cyberspace to achieve national objectives.[68] The 12-unit program covers 679 academic hours of instruction over 85 training days (approximately 16 weeks) and is skewed more toward theory and less toward practicum.

Table 6 shows the syllabus for the 12 units of initial cyberspace defense operations training, which begins with an overview of skills needed for cyberspace defense, such as network warfare principles and information assurance. The course progresses through other key elements—including various operating systems, network exploitation, industrial control systems, and cyber threats and defense—culminating with its capstone event of fighting through a cyber attack. At the end of each block, except the capstone block, students are challenged with a written test. In capstone block 12, the cyber attack is their test.

Table 6. 1B4X1 course of instruction for cyberspace defense operations

Block 1: Cyberspace defense overview	Block 2: Laws and ethics
Orientation Cyberspace defense operations career field Cyber 101 Network warfare principles Information assurance Standardization and evaluation program	Federal laws governing network monitoring International and operations law Ethics regulations and obligations
Block 3: Operating systems (OS) and architecture	Block 4: Advanced information technology
Microsoft Windows OS UNIX/LINUX (*NIX) OS Mobile OS and architecture	Networking principles System configurations Traffic analysis

Table 6 (*continued*)

Block 5: AF enterprise structure and defense	Block 6: Attacking and exploiting cyber networks
Air Force enterprise Tools and applications Cyber operations	Network warfare operations Attacking and exploiting cyber networks Wireless communication attack/defense
Block 7: Telephony networking	Block 8: Mobile, space, and satellite networks
Telephony networks	Mobile networks Satellite and space communications
Block 9: Battlefield networks	Block 10: Industrial control systems
Integrated air defense networks Combat support (command and control) / tactical data link (TDL) networks	Industrial control networks
Block 11: Cyber network threats and defense	Block 12: Fighting through a cyber attack (capstone)
Cyber network threats and defense	Fighting through a cyber attack Course feedback and graduation

Reproduced from 81st TW, Tentative POI, Cyber Defense Operations, E3ALR1B431 0A1A, 7 November 2013.

Once students graduate from the Keesler course, they move on to AFSPC's 39 IOS eight-week INWT at Hurlburt. INWT is an advanced course providing IQT to cyber operators. Students at INWT take the basic skills learned in initial cyberspace defense operations training and dive deeper with more hands-on activities—comprising about 40 percent of the course.

Students are taught a variety of skills to build their foundation for network programming and operations. These skills include the following:

- Building a virtual network interacting with firewalls, servers, and routers as well as other networks.
- Handling incidents and conducting forensic analysis.
- Mastering hacking and attacking techniques.
- Working with the various intelligence disciplines that cyber operators are likely to encounter during operations.

- Developing a cyber-operations strategy and mission planning.
- Understanding the responsibilities of the network warfare operations cell.
- Employing offensive cyber operations capabilities against IP and functional networks such as IADS.
- Understanding the chain of command for network defense and the devices used to protect, detect, and defend the network.

The course concludes with a capstone mission evaluation. Students divide into offensive and defensive roles, depending on the mission of their follow-on assignment, and respond to a series of injections to demonstrate their grasp of course objectives (table 7).

Table 7. Intermediate Network Warfare Training

Module 0	Module 1
Core concepts	Hacker techniques, exploits, and incident handling—SANS 504.MIL
Module 2	Module 3
Intel	Planning
Module 4	Module 5
Offensive cyber operations and methodologies	SANS NETWARS
Module 6	Capstone
Defensive cyber operations and methodologies	Exercise

Developed from 39 IOS, Intermediate Network Warfare Training, IOS-INWT 001, PDS CODE 06S, Initial Qualification Training Version 1.2, February 2014.

Upon completion of INWT, 1B4s report to their gaining unit for OJT. For the few students selected for national-level positions on one of the NMTs, the NSA and USCYBERCOM provide about two years of OJT and mission qualification training. 1B4s receive OJT at their gaining unit. If that unit is USCYBERCOM, the training is extensive and can last more than an additional 18 months. Those assigned to other systems can become mission ready in as little as one year from the date they entered training at Keesler (fig. 15). The 1B4 Airmen are certified as 5-level cyberspace defense operations journeymen once they have completed their career development courses (CDC) and OJT training, passed a single scope background investigation (SSBI), and received a Top Secret clearance.

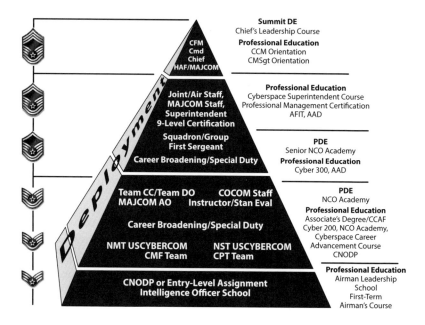

Figure 15. 1B4 enlisted cyberspace defense operations career development

After promotion to staff sergeant, the next step in upgrading one's qualifications begins. Staff sergeants are eligible for the Cyberspace Career Advancement and Cyberspace 200 courses, which educate new staff sergeants so that they may successfully demonstrate mastery of the equipment at their location and lead to a "craftsman" or 7-level certification.[69]

Staff sergeants, as NCOs, develop leadership skills through their positions and assignments. Special duty assignments as an instructor and supervision of more junior Airmen and journeymen in the field are all part of developing the leadership skills necessary to serve at a higher level. Further, at this point, those staff sergeants serving in the field supporting Air Force units will have their final chance to attend the CNODP and gain specific expertise in cyber issues relevant to the NMTs. This training lasts approximately two years and generates less payback at the more senior grades. Personnel interested in pursuing this aspect of cyberspace defense should do so by their 10th year in service or before sewing on technical sergeant.[70]

NCOs should consider which degree to pursue as they continue their education. The Community College of the Air Force (CCAF) offers associate's degrees, and most bases with cyberspace missions have nearby universities that offer bachelor's or higher degrees in the computing sciences. Because these courses of instruction are multi-year and such degrees are not required for leaders at more junior levels, the promotion system for enlisted cyberspace leaders does not consider these education accomplishments until the senior grades.

Technical sergeants have the opportunity to attend the NCO Academy in preparation to lead at higher levels. As enlisted members in this career progress further, leadership opportunities will abound as NMT noncommissioned officer in charge (NCOIC), squadron first sergeant, group first sergeant, and staff positions at the wing, NAF, MAJCOM, and joint command headquarters.

Prior to becoming a senior master sergeant, members of this career field must attend the Cyberspace Superintendent's Course. At this point, enlisted leaders are ready for senior supervisory duties that will enable them to supervise larger-scale cyber operations. Beyond this point, capstone professional development education and selection to chief master sergeant open doors to become wing, NAF, and/or MAJCOM command chief master sergeant. Other senior positions of great importance include functional managers for the career field at the MAJCOM and HAF levels, commandant of the NCO and Senior NCO Academies, and potentially serving as the chief master sergeant of the Air Force.

The research team makes the following observations and recommendations for the 1B4 career field. The team found that the training to be a fully capable cyberspace defense operator at the national level is as long as or longer than that for most aircrew members. Recent implementation of a six-year ADSC for operators who are trained for the national mission is appropriate because it guarantees at least a reasonable payback to the Air Force for time spent in training. The study also found widespread agreement among the operating agencies that advanced degrees in the computer sciences are helpful to achieving success in this field. This study thus recommends that the 1B4 career field be given priority in allocation of tuition assistance and other academic programs in those fiscal years where resources are tight (OPR: A1).

We have also found evidence that retention is correlated with IT business expansion, which in turn is correlated with growth in the US economy. Given that it takes up to three years to create a fully trained cyber defense operator, a system that is reactive to retention trends could result in the creation of "manpower bathtubs" as a result of delayed reactions to attrition that takes years to fill. Therefore, this study recommends that the A1 make deliberate use of the Conference Board Leading Economic Index (often called the index of leading economic indicators) in combination with existing manning and retention statistics to adjust selective reenlistment bonuses and other retention incentives to curb adverse manpower trends before manning reaches crisis levels (OPR: A1).[71]

Enlisted Cyberspace Intelligence Analyst

1NXXX—Highly Specialized Cyberspace Intelligence Analyst

The enlisted intelligence career field 1NXXX is the baseline for all cyber ISR positions within both the national and USCYBERCOM infrastructure. As new cyberspace ISR mission forces were created and the demand for cyberspace ISR analysts increased in the early 2010s, the intelligence field drew upon several AFSCs to fill cyberspace positions. These included the 1N0XX operations intelligence field to fill all-source intelligence analyst positions across the cyber force, the 1N2X1C signals intelligence analysts to bolster cyberspace manpower in the national mission community, and the 1N3XXX cryptologic language analysts who were also used in the national and cyber mission force structures.[72]

With the exception of the 1N3XXXs, the intelligence career field is moving those Airmen trained as highly specialized cyberspace ISR personnel into the newly designated 1N4X1A (fusion analyst / digital network analyst) AFSC. Traditional 1N4X1B fusion analysts (analysis and production) who can move between missions will be designated with the 1N4X1B AFSC. It is the "A" shred, the 1N4X1As, that is of greatest interest to the cyberspace community, and that is the specific career field examined here.[73]

1N4X1A—Highly Specialized Cyberspace Intelligence Analyst

New recruits into the intelligence career field begin their careers at the 3-skill-level in-residence course at Goodfellow AFB.[74] Unlike the

1B4 career field, 1N4X1A is open to direct accessions coming straight from basic training. Combined, the general intelligence (1NX) and 1N431A/B courses total 106 contact days. Completion of these academics results in the award of an apprentice AFSC 1N431A/B. Those who continue along the cyberspace ISR 1N4X1A path attend the Joint Cyber Analysis Course (JCAC) at Corry Station, Florida.[75] The JCAC—120 contact days, or approximately 24 weeks—exposes students to a broader range of experiences and teaches them tools and techniques to overcome adversaries.[76] When all the training time for a new cyberspace ISR recruit is added together—including the eight-and-a-half-week BMT course, the courses at Goodfellow, and JCAC—it is about one year before a new recruit arrives at his/her duty location, where OJT will also be provided (see fig. 16 for the proposed 1N4X1A career pyramid).

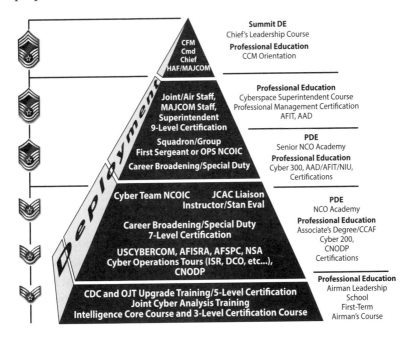

Figure 16. Proposed 1N4X1A fusion analyst / digital network analyst career pyramid.

If the 1N4X1A's initial assignment calls for working on national or cyber mission systems with the NSA or USCYBERCOM, then more robust training is necessary. For individuals in this field whose first assignment is outside the NMTs, this training becomes required upon first assignment to the team. Since this training is tailored to the individual, especially in later phases, it can last up to 18 months.

For promotion to staff sergeant, Airmen must complete the Airman Leadership School. Once promoted, they pursue upgrade to 7-level (craftsman). At this level, assignments generally remain operational as new NCOs increase career proficiency. To this end, the Center for Cyberspace Research offers the Cyberspace 200 course.[77] In addition to Cyberspace 200, staff sergeants should consider additional education via the CCAF (required for senior rater endorsement) or through a separate, accredited academic degree program.

Upon promotion to technical sergeant, craftsman 1N4X1As may broaden their careers into a variety of PME and technical training instructor positions.[78] At this point, attendance at the NCO Academy is mandatory for senior-rater endorsement to be considered for promotion to senior master sergeant.

As the cyberspace intelligence analyst reaches the senior enlisted ranks, additional education and leadership opportunities are available. Educational opportunities include the Cyberspace 300 course and continued work on academic degrees and certifications. Leadership opportunities for master sergeants include NCOIC positions at the squadron level and cyber and national mission force teams. Senior master sergeants may compete for squadron and group NCOIC positions, and the chief master sergeants have wing- and command-level chief positions available. The 9-level (superintendent) development in the career field should be completed at the rank of senior master sergeant. In addition to the operational unit NCOIC positions, senior staff positions at the NAF, MAJCOM, combatant command, and Air Staff are also positions for which senior NCOs may compete.

Enlisted Intelligence Career Field Observations and Findings

This study finds that the intelligence career fields related to the national and cyber mission forces are developing quickly. HAF/A2 has consistently been proactively working issues uncovered by the research team, whether as a result of our discussions or simultaneous discovery of issues by their staff.[79] Over the course of this study, retention bonuses were instituted in fields where cracks in retention appeared, and six-year enlistments were implemented for positions requiring extensive training. In response to discussions on the enormous cost of training an intelligence analyst for cyberspace, career field managers have aligned the 1N4X1A specialty in such a manner that they routinely move from one cyberspace ISR assignment to another, thus minimizing the training bill the Air Force will have to pay to keep these analysts current in their operational field. The only exception to the "cyberspace ISR to cyberspace ISR" assignment rule will be for selected career broadening and instructor opportunities.[80]

13NXXX Cryptologic Language Analysts and Foreign Language Requirements for the Cyber Mission Force

An unanticipated finding during this research project concerned the nature of formal requirements for cyber linguists. The Joint Staff's Human Capital Division (JCS-J1) approved over 300 new DOD linguist billets in support of the cyber mission following workshops with USCYBERCOM in late 2012. Of these billets, 105 were earmarked for the Air Force to support the buildup of its Cyber Mission Force through 2016.[81] The geographic locations mirror those for the SIGINT mission, but the cyber language requirements are separate and distinct from those for SIGINT.

Language Needs for Cyber Operations

Interviews with 1N3XXXs supporting USCYBERCOM on cyberspace ISR teams and their supervisors reveal that language skills are only part of the cryptologic language analyst puzzle.[82] Just as in English, computer coding is not intuitive even if one is fluent in a particular language.[83] Although the Air Force tests cryptologic language analysts to codify listening, reading, and speaking skills, writing skills are less well evaluated. Writing skills in computer code are not tested at all.

Linguists embedded within teams supporting cyberspace ISR missions must not only be fluent in their respective languages but also be able to occasionally draw upon the skills of reading computer code in those languages. Most computer code, even that in a foreign language, will decompile into a machine language that most cyber experts can readily understand. In most cases, the comprehension of machine language instructions is sufficient for the Air Force's cyber defense needs. However, the research team learned of operational instances in which cyber operators encountered computer instructions not in English that required interpretation. Though uncommon, such events suggest that more needs to be done to ensure that our cyber ISR operations locations maintain a readily available cadre of people who not only speak foreign languages but also can program or understand programming that uses these languages. Further, even when the programming itself may decompile into binary or computer code, the documentation and notes in the programming code are usually in the programmer's native tongue.

Based on initial estimates of language needs, the Air Force A2 staff (HAF/A2D) has filled the training pipeline with the needed Airmen.[84] Training of this cohort, however, will take up to two years from accession to first assignment. In the interim, the Air Force's 1N3X0 community must perform both the SIGINT and cyber linguist missions with its available resources. Figure 17 depicts this initial language laydown.

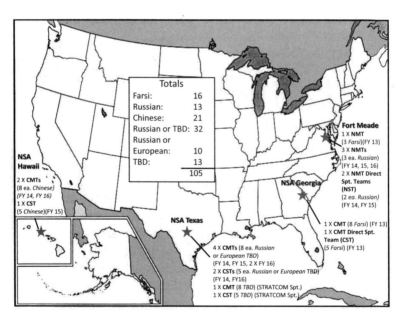

Figure 17. Air Force NMT/combat mission direct support team (CST) language requirements. (Developed from data provided by JCS/J1 [Manpower and Personnel], Pentagon, Washington, DC.)

Cyber events occur everywhere in the world, and the use of local languages and street slang in native dialects in chat rooms and on social media continues to rise.[85] Local patois will be an impediment to quick US analysis and understanding, requiring more language expertise in the future rather than less. Because language is developing into a greater cyber enabler, this study recommends that Air Forces Cyber (AFCYBER) evaluate the various languages in which programming is currently found and establish requirements for programming-proficient linguists. Once these standards are established, this study further recommends conducting an analysis of alternatives to determine whether this need—often episodic—is best met by military, civilian, or contract personnel and whether physical or virtual availability is sufficient.

As AFCYBER conducts this review, the research team noticed that of the existing language requirements, none apply to most of Africa.[86] In fact, the current language plan focuses on just a few languages for the force, to the exclusion of many others. The Air Force plans for nine language shreds as categories for managing its linguists, using a 10th shred for all others, characterized as "low flow" languages. Although French is the principal language used throughout almost all of Africa, it is among the low-flow languages. Such is the case despite the fact that French is an official language in 33 foreign countries—more than any other language except English. It is the sixth most commonly spoken language on the planet—with 292 million speakers—and the third most used language on the Internet.[87] When the research team asked why the Air Force has this management focus, respondents replied that it was because many francophone countries don't have air forces. From this discussion and others, this study finds that although the Air Force has committed to supporting language requirements for the air domain, it has not done so for the cyber domain, which is less defined by nation-states, boundaries, or even the presence or absence of an air force.

Lastly, a consideration for cyber operations entails developing a database of individuals proficient in required languages. Our most recent conflicts have not given the United States the years of warning necessary to fully train cyber linguists. Therefore, AFCYBER should evaluate the utility of establishing an on-call language assistance capability. The Military Personnel Data System (MilPDS) is an often-used resource to locate people with hard-to-find language skills for a variety of customers, but this database is populated only by individuals receiving Foreign Language Proficiency Pay (FLPP). To receive FLPP, an individual first must take the Defense Language Proficiency Test (DLPT), which offers a fairly accurate view of proficiency. But not everyone who has skill in another language chooses to take the test, creating gaps in the Air Force's total language proficiency picture.[88]

Even for those who do take the tests, this study found deficiencies in our linguist testing modality to identify prospective cyberspace linguists. Our current testing for language skills does not address cyber expertise and includes only simple speaking, listening, and reading.[89] This study recommends that the DOD senior language authority initiate planning for a DLPT Writing Test that uses the existing American Council on the Teaching of Foreign Languages (ACTFL) 2012 Writing Proficiency Test as a guide.[90] In addition, this study recommends that a computer coding component be added to this linguistic testing to identify potential cyberspace linguistic analysts.

Upon identification of individuals with these skills, this study recommends establishing a special cyber experience identifier for cyber linguists to enable tracking them in the various personnel databases. In addition, since the ability to read programming language in a foreign tongue is not a skill for which all linguists are suited, this study further recommends that those who develop this skill be managed similarly to their 1N4X1A counterparts, with an emphasis on—but not necessarily exclusive use of—service in cyberspace roles and missions.[91]

The ANG and AFR have a resident language capability—a natural fit for ad hoc and surge support. This study recommends that until the new cyber linguist cohort is fully established, Guard and Reserve assets should be used to address any short-term manning deficits. As the cyber linguist mission matures, Guard and Reserve support in this area may also grow. To fill this role, these components will need to implement tracking procedures for foreign language expertise as indicated above.

Whether a database uses SEIs for military personnel or other identifiers for contract help, this specialized cadre of linguists needs to be tracked and available to all cyber operations everywhere. Thus, this study recommends that a tracking system of this expertise be maintained on all operational cyberspace floors to ensure that, when needed, these experts can be called upon in a short period of time—a condition analogous to quick-reaction alert status. Due to the rapidly changing nature of the cyber domain, the study also recommends that AFCYBER review these language requirements and the tracking mechanism no less frequently than once every two years as part of the formal POM cycle.

Regaining Proficiency through a Cyberspace Transition Course

Cyberspace ISR currency is an ongoing concern across both the 1N4X1A and 1N3XXX career fields. The planned back-to-back cyber ISR assignments process for 1N4X1A Airmen will largely alleviate these concerns but not completely. As with their cyber counterparts, should our Airmen in the cyberspace intelligence specialty leave for a career broadening or training assignment, the Air Force will need a planned approach for these Airmen to regain proficiency in the rapidly moving cyber field as they reenter the specialty. This study recommends establishing a formal transition course, analogous to what is done in the flying career fields, for those enlisted and officer specialties requiring high-end cyber operations. Such a course would be used for those who have left cyberspace operations for more than 12 but fewer than 48 months to reenter the field. For personnel who have left this field for more than four years, retraining may need to be at a more basic level, analogous to the "basic" course used to retrain aviators who have left the cockpit for more than five years. Because cyberspace-specific skills overlap several specialties, this study recommends that HAF/A2 and HAF/A6S examine the prospects of establishing a single cyberspace transition course for everyone returning to the cyberspace field after lengthy periods away or that they work with USCYBERCOM and the associated joint community to create such a course.

Big-Data Analysts

As its capabilities become better known, "big data" will increase in importance to the Air Force and US government in the years ahead. The *Blue Horizons III* study concluded that perhaps over 80 percent of future ISR will be conducted in or through the domain of cyberspace. With over 75 million photos per day shared on Instagram alone, it is now possible to construct near-real-time, three-dimensional walk-throughs of cities and major buildings of interest around the world.[92] The key to making ISR work in and through cyberspace—both to deter new weapons of mass effect and to target adversaries—is the use of big data.[93]

Federal spending on big-data-related services will climb 45 percent in the next three years, rising from $1.55 billion in 2014 to approximately $2.25 billion by 2018.[94] The pattern for DOD spending is likely to be similar. Alex Rossino, an analyst at Deltek, states that "DOD spending on Big Data–related software and services is projected to jump from $670 million in 2013 to $880 million in 2018."[95] As the DOD moves to more automated systems and services, these numbers will likely increase because much of the actual future investment has yet to be captured.

In examining the Air Force cyber force structure and personnel systems, this study finds that despite the expanded role of big data in the Air Force's future, we have no mechanism to identify personnel who have the skills to operate these types of data.[96] The research team believes that this emerging field will require greater emphasis in the future and that the Air Force and DOD will need to be able to recruit, train, and track analysts capable of manipulating big-data sets in the near term. For these reasons, the study recommends that AFCYBER and Twenty-Fifth Air Force collectively and comprehensively examine the needs for big-data analysts, establish formal requirements to address these needs, and then work with A1 to establish a mechanism for the identification and tracking of this specialized expertise within the Air Force personnel system.

3DXXX Career Fields

Several career fields in the realm of what is often called cyberspace support bear mentioning even though they are not usually associated with the national or cyber mission forces that are this study's principal concern. The career progression of these cyberspace support fields is examined next. Some career fields are in flux and will be altered between the time this study is presented and its publication. As of mid-2014, these career fields included the following (table 8):

Table 8. 3DXXX career fields

Career field designation	Career field description
3D0X1	Knowledge operations
3D0X2	Cyber systems operations
3D0X3	Cyber surety
3D0X4	Computer systems programs
3D1X1	Client systems
3D1X2	Cyber transport systems
3D1X3	Radio frequency transmission systems

Table 8 (*continued*)

Career field designation	Career field description
3D1X4	Spectrum operations
3D1X5	Radar
3D1X6	Airfield operations
3D1X7	Cable and antenna systems

This table and subsequent graphs are compiled from research team findings and individual career field education and training plans (CFETP) for the career fields listed. For CFETPs, see the Air Force e-publishing website, http://www.e-publishing.af.mil, and enter "CFETP" in the search engine.

Of note, recent manpower discussions determined that the knowledge operations career field would be split into two pieces, one of which will become a personnel career field. In addition, the radar and airfield operations fields listed above will be moved out of the cyberspace classification and into a more general mission support category.

Developed and managed by a single functional management system within HAF/A6, these 11 enlisted career fields share remarkably parallel career paths (fig. 18). Although the specifics of the technical training required for each specialty are unique, the personnel are managed similarly. With only one exception (spectrum operations), all of these career fields are generally direct entry from BMT. Each has a course of initial instruction taught at Keesler and requires 12 months of OJT and the completion of a set of CDCs and selected specialty courses to be certified as a journeyman, or a 5-level Airman. Each career field recommends Airman Leadership School and a 7-level or craftsman upgrade in the same manner and at the same time, and each has a parallel development through the senior ranks to the level of chief master sergeant. The generic 3DXXX career pyramid captures the commonalities across these 11 specialties (fig. 19).

Initial training across these 11 career fields varies but generally lasts a few months after the completion of basic training. Airmen are then assigned to their first duty stations, typically in a communications squadron supporting a group or wing. Here, new apprentices receive a minimum of 12 months of OJT as they prepare for upgrading to journeyman status. Upon completion of the requisite CDCs, and in some cases additional required courses, the Airman can be certified at the 5-level, or journeyman.

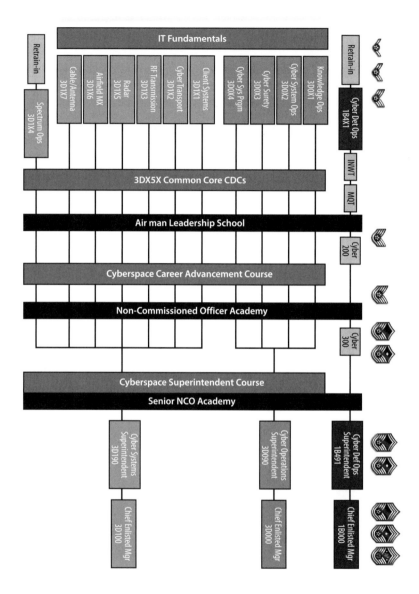

Figure 18. Career development path of 1B4 and 3DX enlisted AFSCs. (Developed by AFRI research team using CFETPs of the individual 3DXXX AFSCs; CMSgt Robert Jackson, USAF 3DXXX career field manager, in discussion with AFRI research team, Air Staff, Pentagon, March–May 2014; and Jackson to Dr. John P. Geis, e-mails, March–May 2014. For CFETPs, see the Air Force e-publishing website, http://www.e-publishing.af.mil, and then enter "CFETP" in the search engine.)

FORCE DEVELOPMENT | 125

Figure 19. Generic career pyramid for 3DXXX career fields. (Developed by the AFRI research team from the synthesis of the CFETPs of the 3DXXX career fields available through USAF e-publishing, http://www.e-publishing.af.mil.)

Before Airmen can be promoted to the first of the NCO grades, they must complete Airman Leadership School, which they may start upon selection to the rank of staff sergeant or after the four-year point of active service.[97] Once Airmen rise to the NCO ranks, the upgrade process to craftsman or 7-level can begin. Again, regardless of which subspecialty the Airman is in, this is the level at which the NCO will supervise journeymen and apprentices as they operate in the field. For 7-levels, career broadening is also a possibility in a variety of positions, including recruiting or formal instructing. Additionally, junior NCOs are encouraged to complete CCAF associate's degrees, which are desired at the rank of technical sergeant and are a prerequisite for senior rater endorsement for promotion consideration to senior master sergeant. Academic degree programs, including those leading to advanced degrees, are also offered through AFIT and a variety of universities with local and on-base programs open to military personnel. In many of the subfields, pertinent certifications can be earned through a combination of education, experience, and the passing of professional examinations. Airmen are encouraged to pursue these certifications in addition to academic degrees.

As technical sergeants, Airmen train for more senior leadership positions by attending the NCO Academy. Attendance is prerequisite to sewing on the rank of master sergeant—normally around the 15-year point in service (although very rarely occurring as early as the 8-year point). By this stage, senior NCOs are ready for leadership positions on various staffs or as a squadron first sergeant. Master sergeants must attend the Senior NCO Academy prior to promotion to senior master sergeant.

Upon promotion to senior master sergeant, 9-level superintendent upgrade training begins. Senior master sergeants are placed in senior NCOIC or leadership positions on wing, NAF, MAJCOM, or joint staffs. Upon the individual's promotion to chief master sergeant and completion of requisite capstone education requirements, potential assignments include functional manager on the Air Staff and command chief master sergeant at the wing, NAF, or MAJCOM level. With only minor variation among the subspecialties, promotion to chief master sergeant averages between the 22- and 23-year point of an Airman's career.

Summary

This discussion addressed the development of the USAF force structure for cyberspace career fields—specifically the 14- and 17-series officer career fields; the 1B4, 1N4, and 3D enlisted career fields; and the civilian 2210 IT management series. The detailed analysis of the cyber force education and training structure is of most interest to individuals involved in personnel management. To that end, we have included minor modifications to career developmental pyramids and changes within the developmental processes of specific AFSCs.

However, from our examination, this study makes several recommendations applicable more broadly than just to the personnel management community:

- The Air Force should create and implement a cyber hygiene developmental program for new accessions before they touch an Air Force cyber system. All new accessions—whether officer, enlisted, or civilian—must achieve an analysis level of understanding of potential cyber threats to their information systems prior to becoming authorized users on Air Force networks.

- The service should conduct a full curriculum reevaluation of the Intelligence Officer Course at Goodfellow AFB for the purpose of increasing the concentration in cyberspace systems for 14-series initial development.

- Because experienced cyberspace operators are a long time in the making (three years in some cases) and because we can show a strong correlation between a strong US economy and cyberspace retention problems, this study recommends that HAF/A1 initiate cyberspace retention incentives using a proactive or predictive construct such as the index of leading economic indicators rather than waiting for cyberspace attrition issues to emerge.

- The Air Force senior language authority should devise and implement specific language standards and testing for cyberspace linguistic needs. At minimum, such tests should include reading, speaking, listening, writing, and computer coding in the foreign language.

- This study finds that despite the emergence of big data / big-data analytics as a major frontier in business and industry, the Air Force is unable to locate individuals who have these skill sets. AFPC should devise and implement a mechanism for tracking and managing the careers of personnel who have this rare and critical emerging skill set.

- The Air Force should conduct a wholesale overhaul of how it tracks and hires civilians in the cyberspace arena. Presently, Air Force cyber civilians—from data entry operators to keyboard repair technicians to network administrators—are tracked under the 2210 civilian occupational series. This study recommends that the Air Force adopt and implement the DHS classification framework embedded in the National Initiative for Cyberspace Education to categorize and track civilian cyberspace specialization skills.

The following chart summarizes all recommendations from this chapter:

FORCE DEVELOPMENT

RECOMMENDATIONS SUMMARY

- Include a short course in cyber hygiene that achieves analysis-level learning objectives in cyber information assurance operations as part of all accessions programs: BMT, OTS, USAFA, and ROTC.
- Follow-on studies should look closely at the cyber intelligence collection field (1N2) and examine the enlisted 3DXX career field set more thoroughly.
- Although the USAF should continue to work with the DHS in implementing the NICE framework, it should not undertake wholesale changes to the 2210 civilian occupational specialty until the framework is finalized. The OPM will not complete reclassification of the cyber civilian workforce until at least 2018.
- Build a robust 14XX website for the 14N career field, maintained by HQ AFPC, and clearly communicate that website's location to the field.
- The functional manager for the 14XX career field should consolidate all documents and management of the career field at the corporate USAF level and work with AFPC to publish the appropriate USAF-level guidance.
- The intelligence community, including Twenty-Fifth Air Force, should reexamine the Intelligence Officer Course to determine if recent events in cyberspace warrant adjustment of course content and reallocation of time across the various intelligence disciplines and competencies.
- Cyberspace 14Ns should be assigned a minimum of two—preferably three—back-to-back cyberspace tours before career broadening into other areas to reduce the training demand and create more highly experienced cyberspace intelligence officers.
- Because the career-path tool is not currently in active use at AFPC, give 14Ns an SEI that tracks their specialized expertise and makes it easier for the assignment system to manage them as the specialized resource they are.
- Economic trends should be monitored closely, and the personnel community should stand ready on short notice to implement retention and accessions incentives should these trends appear and/or grow worse.
- Develop a cyber-CLEP exam for UCT for personnel with deeper cyber education or experience. This test would create additional on-ramps for individuals to enter the program and potentially help avoid repeated training for officers with technical degrees, such as CS, CE, and EE. Those time savings could shorten the pipeline for some, leaving the UCT course for others without the requisite education or experience.
- Due to the need for stable accessions of technically savvy officers in the cyber domain and the stability that ROTC and the USAFA confer on officer accessions, we recommend that for the time frame of this study the Air Force plan to access all of its cyberspace officers entirely through the USAFA and ROTC.
- The DOD senior language authority should initiate planning for a DLPT writing test using the existing ACTFL 2012 Writing Proficiency Test as a guide.

RECOMMENDATIONS SUMMARY *(continued)*

- Establish a formal transition course for operators on the NMTs, national support teams, CMTs, cyber support teams, and CPTs. This course should be critical, as is true in the rated force, for those who spend more than 12 months but fewer than 48 months away from the operations floor. Beyond a 48-month absence, this study recommends attainment of full mission requalification.
- Make all cyberspace training ranges (including those at Keesler AFB and Hurlburt Field) formal programs embedded within the POM process in the same manner as the training ranges in the air domain. The POM process should be used for maintenance, operations, and upgrade of the facilities on a planned rather than ad hoc basis.
- Prioritize the 1B4 career field for allocation of tuition assistance and other academic programs in those fiscal years when resources are tight.
- The A1 should make deliberate use of the Conference Board's Leading Economic Index (often called the index of leading economic indicators) in combination with existing manning and retention statistics to adjust selective reenlistment bonuses and other retention incentives to curb adverse manpower trends before manning reaches crisis levels.
- Because language is developing into a greater cyber enabler, AFCYBER should evaluate the various languages in which programming is currently found and establish the requirements for programming-proficient linguists. Once these requirements are established, it should conduct an analysis of alternatives to determine whether this need—often episodic—is best met by military, civilian, or contract personnel and whether physical or virtual availability is sufficient.
- Add a computer coding component to this linguistic testing to identify potential cyberspace linguistic analysts. Once individuals with these skills are identified, establish a special cyber experience identifier for cyber linguists to enable tracking them in the various personnel databases.
- Since the ability to read programming language in a foreign tongue is not a skill for which all linguists are suited, manage those who develop this skill similarly to their 1N4X1A counterparts, with an emphasis on—but not necessarily exclusive use of—service in cyberspace roles and missions.
- Until the new cyber linguist cohort is fully established, use Guard and Reserve assets to address any short-term manning shortfalls. As the cyber linguist mission matures, Guard and Reserve support in this area may also grow. To fill this role, these components will need to implement tracking procedures for foreign language expertise as indicated above.
- Maintain a tracking system of this expertise on all operational cyberspace floors to ensure that, when needed, these experts can be called upon in a short period of time—a condition analogous to quick-reaction alert status.
- Due to the rapidly changing nature of the cyber domain, AFCYBER should review these language requirements and their tracking mechanism no less than once every two years as part of the formal POM cycle.

> **RECOMMENDATIONS SUMMARY** (continued)
> - Because cyberspace-specific skills overlap several specialties, examine the prospects of establishing a single cyberspace transition course for all personnel returning to the cyberspace field after lengthy periods away or working with USCYBERCOM and the associated joint community to create such a course.
> - AFCYBER and Twenty-Fifth Air Force should collectively and comprehensively examine the needs for big-data analysts, establish formal requirements to address these needs, and then work with A1 to create a mechanism for the identification and tracking of this specialized expertise within the Air Force personnel system.

Notes

1. HAF/CK (CSAF Strategic Studies Group), on behalf of CSAF, to AFRI/CL (director), memorandum; and discussion between research team and Gen Mark Welsh at AFRI, 2 April 2014.

2. Welsh, discussion. General Welsh asked the AFRI research team to initially conduct research for the national mission teams (NMT), the near-term challenge the Air Force now faces. The CSAF and researchers acknowledge that similar follow-on work must be extended to the rest of the cyber career field.

3. Bloom and Krathwohl, *Taxonomy of Educational Objectives*, 15.

4. SAF/Public Affairs, "Rise of the Cyber Wingman."

5. Currie et al., *Air Force Leadership Study*, 25.

6. Lt Gen Harry D. Raduege, Jr., USAF, retired, interview with AFRI research team, Washington, DC, January 2014. General Raduege is the former director, Defense Information Systems Agency; former commander, Joint Task Force Global Network Operations; and former deputy commander, Global Network Operations and Defense, US Strategic Command Joint Forces Headquarters–Information Operations.

7. Mr. Jason May (HAF/A3C/A6C), interview by John Geis and Pano Yannakogeorgos regarding HAF A3/6 management of civilians, 14 January 2014.

8. Maj Derek Tharaldson (AFPC Analysis Branch chief, AFPC/DSYA), interview with research team, Randolph AFB, Texas, 6 March 2014.

9. OPM, *Handbook of Occupational Groups and Families*, 120–21.

10. NICE, "National Cybersecurity Workforce Framework"; and Mr. Robin Williams (DHS), interview by the research team on the implementation of the NICE framework, 16 July 2014.

11. Led by the DHS, NICE is an outgrowth of the Comprehensive National Cybersecurity Initiative (CNCI) launched by President George W. Bush in National Security Presidential Directive (NSPD) 54 and Homeland Security Presidential Directive (HSPD) 23. This initiative was continued following President Obama's Cyberspace Policy Review, part of which is now NICE. See the CNCI at https://www.whitehouse.gov/issues/foreign-policy/cybersecurity/national-initiative. The seven categories of civilian cybersecurity fields are laid out in NICE, "National Cybersecurity Workforce Framework," 1–3.

12. Department of the Air Force (DAF), *AFSC 14NX Career Field Education and Training Plan* [*CFETP*], 12–13.

13. The enlisted subspecialty 1N4X1A was created in 2014 to address this problem. See ibid. for a better understanding of the reasons the intelligence disciplines are not differentiated in the 14N AFSC.

14. HQ AFPC/Directorate of Personnel Services (DPSIC), *Air Force Officer Classification Directory*, 79–82; and DAF, *AFSC 14NX CFETP*, 22. According to the *Air Force Officer Classification Directory*, once individuals complete staff position assignments, they revert to a 14N2 or 14N3, depending on their previous status.

15. See "14XX Intelligence." By comparison, see for example the 11XX or 12XX career field websites; they contain "Spread the Word" briefings on career force structure, information on force-shaping effects on specific career fields, and complete career field development plans and other associated information.

16. If the 14N community finds value in placing its personnel website outside the MyPers portal, then this study recommends that a link to this site be maintained as a permanent feature of the 14NX page on the portal.

17. AFSPC, "Force Development Roadmap." Note that AFISRA and its associated 14N career force, as Twenty-Fifth Air Force, became part of ACC in early FY 2015.

18. Ibid., 1.

19. Ibid.; and Cook, briefing, subject: Cyber ISR Workforce Development.

20. Cook, briefing, subject: Cyber ISR Workforce Development.

21. Analysis of the AFPC database on officers accessed into the 14N career field from 1995 to 2014 conducted by research team. Embedded in these data is the fact that 74 percent of newly accessed 14Ns come from ROTC, where, theoretically, some direction of student courses of study is possible. Only 11 percent of 14Ns come from OTS, where the degree is in hand prior to accession.

22. 17 TW, Intelligence Officer Course Syllabus, 3 December 2012 (FOUO; information used is unclassified).

23. John Conway, AFRI research team, observations on-site as the cyber segment was taught to a group of students he shadowed, February 2014; and 17 TW, 14N Course Chart/Schedule, 9 September 2013 (FOUO; information used is unclassified).

24. 14N Course Chart/Schedule, 9 September 2013.

25. Ibid.

26. 17 TRG/CC, memorandum.

27. Maj Aaron Cooper (14N assignment team leader), interview by AFRI researchers, 21 November 2013; and Cook, briefing, subject: Cyberspace Workforce Development.

28. Cook, briefing, subject: Cyberspace Workforce Development.

29. The Cyber 200 and 300 courses are discussed more fully in the education portion of this study.

30. SEIs are awarded only if an officer attends the Intelligence Field Training Unit course and spends a minimum of one year on the floor of an operational cyberspace unit. Many people who spend a year in a cyberspace tour do not attend the CIFTU course and, as such, do not receive the cyberspace SEI.

31. DAF, *AFSC 14NX CFETP*, 36. See also "Information Assurance (IA) Development Programs."

32. USCYBERCOM personnel, interviews by AFRI research team, NSA, Fort Meade, MD, February 2014.

33. AFSPC, "Force Development Roadmap," 6; and DAF, *AFSC 14NX CFETP*, 31. The CFETP goes to great lengths to describe the history between the generalist and specialist debate, falling on the side of generalists who "were now on a 'level playing field' and were expected to be leaders, not specialists" (par. 8.4.3).

34. The combined time to attend Intelligence Officer School, the CIFTU course, INWT, and the top-off training at USCYBERCOM can total over two years. To help alleviate this issue, HAF/A2 is now actively working with the various cyber entities (notably AFSPC, Twenty-Fourth Air Force, etc.) to identify 14Ns they want to remain in the cyber realm of operations. AFPC has begun an active process in which 14Ns interested in returning to or remaining in the cyber operations community will work with their commands and gain special tracking in the career path management tool at HAF/A2. HAF/A2 will then work with the units and 14Ns to obtain a cycle whereby the 14Ns will return to cyber for every other assignment. Some of these assignments will take effect in fall 2014, but the first significant effect will be seen during the major move cycle of summer 2015.

35. AFSPC, "Force Development Roadmap," 6–8.

36. This identifier is granted to a 14N-qualified officer who attends an intelligence FTU course specific to cyberspace and then spends 12 months in cyberspace operations. If both of these criteria are met, the 14N officer is credited with the equivalent of having attended UCT. This marker is tracked in the field and not by AFSPC. AFSPC/A3 (Operations) staff, interviews with research team, Headquarters AFSPC, 7 May 2013; and HAF/A3C/A6C staff, Headquarters AFSPC, 13 April 2014.

37. DAF, *AFSC 14NX CFETP*, 21. Personnel can take ISR 300 either via distance learning or in residence (ibid.).

38. Several senior leaders have recommended a minimum of three tours as a result of the intense training demand signal and the institution of cyberspace gate months analogous to flight gate months to maintain expertise and currency in this domain (e.g., Maj Gen Suzanne Vautrinot, USAF, retired, interview by research team, LeMay Center, Maxwell AFB, AL, 24 April 2014).

39. The generalization of the 14N community is an evolution approximately 20 years old. Prior to the mid-1990s, intelligence officers were often developed inside the stovepipes of the separate intelligence disciplines.

40. Bailey, presentation.

41. Ibid.

42. HQ AFPC/DPSIC, *Officer Classification Directory*, 80–82.

43. 17D Officer Assignment Team, Cyberspace Operations "Spread the Word" briefing, slide 9.

44. HAF/A3C/A6C, "Career Field Snapshot."

45. Ibid. The planned accessions of 195 are slightly below this estimate. However, the presentation later talks of future sustainment issues because of a failure to recruit sufficient numbers from 2005 to 2009.

46. 17D Officer Assignment Team, Cyberspace Operations "Spread the Word" briefing, slide 10.

47. Losey, "Leaner Force."

48. StreetAuthority, "Economy Is Finally Approaching Lift-Off." The research team believes that this growth outlook may be uneven in places where the economy is highly dependent on oil revenues in the near term.

49. CareerBuilder's annual hiring forecast for 2015 is the best in nine years, with corporate hiring returning to levels not seen since the onset of the Great Recession in 2007. See CareerBuilder, "2015 U.S. Job Forecast." While other sources suggest that economic problem spots still lie ahead, eventually hiring will increase, whether in 2015 or later. When it does, these issues will appear.

50. HQ AFPC/DPSIC, *Officer Classification Directory*, 80–82.

51. AFIT Graduate School for Engineering and Management, Advanced Cyber Education, "Course Information." The program seeks candidates studying EE, CE, CS, or information operations as well as students with experience in programming, networking, and operating systems. The website states that "ACE teaches the cadets cyber-security principles through intense coursework and internship experiences completed at the Air Force Institute of Technology (AFIT), Air Force Research Laboratory (AFRL), Human Performance Wing and other base organizations throughout their eight-week program. ACE helps students understand why cyberspace is a unique warfighting domain and develops an appreciation for why cyber dominance is a prerequisite for superiority in Land, Sea, Air, Space and now Cyberspace."

52. 81 TW Plan of Instruction, Undergraduate Cyber Training (Phase 1).

53. HQ AFSPC/A3, briefing: subject: AFRI Cyberspace Development Questions, slide 6. See also Vautrinot, briefing, subject: AFCYBER.

54. USCYBERCOM officials, research team interview during site visit, Peterson AFB, CO, 28 January 2014.

55. Analysis of the OTS accessions data sets, 2004–7. The correlation between economic growth and an inability to recruit officers with technical degrees is both substantively massive and statistically highly significant. OTS is an extremely unreliable source of technical expertise. Although a full statistical analysis was not done on other career fields, anecdotally the data appears to show the same dynamic across all disciplines of the hard sciences.

56. HQ AFSPC/A3, briefing, subject: AFRI Cyberspace Development Questions, slide 6; and Vautrinot, briefing, subject: AFCYBER, slides 26–29.

57. USCYBERCOM officials, interview.

58. HQ AFSPC/A3, briefing, subject: AFRI Cyberspace Development Questions, slide 6.

59. Col Dean Clothier (vice-commander, 67th Cyberspace Wing), interview by research team, Lackland AFB, TX, 6 March 14.

60. The focus of this study is on the expansion of the national mission force, which is predominately the 17S field as redesignated in November 2014. The career pyramid presented here is not exclusive of the 17Ds, and, in fact, this study recommends some crossflow between 17S and 17D personnel. Experience in cyber warfare provides an enhanced perspective on network operations—the essential element of the 17D career field. Movement between the two suffixes is proposed to be accomplished through professional development. Any omission of potential assignments of the 17Ds in this pyramid reflects the national-level focus of this study and should not be construed as implying that any missions are less important than others.

61. Sanders to Geis, e-mails.

62. Ibid.; and "Selective Reenlistment Bonus Program." These bonus rates went into effect in the spring of 2014. See also Gildea, "45 AFSCs Removed from SRB List."

63. Senior leaders at Headquarters USCYBERCOM and associated field agencies, interviews with the research team, January and February 2014.

64. Sanders to Geis, e-mails.

65. We have insufficient statistical evidence to clearly recommend whether relocating UCT to a more desirable location or offering some zone D or E reenlistment incentive would best stem the drain of experienced cyberspace warriors from the schoolhouse, where the Air Force would ideally want its best and brightest creating and training our new cyber operators. Nonetheless, the anecdotal evidence is disturbing, and cyberspace career force managers should continue to watch these trends with an eye toward uncovering their underlying causes. The remarks above are based on discussions with nearly two dozen senior defense and civilian cyber professionals in a cyberspace advisory group meeting (Chatham House Rules) hosted by AFRI in July 2014.

66. Twenty-Fourth Air Force, vice-commander, briefing.

67. Although our sister services directly access the specialty codes equivalent to the 1B4, this process results in a very high attrition rate in training. In some cases this attrition is upward of 40 percent. Thus, even though creation of a 1B4 cyberspace defense operator takes a long time because of the initial developmental assignment, the cost-benefit of moving toward direct accessions with extreme attrition is unclear, as are the second-order effects of that attrition. Any movement toward direct accession of 1B4 Airmen should proceed with caution.

68. 81 TW Tentative Plan of Instruction, Cyber Defense Operations.

69. The availability of the Cyberspace 200 course is problematic because course demand greatly exceeds the supply of potential slots. This issue is raised again in this study and becomes the genesis of a recommendation to expand Cyber 200/300 throughput capacity.

70. If the Air Force is to receive a proper return on its training investment, this study recommends that midlevel and more senior NCOs not go through the CNODP, given the limited part of their career that remains. Of note are the numerous positions for senior NCOs to lead in the mission support community and somewhat limited opportunities in the national mission units. As such, this study finds that the cadre of personnel from which the senior leaders for the national mission units will be chosen should be groomed from an early to a midpoint in their career.

71. Conference Board, Leading Economic Index.

72. Watson to Geis, e-mail. This communication dealt with the history, evolution, and future intent of the cyberspace intelligence career fields.

73. Ibid.; and Lacks, bullet background paper.

74. Watson to Geis, e-mail; and DAF, *Operations Intelligence CFETP*, 10.

75. DAF, *Operations Intelligence CFETP*, 10. See also the US Marine Corps Training Command, "Joint Cyber Analysis Course."

76. Twenty-Fourth Air Force HQ staff, interview by research team, Joint Base San Antonio–Lackland AFB, TX, 4 March 2014.

77. As mentioned, the Cyberspace 200 course does not have enough training slots to fulfill the demand requirement; this study recommends that the throughput of this course be adjusted upward.

78. Seven-level craftsmen can occupy a variety of training positions prior to pinning on technical sergeant. However, it is the belief of the research team that for the 1N4X1As, where cyber currency is difficult to maintain and regain, this type of career broadening is best timed after the sergeant's third operational assignment—at around the 10–11 year point, probably at the technical sergeant level.

79. Watson to Geis, e-mail.

80. Ibid.

81. Brokaw to Conway, e-mail.

82. Interviews and observations by the research team at USCYBERCOM and NSA, Fort Meade, MD, February 2014.

83. For example, most people reading this study fluently read and write English, but few of them can program computers, even if they use English-language-based computer code. The same holds true for individuals fluent in other languages.

84. HAF/A2D staff, interview by research team, 23 June 2014.

85. As the number of computer devices manufactured by non-English-speaking companies increases, so will the need for comprehension of foreign languages since many of the instructions and the back-end user interface will be non-English as well.

86. Senior Language Authority (SLA) roundtable participants and SLA Roundtable, NSA, Fort Meade, MD, interviews by the research team, 11 March 2014.

87. French is also the language in which nearly 20 percent of global commerce is conducted. See French Ministry of Foreign Affairs, "Status of French"; and Organisation Internationale de la Francophonie, "Benchmarks."

88. AFI 36-2605, *Air Force Military Personnel Testing System*, and att. 14.

89. Scott C. Brokaw (JCS/J1) and Ms. Amy Brown (USCYBERCOM Senior Language Authority), interview by John Conway (AFRI), Fort Meade, MD, 23 July 2014.

90. The ACTFL writing test and proficiency guidelines test can be found at http://www.actfl.org/sites/default/files/pdfs/ACTFLProficiencyGuidelines2012-Writing.pdf.

91. Among the concerns the research team wrestled with was whether cyberspace linguists can be recruited or need to be created. The latter is extremely manpower intensive and would require educating/training a linguist through a curriculum similar to that of the CNODP. Although the CNODP may not be the ideal vehicle, if we cannot find cyber-savvy linguists, a method of educating linguists in detailed computer programming may need to be created. However, until we know whether we can access the necessary skills into the Air Force, making a recommendation to stand up formal, lengthy education programs to create a set of cyber-savvy linguists may be premature.

92. Smith, "By the Numbers"; and Hailes and Geis, "Observer Warrior," 147–66.

93. Geis et al., *Blue Horizons IV*.

94. Watkins, "Federal Big Data Spending to Increase."

95. Ibid.

96. The research team found anecdotal conflation of the concepts of data fusion and big data among some analysts. It is important to note that although data fusion is a part of how big-data sets are manipulated and analyzed, the skill sets needed to manipulate, program, and ply big-data sets to obtain meaningful information are not found in a typical data-fusion analyst.

97. "Airman Leadership School." These requirements are also located in the CFETPs for the various career fields.

Chapter 6

The Air National Guard, the Air Force Reserve, and Cyber

Cyber is the Air Force's newest mission and its least understood; nevertheless, politicians, commissions, and well-meaning supporters of this or that military affiliation claim that their troops can easily handle cyberspace. In the past two years, think tanks, commissions, and even Congress have focused on the reserve components' (RC) cyber roles.

A September 2013 Institute for Defense Analyses (IDA) report, *A New Approach to Force-Mix Analysis* (later referenced in the 2014 National Commission on the Structure of the Air Force [NCSAF] report), called for additional days of active duty for Air National Guard and Air Force Reserve cyber personnel beyond the "normal 39 days." Extra days, the report claimed, would increase personnel currency, better use their advanced education and training, and "lower RC hourly costs by adding in more workdays at less than drill pay rates and increasing [the] percent of time performing useful work."[1]

In May 2014 a Reserve Forces Policy Board (RFPB) report for the secretary of defense, *Reserve Component Use, Balance, Cost and Savings*, included the recommendation to "expand RC in key skill areas." The board proposed that the DOD examine skill sets where the RCs clearly excel because of their members' "civilian acquired skills and exposure to new technologies in the workplace."[2]

Finally, in late 2013, the National Defense Authorization Act for Fiscal Year 2014 (FY 14 NDAA) called for even more reports on the RCs and cyber "requir[ing] the Secretary of Defense to conduct a mission analysis of [DOD] cyber operations," including "an evaluation of the potential roles of the reserve components [in] . . . cyber operations" and a separate assessment by the chief of the National Guard Bureau of "the role of the National Guard in supporting the [DOD] cyber operations mission."[3]

The conclusions of all three reports have common themes:

1. The RCs are cheaper.
2. The RCs have relevant and exploitable civilian skills for this mission.
3. Therefore, the Air Force should expand its RC roles for cyber.

Not surprisingly, the congressionally chartered NCSAF *Report to the President and the Congress of the United States* (January 2014) reached the same conclusions. Recommendation 25 regarding cyberspace Airmen states, "As it increases the number of Airmen in career fields associated with Cyberspace, the Air Force should fill much of that demand with the Reserve Components, which are well situated to recruit and retain from the specialized talent available in the commercial cyber labor market."[4] In April 2014 the commission appeared before the Senate Armed Services Committee, and its testimony again highlighted increased Guard and Reserve involvement in cyber, the relevant civilian cyber skills in those components, and cost savings.[5]

Cost as the Overarching Factor

Of the three themes above, cost—more precisely cost savings—was cited most often in these reports as the raison d'être for more RC cyber involvement. The most-quoted source for cost comparisons was the RFPB's 2013 report *Eliminating Major Gaps in DoD Data on the Fully-Burdened and Life-Cycle Cost of Military Personnel*. It concluded that "the cost of an RC service member, when not activated, is less than one third that of their AC [active component] counterpart."[6] This revelation quickly became the mantra for calls to transfer many types of missions to the RCs and the source for several news stories.[7] However, the modifying phrase "*when not activated*" (emphasis added) was ignored.

The Center for a New American Security has observed that "Guard and Reserve Forces generally cost about the same as active forces when they are activated. But when they are not activated—which is the majority of the time—they cost approximately one-third as much."[8] But its report overlooked the full-time support tail that comes with each Guard and Reserve unit: the percentage of the Selected Reserve manning that is full-time support—either Active Guard and Reserve (AGR) or military technicians (dual status).[9] This staffing is a significant cost factor for peacetime support. Since commonly agreed upon RC cost-savings data remains elusive, the lure of cost savings alone should not be the main reason for a significant transfer of cyber missions to the Guard and Reserve.

Recommendation: The cost of active duty "when not activated" should be reassessed, and RC costs upon activation should also be recalculated.

Civilian Cyber Skills in the Reserve Components

A significant body of literature and testimony favors expanding Guard and Reserve cyber missions based on civilian skills they would bring to the fight.[10] However, inconsistencies in nomenclature, problems with projected mission sets, and even legal issues must be sorted out before the citizen-Airman cyber mission should expand. The expertise and experience of Guard and Reserve personnel will be needed and welcomed, but first there must be some cogent plan, and right now that plan does not exist. As one knowledgeable observer noted, "We at CYBERCOM know we have not yet defined a surge requirement, . . . but we have so many moving parts with . . . trying to build existing capability . . . that it's really hard to squeeze a whole heck more out."[11]

Some confusion exists about what constitutes a cyber mission and who performs it. For example, the NCSAF report states that 43 percent of personnel (some 11,000 Airmen) for the cyberspace superiority core mission reside in the Guard and Reserve, calling that mission "among the most integrated of the core functions."[12] A closer look at the numbers reveals that most individuals are in combat communications squadrons—a part of the cyber community but by no means directly involved in cyberspace superiority.[13]

Several names have been proposed for Guard and Reserve cyber missions; among them are *offensive cyber operations*, *computer network attack*, the aforementioned *cyberspace superiority*, and *cyber defense*.[14] However, offensive cyber operations and computer network attack are Title 50 missions, authority for which is held only at the NSA.[15] Moreover, these two are at the far end of the cyber operations spectrum, usually referred to as "computer network exploitation."[16] The term *cyberspace superiority* appears to be more of an end state rather than a mission set and is too vague a term to be of any use.

Cyber defense and *computer network defense* are very similar terms, but *cyber defense* is more inclusive and easily understood. For Title 32 Guard missions and Title 10 Reserve missions, *cyber defense* is a good fit: it is within the guidelines of Titles 10 and 32, blends with the efforts of the DHS and the Federal Bureau of Investigation, and does not overstate what the RCs can legally undertake.

Recommendation: Clarify which missions are currently being performed by the Guard and Reserve by providing categories of cyber work, including combat communications, for each RC unit.

Recommendation: Discontinue the use of the term *computer network attack* (as well as any other terms associated with offensive cyber missions) to describe a cyber mission. Explicitly define those missions within cyber (computer network defense, etc.) that can be performed by Guard and Reserve personnel. In particular, clearly define the functions that Guard personnel can perform in Title 32 or state active duty (SAD) status.

During its 2013 hearings, the NCSAF heard much testimony about the crossover of civilian cyber skills to military cyber missions. For instance, Maj Gen Arnold Punaro, USMC, retired, stated, "I guarantee you you're going to have better cyber-skills in the Guard and Reserve than you're going to be able to sustain in the Active Component. . . . As soon as they [active duty] finish their training they're going to go to work for Microsoft and Google, . . . so why can't we put them into Guard and Reserve units?"[17]

Similarities between Air Force cyber needs and civilian cyber experience do exist, and there is a solid case for more RC personnel in the DOD cyber mix. However, the service faces issues concerning civilian cyber employees as military cyber warriors:

- *Geography.* Most civilian cyber companies are clustered in the metropolitan DC area, near Seattle, in Silicon Valley, or in San Antonio (location of Twenty-Fourth and Twenty-Fifth Air Forces).[18] What about cyber missions elsewhere? Cyber protection teams are being proposed for each of the country's 10 Federal Emergency Management Agency (FEMA) regions, but populating these units will require a fairly substantial training tail (see next page).[19] Without a cadre of experienced computer personnel nearby to populate these units, training and accession issues will significantly slow stand-up and initial operational capability.

Recommendation: Collocate these CPTs at each FEMA regional headquarters—all located in highly populated urban areas—to aid in recruiting a trained cyber workforce and help mitigate sourcing problems (fig. 20).

Figure 20. FEMA regional headquarters. (Reproduced from Federal Emergency Management Agency, "Fire Management Assistance Grants: Regional Contacts," 30 January 2015, http://www.fema.gov/fire-management-assistance-grants-regional-contacts.)

- *Training.* Elsewhere in this study is a discussion of the significant amount of training necessary to obtain proficiency and remain proficient in the cyber world. Individuals in cyber units undergo refresher training roughly every 90 days to stay current with changing technologies. Given the part-time nature of the RC cadre, numerous extra days beyond the normal 39 duty days per year would be needed just to maintain currency. The IDA reported that workers at one civilian cyber company needed refresher training "every few weeks to keep up with the dramatic increases in the sophistication of cyber attacks." It also reported that an Air Force Reserve Command (AFRC) analysis of a 2011 cyber business case indicated that reservists serving for only 60 days at a time in cyber jobs "provide low benefit."[20] Cyber skills, tactics, techniques, and technology are constantly evolving, and 90-day upgrades are a civilian industry norm. The training tail for any cyber unit is significant; it is even more so for a part-time force.

Recommendation: Increase training funds to assure cyber reservist currency.

- *Numbers.* How big should the current force of RC cyber warriors become? In 2014 six cyber squadrons were in the ANG and two in the AFRC.[21] In early 2014 the NCSAF recommended more, and the FY 2014 NDAA called for an immediate review to determine an exact growth number.[22] As described above, though, USCYBERCOM is still trying to define the exact end state it desires.

Recommendation: The NSA and USCYBERCOM should clearly articulate in formal planning documents the cyber missions for the Guard and Reserve. In the interim, designate projected CPTs as Guard units (per the Council of Governors) for each FEMA region. Otherwise, halt further expansion until formal planning is accomplished.

- *Defense Support to Civil Authorities* (DSCA). One of the least understood roles of the military is DSCA. Homeland security and homeland defense are not DSCA but are often confused with it.[23] Simply put, DSCA occurs after a disaster and at the request of local and state authorities whose capabilities for disaster mitigation have been overwhelmed. Under the aegis of DSCA, the ANG (plus the Army National Guard and the RCs of the other services) would play a large role in the mitigation of any cyber disaster. USCYBERCOM has suggested that 10 of its planned 20 CPTs be Guard units assigned to FEMA regions to work with local and state officials.[24] However, the legality of the Guard's performing domestic cyber activities in SAD or Title 32 status will need to be determined on a case-by-case basis. Judge advocate general guidance may be required to make these calls, and adding a lawyer to each CPT would be a wise idea. Funding for such missions is another thorny issue. One possible solution is to seek funding from the DHS in the same manner that funding for the Guard and Reserve flows from the Office of National Drug Control Policy (ONDCP) for counterdrug support.[25]

Recommendation: Cyber missions performed by the Guard in support of the DHS should be funded by the DHS. Use the ONDCP counterdrug funding example as a guide.

- *Availability.* Like many other trained RC first-responders (who are civilian police, firemen, and emergency medical services personnel), Guard and Reserve cyber warriors are citizen-Airmen who, for the most part, have full-time careers. If they are employed in a cyber capacity as civilians, they may not be available for duty beyond their required days because of their other responsibilities. Further, in a cyber emergency, they may be needed at their civilian jobs as much as or more than on active duty. Using the civilian sector cyber expertise of Guard and Reserve personnel as a force enhancer/multiplier is an excellent option, but as a sole manning option, its effectiveness may be blunted by RC personnel's civilian demands.

Recommendation: Guard/Reserve recruiting for cyber units should not focus exclusively on employees from the computer/cyber security industry. Although they may have the proper background, conflicts of interest could inhibit their full utilization in an emergency.

Summary

The Guard and Reserve partnership with the active Air Force should extend to the cyber domain, just as it does for air and space. However, the rapid growth of RC cyber units, coupled with the recent (2010) stand-up of USCYBERCOM, means that the roles and missions of both the Guard and Reserve are only now being understood. Cost savings alone is an invalid reason to stand up more RC cyber units. Solid requirements must drive force presentation, and policy makers and military planners alike must have access to accurate cost calculations. Using the civilian expertise of RC cyber warriors is an attractive selling point for RC cyber units, but people in civilian cyber first-responder jobs or in damage-mitigation roles cannot be counted on to choose between their civilian careers and activation. Specific missions in support of USCYBERCOM naturally fall into its funding line. However, the DHS must be a source for funding when the task clearly supports its activities.

RECOMMENDATIONS SUMMARY

- Reassess the cost of active duty "when not activated," and recalculate RC costs upon activation.
- Clarify missions that the Guard and Reserve are currently performing by providing categories of cyber work, including combat communications, for each RC unit.

> **RECOMMENDATIONS SUMMARY** (continued)
>
> - Discontinue the use of the term *computer network attack* (as well as any other terms associated with offensive cyber missions) to describe a cyber mission. Explicitly define those missions within cyber (computer network defense, etc.) that can be performed by Guard and Reserve personnel. In particular, clearly define the functions that Guard personnel can perform in Title 32 or SAD status.
> - Collocate CPTs at each FEMA regional headquarters—all located in highly populated urban areas—to aid in recruiting a trained cyber workforce and help mitigate sourcing problems.
> - Increase training funds to assure cyber reservist currency.
> - The NSA and USCYBERCOM should clearly articulate in formal planning documents the Guard and Reserve cyber missions. In the interim, designate projected CPTs as Guard units (per the Council of Governors) for each FEMA region. Otherwise, halt further expansion until formal planning is accomplished.
> - The DHS should fund the Guard's cyber accessions in support of the DHS. Use the ONDCP counterdrug funding example as a guide.
> - Recruiting for cyber units should not focus exclusively on employees from the computer/cyber security industry. They may have the proper background, but conflicts of interest could inhibit their full utilization in an emergency.

Notes

1. Miller, Levine, and Horowitz, *New Approach to Force Mix Analysis*, iii, 5, 59.
2. Reserve Forces Policy Board, *Reserve Component Use*, 17.
3. House, *National Defense Authorization Act for Fiscal Year 2014*, subpars. (a), (b)(8), and (e).
4. NCSAF, *Report to the President*, 62.
5. Senate, *Appropriations for Fiscal Year 2015*, 15, 22–23.
6. Reserve Forces Policy Board, *Eliminating Major Gaps in DoD Data*, 5. The report further states, "According to RFPB analysis of the Fiscal Year 2013 budget request, the RC per capita cost ranges from 22% to 32% of their AC counterparts' per capita costs, depending on which cost elements are included" (ibid.).
7. National Guard Association of the United States, "It's Official: Guard a Bargain."
8. Bensahel, *Beyond the QDR*, 3. As an overall percentage of the ANG's end strength (FY 2014 NDAA), technicians and the Active Guard and Reserve comprise more than one in three (34.73 percent) of the force. The Air Force Reserve Command (AFRC) has a little fewer than one in five in those two categories (18.95 percent). These totals create significant additional costs beyond those of the traditional 39-day-a-year reservists who make up the rest of the force. The cost of active duty "when not activated" should be reassessed, and RC costs upon activation should also be recalculated.
9. Per 10 *USC*, sec. 10216(a)(1), a military technician (dual status), is "a Federal civilian employee who . . . (B) is required as a condition of that employment to main-

tain membership in the Selected Reserve; and (C) is assigned to a civilian position as a technician in the organizing, administering, instructing, or training of the Selected Reserve or in the maintenance and repair of supplies or equipment issued to the Selected Reserve or the armed forces."

10. There will be more missions, and in the case of the Guard, those already in existence could not be cut in FY 2014. House, *National Defense Authorization Act for Fiscal Year 2014*, par. (c).

11. Zuehlke to Conway, e-mail.

12. NCSAF, *Report to the President*, 36–37.

13. Miller, Levine, and Horowitz, *New Approach to Force-Mix Analysis*, 16. See also McKinney, "National Solution," 12.

14. The NCSAF's *Report to the President* and the IDA report (Miller, Levine, and Horowitz's *New Approach to Force-Mix Analysis*) use all of these terms at various points in their discussion of RC cyber missions.

15. 50 *USC*, War and National Defense. For an exhaustive treatise on Title 10 / Title 50 cyber issues involving the military, see Chesney, "Military-Intelligence Convergence," 541, 580–81, and 607–8.

16. Brown, CYBERCOM senior language authority, interview.

17. Punaro, testimony, 74–75. NCSAF recommendation 25 (quoted previously in this chap.) asked precisely the same question.

18. Gen Mark Welsh points out that there is a "very rich recruiting pool for a cyber workforce that the Guard and Reserve can actually take advantage [of] much easier than the Active component can take advantage of *in some parts of the country*" (emphasis added). Senate, *Appropriations for Fiscal Year 2015*, 15.

19. Zuehlke to Conway, e-mail.

20. Miller, Levine, and Horowitz, *New Approach to Force-Mix Analysis*, 12. The AFRC business case analysis referred to is "Total Force Integration, 24th Air Force, 624th Operations Center Air Force Space Command (AFSPC) / Reserve Associate Unit (RAU), Air Force Reserve Command, Lackland Air Force Base, TX," AFSPC A8, January 2011 (ibid., 12n11).

21. Two examples illustrate the patchwork approach to RC cyber unit stand-ups. First, the 118th Airlift Wing at Nashville is converting some elements to form a cyber unit. During an interview with HAF/A2D (ISR Strategy, Integration, and Doctrine), we were told that the unit called their office, announced that the unit was "converting to cyber," and asked for "paperwork" for cyber positions (23 July 2014). Second, the AFRC activated a classic associate unit in support of the 70th Intelligence Wing (IW) at Fort Meade last fall. This squadron was created at the request of the 70 IW/CC to resolve the "administrative problems" associated with the management of its individual mobilization augmentee (IMA) force. To stand up the 100-person unit, 189 IMA billets were traded for 100 traditional reserve drilling positions, including a full-time cadre of 10 AGRs. Heikkinen to Conway, e-mails.

22. The NCSAF's *Report to the President* proposes a shift of 450 positions of planned growth in the cyber core function to the RCs (p. 101). The commission also recommends moving some "3,875 Offensive Cyber Operations (OCO)–type intel and data analysis positions" to the Guard and Reserve within the global integrated ISR core function (ibid.). This latter shift—about eight times larger than the one

from the cyber core function—is particularly troubling, given that OCO is a Title 50 function not delegated to the states.

23. The DOD is the lead federal agency for homeland defense, and the DHS is the lead federal agency for homeland security.

24. For the number of proposed USCYBERCOM CPTs, see the briefing "USCYBERCOM Cyber Mission Force," slide 5. The number of CPTs that the Council of Governors has projected for the Air Guard / FEMA region beddown comes from Zuehlke to Conway, e-mail.

25. McKinney, "National Solution," 11.

Chapter 7

Educating and Training Cyber Forces

Leadership tomorrow depends on how we educate our students today—especially in science, technology, engineering and math.
—President Barack Obama, 16 September 2010

To compete with both advanced nation-state and nonstate adversaries, the Air Force and DOD at large require a cadre of cyber operators capable of reacting to novel threats in novel situations. Education is the foundation on which the Air Force can build a cyber force to achieve this objective. Ideally, the Air Force would reach this goal by selecting individuals who have specialized in the science, technology, engineering, and mathematics fields; training them in the art and science of cyber warfare; providing them experience in operations; and then continuing their education with an advanced academic degree (AAD) in a STEM discipline. Unfortunately, we are not there yet. A significant concern discovered during our research is the Air Force's emphasis on ramping up the cyber workforce with trained operators who are commercially certified. At first blush, this approach seems prudent. However, the training path tends to produce officers with rote-memorized skills versus flexible, critically thinking cyber warriors prepared to meet adaptive adversaries. The Air Force, DOD, and national security community at large must focus efforts to attract personnel educated in STEM fields as well as those in the arts with a proclivity for cyber operations (STEAM) for missions in a contested environment.

When considering the skills that a student learns in a CS curriculum, a CE or systems engineering (SE) degree might be better suited for the OCO and DCO mission sets while CS may be preferable for the DODIN mission space. The fields of computer, electrical, and systems engineering differ from CS, which involves the methods for representing, transforming, and transmitting information. The somewhat overlapping fields of CE, EE, and SE address the mapping of computing processes onto mechanisms that control platforms or physical infrastructure. Assuring Air Force core functions and missions entails the understanding of mission dependence on cyberspace. This dependence goes beyond traditional CS disciplines of computer networks. The embedded processes and controllers on weapons platforms, design of resilient computing architectures, and protection of the USAF's critical infrastructure require an interdisciplinary understanding of computer systems and their interactions with humans. An emphasis on training in traditional CS disciplines (explored in depth throughout this chapter) is a significant point of concern in our study. An overview of the differences between education and training is therefore our starting point. We then assess the United States' place in the world in terms of STEM education while understanding the levels of education within the current USAF cyber workforce and the curricula and facilities that exist to support the education and training of our cyber warriors. Overall, the Air Force needs to recognize that an educated cyber workforce is imperative to assure Air Force missions beyond current IT paradigms and embrace education as an integral aspect of the career development of cyber operations personnel.

Education versus Training

Distinguishing between cyber education and training is important. We use Bloom's Taxonomy as the representative model of the stages of higher-order thinking.[1] Civilian and military curriculum developers use this taxonomy to create material that will expose students to activities requiring them to acquire and remember information and then demonstrate and practice their understanding of the knowledge by applying it to create new knowledge. Figure 21 shows examples of cyber tasks that would be demonstrated at the levels of Bloom's Taxonomy.

Cyber education, as defined here, consists of academic degrees in related disciplines and actual time spent in the discipline itself. For purposes of simplicity, we defined a cyber-trained officer as one certified in following procedures and tested on skills offered through certification programs accredited by various vendors. These certificates are indicators of the knowledge and perhaps comprehension levels in the taxonomy and of who may be able to follow a script—useful in gaining awareness of the cyberspace arena. This training is touted as industry best practice and is currently used to measure skills within the career field. The reality is that industry-standard training is inadequate in today's threat environment. A case in point is the North Korean data theft at Sony revealed in November 2014. A crew of trained operators could not protect the core cyber infrastructure of the corporation against a nation-state adversary.[2] This case demonstrated that "trained personnel" do not necessarily equate with personnel who can react to novel threats and apply their knowledge in new situations. The hacking of Anthem, Inc. is another case in point on the limitations of risk mitigation frameworks, such as the NIST Cybersecurity Framework. In that case, the industry "best practices" implemented on complex systems by trained personnel to defend against advanced adversaries did not fit the bill and gave a false sense of security.[3] Unless educated with critical thinking skills and a formal course of study in a cyber specialty, personnel will not reach the levels of evaluation and creation (synthesis) in Bloom's Taxonomy to compete with nation-state-level adversaries.

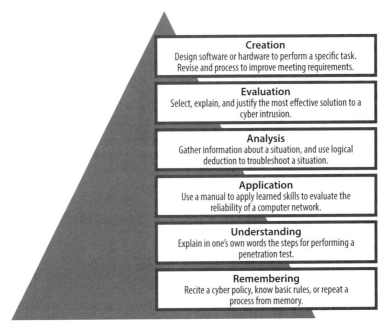

Figure 21. Cyber tasks at levels of Bloom's Taxonomy. (Adapted from Benjamin S. Bloom and David R. Krathwohl, *Taxonomy of Educational Objectives, Book 1: Cognitive Domain* [Reading, MA: Addison Wesley Publishing Company, 1984].)

In comparisons with foreign countries, we found that allied and adversarial nations alike seek to craft a cadre of cyber warriors who hold master's degrees rather than trained cyber automatons. This desire becomes apparent when one compares the profile of cyber officers. In France, for example, the ideal cyber officer is a "holder of [a] Masters in Cyber Defense, is an expert in cyber operations and crisis management, . . . controls [the] environment in the humanities and social sciences in his field and has gained a good technical knowledge of networks, with systems information and their related materials."[4] This statement indicates that France is in the process of developing well-rounded cyber warriors with an interdisciplinary background. Such education allows operators to holistically appreciate the policy behind the kinetics as well as create innovative solutions not stovepiped in one discipline.

Unlike our adversaries, the United States faces a void of cyber-educated personnel able to think dynamically in unusual situations. When combined with the declared doctrinal intent of Russia, China, and Iran to operationalize the cyber domain for military purposes, this situation is worrisome (fig. 22).

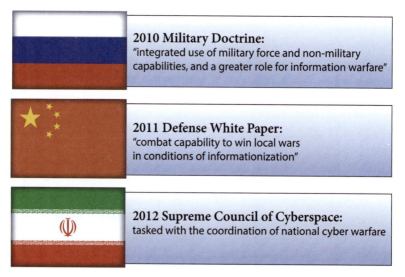

Figure 22. Cyber in foreign military doctrine and strategy. (Compiled from Carnegie Endowment, "The Military Doctrine of the Russian Federation," 5 February 2010, http://carnegieendowment.org/files/2010russia_military_doctrine.pdf; "China's National Defense in 2010," Information Office of the State Council, People's Republic of China, Beijing, March 2011, http://news.xinhuanet.com/english2010/china/2011-03/31/c_13806851.htm; and Gabi Siboni and Sami Kronenfeld, "Iran's Cyber Warfare, *INSS* [*Institute for National Security Studies*] *Insight* No. 375, 15 October 2012.)

International CS competitions demonstrate that the recruitment pool within these countries is deeper in STEM expertise. Thus, as indicated in the performance of US teams in international programming competitions, those who may seek to disrupt Air Force missions and destroy critical infrastructure will be drawing from this pool of students steeped in STEM and cyber. On the adversarial side, Timothy Thomas describes the Chinese Information Security University, which specializes in military information security with a rigorous emphasis on science, technology, and mathematics in cyber operations.[5] Simply put, a trained Air Force operator will not be competitive on the cyber battlefront against an adversary trained in the military arts and sciences and educated in the mathematics and science of cyber operation.[6] Advanced mathematics, computer programming, and teamwork provide the theoretical foundation essential to maneuvering and adjusting to the dynamic cyber domain.

This point is quantified in figure 23 with the results of the Association for Computing Machinery International Collegiate Programming Contest (ACM-ICPC). Such competitions offer insight into the divergence between the level of cyber education and prowess of students internationally versus that of students at US universities. The ACM-ICPC results are of particular interest as the competition takes "teams of three students represent[ing] their universities in multiple levels of regional competition. Volunteer coaches prepare their teams with intense training and instruction in algorithms, programming, and teamwork strategy."[7] Russia and China dominated the 2014 competition while the United States failed to break into the top 10.

The International Informatics Olympiad is yet another benchmark that "offers an opportunity to bring together the accumulated knowledge and experiences from a number of events on teaching algorithms and programming."[8] At first glance, figure 24 appears to indicate that the United States fares quite well against Russia and China. However, a further look reveals that this chart shows total medal count and not a placement within the group based on top performers. For example, Iran has a considerably higher total of silver and bronze medals. This figure also shows that other countries are rapidly achieving, if not surpassing, US levels of cyber-savvy performance. As a national snapshot, the picture is grim. When one delves into levels of STEM education within the current Air Force cyber workforce, the picture becomes bleaker given that if the service's missions fail, loss of life could be the consequence.

Figure 23. 2014 ACM programming competition. (Compiled from Association for Computing Machinery International Collegiate Programming Contest, "World Finals," 2014, http://icpc.baylor.edu/worldfinals.)

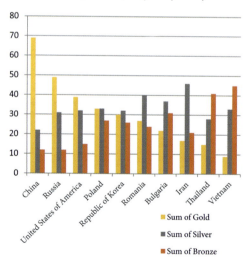

Figure 24. Informatics Olympiad medal totals, 1988–2014. (Developed from data from International Olympiad in Informatics website, http://www.ioinformatics.org/index.shtml.)

Levels of Education within the USAF Cyber Workforce

This study found a severe lack of cyber-related degrees within the core cyberspace operations cadre of 17D network operations officers, 14N intelligence officers, and the 1B4, 1NXXX, and 3DXXX enlisted fields. Of those accessed into the cyber career field, only one in three (35 percent) have a cyber-related bachelor's degree. A majority of 17-series career field majors and colonels have AADs, but historically only 10 percent of those degrees are cyber related.[9] A breakdown of bachelor's degrees and AADs follows (tables 9 and 10, fig. 25).

Table 9. 17D bachelor's degrees

Subject	Percentage of total
Computer science	8.7%
Electrical engineering	1.5%
Computer engineering	0.4%
Any cyber degree	10.6%
Of these, NSA accredited	43.5%

Developed from Air Force Personnel Center, Personnel Database, Extracts of Officer Data, 1995–2014.

Table 10. 17D master's degrees

Subject	Percentage of total
Computer science	24.7%
Electrical engineering	8.4%
Computer engineering	2.0%
Any cyber degree	35.0%
Of these, NSA accredited	1.4%

Developed from Air Force Personnel Center, Personnel Database, Extracts of Officer Data, 1995–2014.

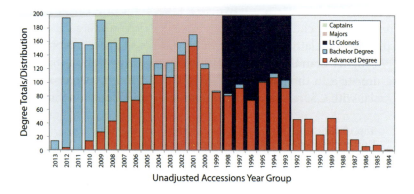

Figure 25. 17D overall degrees. (Reproduced from Air Force Personnel Center, Personnel Database, Extracts of Officer Data, 1995–2014.)

The United States has the greatest higher education system in the world. Research universities continue their lead in developing advanced information and communication technology. Unfortunately, very few Air Force accessions come from universities with top cyber programs (fig. 26). Of all officers brought into the cyber profession, the Air Force has averaged about three officers per year from highly recognized universities in the field (table 11). We judge that this problem can be addressed with the right policies and procedures in place.

United States Air Force Academy

Two years ago AFPC was given responsibility for determining AFSCs for ROTC and USAFA cadets. Preference, academic rank, and major are the three main determinants of AFSCs—along with the needs of the Air Force. Currently, the Air Force is asking the USAFA to produce 50 17D-series Airmen per year. EE/CE is the third-least-popular major, and CS is the fifth-least popular.

We wanted to determine both USAFA cadet interest in cyber career fields and the quality of students interested as measured by GPA. We found the number of cyber-degreed cadets who chose 17D first among nonrated AFSCs and divided it by the number of 17Ds the Air Force has accessed from the academy (currently, all cadets can become 17Ds, at least theoretically) from 2011 to 2014. Figure 27 shows the percentage of USAFA cyber majors who selected 17D as their first choice. Figure 28 indicates that those with a 17D preference at the USAFA generally have a lower GPA than other nonrated line officer career fields and, even more worrisome, that the 17D career field is among the last choices of nonrated officers. This finding cannot be explained by relative difficulty of major because cyber majors have GPAs higher than the average GPAs of the academy (table 12). Delving deeper into the data, one discovers that the 17D career field is popular with CS majors but unpopular with CE/EE majors (fig. 29).

Figure 26. Top-ranked cyber programs worldwide. (Developed from [*left*] *Times Higher Education* World University Rankings, "Subject Ranking 2013–14: Engineering and Technology," 2014, https://www.timeshighereducation.co.uk/world-university-rankings/2014/subject-ranking/engineering-and-IT#; and [*right*] NSA, "List of Centers of Academic Excellence for Cyber Operations," 2014, https://www.nsa.gov/academia/nat_cae_cyber_ops/nat_cae_co_centers.shtml.)

Table 11. Cyber-educated accessions from top universities

2009	2010	2011	2012	2013
4	3	2	3	5

Developed from Office of the Registrar, Holm Center, Maxwell AFB, AL, March 2014.

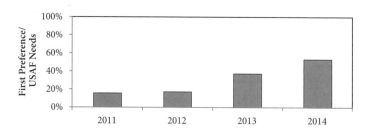

Figure 27. USAFA cyber major preference for 17D. (Developed from Cadet Administrative Management System, Office of the Registrar, United States Air Force Academy, Colorado Springs, CO, August 2014.)

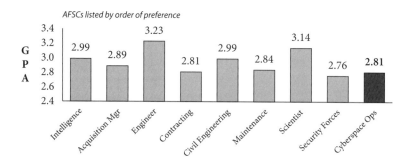

Figure 28. USAFA nonrated preferred AFSC and GPA. Chart indicates decreasing order of preference from left to right. (Developed from Cadet Administrative Management System, Office of the Registrar, United States Air Force Academy, Colorado Springs, CO, August 2014.)

Table 12. Average GPAs of USAFA cyber majors versus all USAFA cadets

Major	Average GPA
Electrical engineering	3.25
Computer engineering	3.09
Computer science	3.02
Average of all USAFA cadets	2.97

Developed from Cadet Administrative Management System, Office of the Registrar, United States Air Force Academy, Colorado Springs, CO, August 2014.

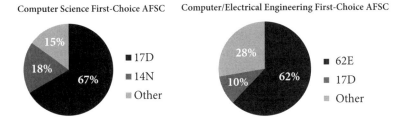

Figure 29. USAFA cyber majors' first-choice nonrated AFSCs. Computer science major (*left*) and CE/EE major (*right*) first-choice AFSCs. (Developed from Cadet Administrative Management System, Office of the Registrar, United States Air Force Academy, Colorado Springs, CO, August 2014.)

The AFSC choice is not an easy fix. All USAFA cadets are free to select any major they desire, making it difficult to push cadets into specific disciplines. Cadets complete their dream sheet during their senior year, and about half of all USAFA graduates choose a rated AFSC. This statistic holds true for CS, CE, and EE majors. Top-performing students are given preference in the assignment process; those choosing to fly, if medically qualified, generally get their wish. In addition, many technical majors essentially wash out and are directed to broader majors. Consequently, graduates from technical majors who are more apt to fill 17S slots tend to have lower GPAs than their classmates who fill rated slots, resulting in the cyber career field receiving, on average, a lower-quality graduate.

The USAFA is creating a new computer and network security (CNS) degree that will combine CS, computer operations, and software development. The degree is tied to NSA requirements, and the academy is seeking recognition as a cyber operations center of excellence. Before the new major was advertised, 19 cadets showed up to enroll. The CS faculty is understandably excited about this unsolicited demand signal. As of spring 2014, the USAFA had 58 declared majors in CS and CNS for the class of 2017. If normal attrition rates hold, the USAFA expects over 40 of them to graduate—with half of these graduates filling rated slots, leaving approximately 20 CS and CNS graduates to fill the USAFA's 17S quota. The hope is that the rest of the USAFA quota will be filled by CE/EE and other departments.

The consensus among USAFA faculty is that cadets majoring in fields other than CS/EE/CE are unprepared for the complex side of cyber. Although they can handle the management of base communications, they do not have the necessary educational background to operate successfully in the cyber domain. The 17D/17S split should help if it keeps personnel in proper billets. Otherwise, the attrition problem and the desire to avoid 17D/S will not get fixed.

The USAFA has several initiatives to generate more interest in the 17D/S career fields. To improve cadets' interest in the cyber-focused majors, the CS department has revamped its Introduction to Computing course, which all cadets take. It has incorporated simulated OCO and DCO into the course—making it much more popular and increasing the number of students who choose a cyber-focused major. Moreover, cadets are offered some summer opportunities. Anually, the NSA, National Reconnaissance Office (NRO), and MIT's Lincoln Labs each receive two cadets who complete summer research projects. Other summer cyber research opportunities include Twenty-Fourth Air Force, Nellis AFB, and the DHS Cadet Summer Research Projects program. This program allows cadets to conduct cyber research alongside industry leaders such as Intel, IBM, and Sharp at the DHS Center of Innovation on the USAFA campus. Interestingly, every CS cadet sent to the NSA for the summer has come back and selected 17D as his/her primary AFSC choice.

One roadblock to the daunting problem of filling 17-series career fields is a career field perception problem at the USAFA. As of this study, it was unclear whether this problem will persist after the career field split. In the past, when CS/CE/EE students were assigned to 17D involuntarily, enrollment in those majors declined 30 percent. Thus, such a practice has severe repercussions for those areas of study. Recently, of 30 graduated or graduating students from the USAFA cyber program, only 5 chose the 17-series AFSC, and faculty described the year as a "banner" one. Therefore, in most years, the percentage of cadets with technical degrees who choose the 17 series is even lower.

USAFA students do not view the 17-series career field as an attractive long-term career choice. Interviews with cadets offered insights into their motivations and perceptions about the 17-series AFSC. The only less-popular AFSC is 13N (nuclear and missile operations). Most CS/EE/CE cadets are afraid they will get "stuck" serving as a base communications squadron officer instead of doing 17-series work, and getting a (formerly) "A" or "B" shred is not necessarily based on skill but oftentimes on many other factors. The CS and CE departments verified this perception as widespread.

That belief may have some truth behind it. A general agreement exists among interviewed USAFA faculty that 17-series cadets tend to lose their desire to stay on active duty around the six-year point. At this point—after 17-series cadets have been assigned to base communications and their cyber warfare skills have eroded—they cannot return to a cyber-operations floor. As noted earlier, the 17D/17S split may help overcome the negative perception of the career field among technical majors, but more should be done to combat how the career field is viewed.

Recommendation: The best way to increase interest in the 17-series AFSC is for USAFA customers to tell, and then prove to, cadets that they have good jobs for them. Knowing that challenging jobs exist in the field will drive up interest.

Recommendation: Creating a summer course for cadets would be useful as a means of enticing them into the career field. Currently, one does not exist (it was eliminated once the 110 course was updated and offered to all cadets in their first year).

US Air Force Academy Cyber Range

The academy's range receives extensive use. The freshman Introduction to Computing class is now taught at the range, and the USAFA's cyber competition team also competes there. Generally under the name Delusions of Grandeur, the team competes against teams of graduate students and industry professionals worldwide and is generally in the top 15 percent of competitors.[10] The training range currently consists of four classrooms with raised floors and computers, each holding approximately 23 students. An isolated network includes 92 workstations, with commercial Internet access to sites inaccessible on the Defense Research and Engineering Network (DREN) and Nonsecure Internet Protocol Router Network (NIPRNet). This configuration allows academy cyber teams to participate in competitions that run on ports usually blocked by USAFA firewalls. The "server room" that supports the cyber training range is storage space underneath a lecture hall with upgraded power and a portable air conditioner. Equipment refresh and software licenses are estimated at $150,000 per year. Key software used on the cyber range includes Citrix XenServer (virtualization), VMWare Workstation (virtualization), FTK (forensics), and IDA Pro (reverse engineering). IDA Pro is expensive (the USAFA spent $62,000 to acquire licenses in FY 2013), but it is the best in its class and is used by industry professionals.

The high utilization rate of the range has led to a planned expansion with a fifth classroom, contingent on FY 2015 funding. Funding for the USAFA range, similar to that for Keesler or Hurlburt, is not in the USAF POM. The money to put in raised floors, purchase computers, and so forth, originally came from the Defense Information Assurance Program (DIAP) and the NRO, enhanced with USAFA fallout money. Because the cyber range has no POM and it is no longer DIAP funded, there is no sustainment plan. Without periodic updates, the USAFA's cyber range is not running the most current equipment. One faculty member interviewed by the team suspects that this shortfall affects Air Force retention because officers cannot work with the latest tools on the job. A long-term sustainment plan is critical since without the cyber range, instructors would be at mission failure due to the limitations of standard desktops. For these reasons, the study reiterates the recommendation for the USAF to POM for all cyber ranges in the same manner it does for operations, maintenance, and sustainment in the air and space domains.

Reserve Officer Training Corps

Overall, since accession targets for 17-series personnel with cyber degrees are going to rise markedly, USAFA cyber majors will be inadequate to sustain the educated cyber workforce the Air Force needs to compete with adversaries. Despite the positive trends above, USAFA production numbers are a small fraction of what the USAF has indicated it needs in the near future. Thus, ROTC must become a focal point for accessing cyber-educated officers.

The question behind the issue of the poor number of STEM graduates we get from top schools is, Where do we aim the ROTC scholarship dollars? Many recipients of ROTC four-year scholarships will not apply to expensive private schools because of the cost—scholarships are typically awarded after one accepts a university's offer of admission. Prospective students from poor or middle-class backgrounds will head to schools they can afford should the scholarship not come through. Aiming scholarship dollars toward high-quality state schools (and there are many) will work not only in cyber but also across many STEM fields. The challenge then becomes how to choose the schools that will best meet the needs of the Air Force. This study finds that the NSA's Cyber Operations Center of Academic Excellence (CAE-Cyber Operations) is a solid basis on which to direct

ROTC scholarship dollars. Schools selected into the CAE-Cyber Operations program must demonstrate that their curricula are interdisciplinary and technically centered and founded on CS, CE, and/or EE; moreover, they must provide abundant opportunities for practicing skills in hands-on labs and exercises. This program is intended to support the president's initiative to "broaden the pool of skilled workers capable of supporting a cyber-secure nation."[11]

At present the USAF does a poor job of recruiting cyber officers from top schools regardless of how quality is measured. Table 13 tallies the number of cyber accessions from the top 10 schools on both the *US News and World Report* list and the NSA accredited schools list. Of nearly 200 cyber accessions per year, the best the USAF has done in recruiting this top-tier talent has been five, or approximately 2 percent. These numbers drive this study to recommend that applicable ROTC detachments be permitted to recruit students into the USAF from top schools using three-and-a-half-year AFROTC scholarships to improve the quality of education of USAF cyber accessions.

Table 13. USAF cyber accessions from the top 10 schools

2009	2010	2011	2012	2013
4	3	2	3	5

Developed from data provided by Office of the Registrar, Holm Center, Air University, March 2014.

Amazingly, the USAF recruits large numbers of cyber operators from schools with weak computer programs through ROTC. Table 14 shows the schools that produce the most cyber warriors and their Accreditation Board for Engineering and Technology (ABET) accreditation status. Seven of the top 11 schools have programs too weak to even make the ranking list (below 115th) in the discipline. Nonetheless, the USAF accepts its inbound officers from these institutions. Of the schools listed, only Penn State is a top-tier program. Many of the schools on the CAE-Cyber Operations list are cost-effective state schools with ROTC programs. Therefore, targeting AFROTC scholarship dollars to these schools would allow the Air Force to gain cyber talent educated to the NSA educational standards.

Recommendation: Steady ROTC budgets to hedge against the risk of OTS not producing adequate quality/quantity of 17D accessions when the economy picks up.

Table 14. ROTC cyber degree production by school and ABET accreditation status

University	Graduates	ABET Accredited
Embry-Riddle (FL and AZ)	99	Y
Troy University	43	N
University of Notre Dame	37	Y
Clarkson University	34	Y
Illinois Institute of Technology	31	Y
Angelo State University	31	N
Pennsylvania State University	30	Y
Virginia Military Institute	29	Y
The Citadel	27	Y
Iowa State University	26	Y
Brigham Young University	26	Y

Developed from Air Force Personnel Center, Personnel Database, Extracts of Officer Data, 1995–2014.

Cyber Advanced Courses in Engineering: In-Sourcing Educational Force Multipliers

The Air Force currently has two Cyber ACE programs. The AFRL's Advanced Course in Engineering Cyber Security Boot Camp (now called the ACE Information Assurance Internship Program) in Rome, New York, came first. The other is AFIT's ROTC Advanced Cyber Education program at Wright-Patterson AFB, Ohio. Both are lauded by the Air Force; however, pedagogically they are not the same. The similar names create confusion, a fact that may appear to the reader as the description of the two programs is expanded below. Using the same acronym for two distinct programs that can each serve to ramp up the numbers of educated Airmen creates confusion. We therefore strongly recommend changing the name and acronym of AFIT's program to help differentiate between the two programs.

Advanced Course in Engineering Cyber Security Boot Camp, Air Force Research Laboratory, Rome, New York

According to AFIT's website, the AFRL founded the ACE Cyber Security Boot Camp "in response to President George W. Bush's National Strategy to Secure Cyberspace." To help fulfill the president's strategy, the program was created in 2003 to develop top ROTC cadets into future cybersecurity leaders by designing an educational curriculum to train the cyber workforce. The content of the AFRL Cyber ACE program originated from the 80-year-old General Electric (GE) ACE known as the Edison Engineering Development Program model to educate students. The ACE Program condensed GE's three-year course into a 10-week summer course designed to develop and enhance an engineer's technical problem-solving skills. The ACE combines advanced academic training, hands-on internships, officer development, and weekly eight-mile runs into a formidable cybersecurity boot camp. The ACE was designated a special-interest item for its role in developing officers for the new Air Force Cyberspace Command. The program consists of advanced engineering coursework, reports, internships, and team presentations and concludes with a cyber defense exercise.

The ACE sought students who completed at least three years in a computer-related discipline (EE, CE, CS, or information studies) and had experience in programming, networking, and operating systems. In 2010 the National Defense Authorization Act nationally recognized the ACE as a program "vital to ensuring a robust information technology workforce that is capable of handling cyber threats to our systems" and requested additional funding to support the ACE effort.[12] The ACE Cyber Security Boot Camp receives no Air Force funding (as of September 2014) but has received funding from the Army to do research on Army issues. In addition to the rigorous cyber engineering semester, the Crisis Decision Making course enhances student awareness of military mission analysis and planning by exposing students to case studies ranging from the Civil War, *Apollo 13*, and the *Columbia* and *Challenger* disasters to Blackhawk Down.[13]

The Air Force Institute of Technology's Advanced Course in Engineering Program

In 2011 the AFRL's ROTC-focused ACE program (i.e., POM funding) was transferred to AFIT to run a summer cadet program for

AFROTC students (some Army and Navy cadets attended as well). Unfortunately, ROTC ACE was a victim of recent budget battles, and the program was not offered in 2013 and 2014 although it should be an option again in 2015.

Although the AFRL-ACE program develops information assurance leadership skills for precommissioned officers for the DOD (and now the British), AFIT's ACE program concentrates on ROTC summer internship programs. We therefore recommend that AFIT change the name of its program to avoid confusing it with that of the AFRL's.

AFRL-ACE
• Solid track record of producing top USAF cyber warriors.
• All 2013 CNODP students were ACE graduates.
• Graduates have gone on to command, receive the Von Karman Award, and help lead Twenty-Fourth Air Force and USCYBERCOM.
• However, funding is erratic despite program's small cost.
• Recommend that the USAF submit annual request for $1.2M via POM for student throughput.

A timeline outlining the history of the programs illustrates the issue:

2003: AFRL/RI (Information Directorate) created the ACE program as a research internship program—largely funded from AFRL sponsor funds.

2008: AFRL/RI obtained funding from ROTC and made the program available to ROTC cadets.

2009: ROTC began canceling its summer internship programs, but ACE continued at Rome because the organization had other funding sources.

2010: AFRL/CC, AETC/CV, and AU/CC agreed to move the ROTC cyber program, along with POM funding, to AFIT. Consequently, AFIT kept the ACE acronym, but the course was titled Advanced Cyber Education.

2011–12: AFIT ran a version of the ROTC ACE program.

2013: AFIT cancels the ROTC version of ACE because of sequestration and budget issues.

2014: AFIT cancels the ROTC version of ACE, again due to budget issues.

2011–14: AFRL continued running its ACE cyber research internship program, but it returned to its pre-ROTC focus of providing students unique cyber engineering problems to solve while giving them leadership and risk-management lessons. However, in 2013–14, in cooperation with AFIT, it expanded its student base to include ROTC cadets. Some of the AFIT faculty go to Rome and teach/mentor classes.[14] Figure 30 illustrates the overlap of the two programs.

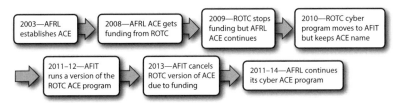

Figure 30. Timeline of AFRL ACE and AFIT ACE development

Certainly, both Cyber ACE programs are force multipliers in that they emphasize the development of educated cyber warriors who can then be trained in the art of cyber warfare for national security objectives. Group discussions with officers at UCT resulted in a consensus that ACE alumni were by far the most qualified of their cohorts in terms of hands-on keyboard portions of the course. One student claimed that Cyber ACE graduates could do the work of four noncyber ACE graduates.

Therefore, we recommend that the Air Force review how it can better leverage the two programs to help meet its cyber needs. Other recommendations in this area include fully funding the AFIT and AFRL ACE programs in the POM cycle and mandating (AU commander) that the AFIT ACE program be renamed to avoid confusion with the AFRL/RI program.

Officer Training School

Since 1971 OTS has accessed about 27 percent of the Air Force's officers. Except for an uptick between 2000 and 2003 in the ramp-up of Operations Enduring/Iraqi Freedom, OTS's percentage of the entire complement of new officers has been running below its historical average for the past 25 years as manning end-strengths have been reduced. However, in 2013 OTS accessions again made up 27 percent of newly minted officers.[15] With the ROTC budget under constant pressure, this recent reliance on OTS's production of new officers is a potential problem. This study determined that when the US economy is robust, skilled cyber professionals—such as the Air Force's 17Ds—

become especially hot commodities and that OTS's ability to recruit and access these skills drastically decreases. Because of the Air Force's current disinclination to direct USAFA cadets to certain majors, the academy cannot be counted upon to deliver more cyber-educated graduates. With both OTS and USAFA unable to reliably populate the Air Force officer cyber corps, ROTC must bear most of the burden. Consequently, there is reason to be concerned that continued hits to ROTC's budget will adversely affect the Air Force's ability to produce officers to fight cyber conflict. The available empirical evidence on the effect of the economy's overall health on accessing cyber-educated officers through OTS can be enlightening when one answers the two questions below.

One question arises during attempts to link the country's economic vitality and new cyber officer production. First, how is economic vitality most effectively captured? Since the emphasis is on the job market, the most natural metric might be the nation's official unemployment rate. As the Congressional Research Service has pointed out, "the main driver of the unemployment rate is the pace of output growth," so the unemployment rate appears to be a good, though lagging, proxy for overall economic well-being as measured by real gross domestic product (GDP).[16] Second, how can high-quality cyber officers be identified at the beginning of their careers? Since the ability to conduct cyber operations at the highest level depends on technical expertise, a "cyber degree" (a bachelor's degree in CS, CE, or EE) can serve as an indicator of technical merit.

The strength of the relationship between cyber-degreed officer accessions and the unemployment rate can be evaluated through measuring their correlation. Based on data provided by the Holm Center and the Bureau of Labor Statistics, the correlation between the average yearly national official unemployment rate and the percentage of cyber-degreed officers accessed from OTS was 0.772 for the period 2005–12 (table 15).[17]

Table 15. Average yearly unemployment rate and percentage of 17D/33S cyber degree holders accessed from OTS (2005–12)

Type of correlation	Coefficient	t-Stat	p-Value
Pearson	0.772	2.215	0.018
Spearman	0.881	4.56	0.004

Developed from data provided by the Holm Center and the Bureau of Labor Statistics.

Meanwhile, the total number of cyber-degreed officers accessed between these years had a correlation of -0.472 with the unemployment rate.[18] This finding means that although more cyber officers have been accessed during times of low unemployment, OTS's production has declined during these periods. It is clear that the Air Force should not depend too heavily on OTS for highly specialized cyber talent.[19] Although this trend does not necessarily mean that the entire ROTC budget must be spared, the number and generosity of scholarships for students pursuing cyber-related degrees should be preserved and quite possibly increased. When one considers the difference in the quality of institutions granting cyber-related degrees to ROTC cadets versus OTS graduates (see the previous discussion in this section), this argument becomes even more powerful.

The correlations show that OTS production of cyber graduates falls during robust economic times. The data suggests that in times of economic growth, OTS is not a reliable producer of cyber warriors. In addition to its problematic nature of recruiting in a prospering economy, OTS's accessions come from a pool of educational institutions inferior to those of ROTC graduates.[20] This finding is based on the fact that 82 percent of ROTC accessions are from schools with ABET accreditation compared to only 26 percent of OTS accessions (fig. 31). ROTC thus provides not only a more reliable source for filling the cyber-officer void but also better quality.

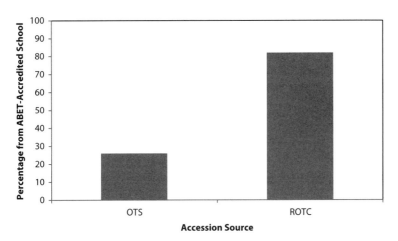

Figure 31. ABET-accredited program graduates from top-producing colleges. (Developed from Air Force Personnel Center, Personnel Database, Extracts of Officer Data, 1995–2014.)

Therefore, this study recommends that the Air Force fully fund the ROTC Scholarship Program to ensure a reliable, quality source of cyber accessions. Moreover, the Air Force should use these scholarship dollars to target recruiting at institutions superior in quality to those from which we have historically drawn our new lieutenants.

Adjustments have been made in table 16 to equate average length of service. The 1B4 field was identified as a secondary AFSC because of incomplete data for the population. On the enlisted side, we see no evidence of adverse selection in education for personnel cross-training into 1B4 (at least compared to 1NXs and 3DXs).

Table 16. Percentage of Airmen by career field and educational level

Career field	Associate's degree	Bachelor's degree	Master's degree
1B4	41.2%	8.48%	0.6%
1NX	21.1%	7.1%	0.4%
3DX	26.2%	7.0%	0.8%

Developed from analysis of AFPC enlisted database, 1998–2014.

Air University and Education at the Operational Level

According to USAF doctrine, operational-level education "assumes a larger role in an Airman's development" and "is intended to enhance professional competence through intermediate developmental education." Education at this level is also "focused on furthering expertise across related specialties and increasing leadership responsibilities" and "continues to build tactical skills and . . . professional competence." For example, "majors will be expected to perform duties as flight commanders or operations officers to gain skills at a higher level in the squadron and complete intermediate developmental education or a selected graduate-level degree program to further their educational needs as maturing professionals." The crux is that development in elite cyber warriors will include a combination of both PME and developmental education. In parallel with their officer counterparts, NCOs attend "relevant specialty schools and pursue professional continuing education [PCE] programs. Civilian personnel at this level fill positions with greater organizational and technical responsibilities. As with their military counterparts, they may be selected to attend an advanced academic degree program . . . or [for] education with industry."[21]

AFIT Graduate Cyber Degree Programs

AFIT, which falls under AU, has the Graduate School of Engineering and Management (EN). The grad school includes departments typically found at any university (e.g., Mathematics, Physics, and Electrical and Computer Engineering [offering the Cyber Operations master's degree]). Students selected are primarily Air Force personnel sent as part of the Air Force Education Requirements Board (AFERB) process and attend for 18 months to earn a master's degree or 36 months for a PhD. In 2013 the Air Force sent a total of three cyber 17Ds to master's programs, and in 2014 it sent eight. These numbers are less than 1 percent of our 17-series cyber force.

In 2007 AFIT instituted the Cyber Warfare Intermediate Developmental Education (IDE) Master's Degree Program for developing midgrade officers. Graduates were to be the USAF's senior cyber leaders within 5 to 10 years of graduation. In 2012 the Air Force decided to stop sending IDE students to AFIT—including all AFIT IDE programs, not just Cyber Warfare—making the 2012–13 academic year the final one that hosted a Cyber Warfare class. During the six years of the program, AFIT produced 45 graduates.[22] Existing capacity and resources (instructors, classroom space, etc.) could have been used to educate 30 additional cyber warfare IDE students without additional faculty or facilities. However, the program was discontinued. Nonetheless, the capacity to restart the program with 30 IDE students remains.

In addition to the now defunct Cyber Warfare IDE program, AFIT has an 18-month cyber operations master's program. Issues with the AFERB process present problems for getting 17-series operators into the program. If units fail to code their billets as requiring advanced degrees, the Air Force doesn't send people to get them. This deficiency affects not only AFIT but also all graduate school opportunities such as universities and the Naval Postgraduate School. The research team found that units are not coding their billets because when they were coded for AADs, the billets went unfilled since no graduates were available. Two or three years ago, during the AFERB meetings to decide how many people were going to go to graduate school, cyber AAD requirements had not been identified, billets were not coded, and then the functional managers were not able to advocate effectively for their needs. The good news is that two years ago, SAF/A6, Maj Gen Earl Matthews, successfully advocated for 35 potential students; they began their master's programs at AFIT in the fall of 2015.

Recommendations: To address the shortage of AAD billets in cyber, this study recommends that the USAF engage in a sequence of actions to undo the destructive effects of previous AFPC actions.

- First, the Air Force should mandate that cyber units review and code their billets for AADs. Newly formed units that are cyber-protection organizations—such as the 624th Operations Center, 39 IOS, and others—must implement this requirement as part of their initial unit manning document.
- Second, AFPC should examine replacing the cumbersome (and always-behind-the-times) AAD-billet-driven system with an inventory-based model. Instead of redesignating billets for AADs every year, the center should assure that "X percent of cyber officers" have advanced degrees (MS and PhD) in cyber.
- Third, the research team believes that the most economical path to fill the void of cyber operation AADs is to send some selects through the AFIT cyber operations master's degree course, which has excess capacity.
- Fourth, AFPC must assign personnel in a way that does not re-create the original problem. When personnel with AADs are not available, AFPC must still fill these billets with the best available talent.
- Fifth, a full reevaluation of the AAD slots and requirements should be embedded within the POM process to effectively update requirements over time.
- Lastly, because a year away from cyber ops results in the need for regaining currency, the USAF should evaluate the merits of creating a two-year PME path consisting of Air Command and Staff College (ACSC) followed by AFIT's cyber operations MS, computer science MS and PhD, or computer engineering MS and PhD, paralleling the current path of ACSC followed by SAASS.

AFIT Professional Continuing Education Programs

AFIT developed and implemented the Cyber 200 and 300 PCE curricula in less than a year after being tasked by AETC/CC. Over 600 officers will have completed these courses in the first year of operation. Cyber 200 and 300 are required for 17-series personnel to obtain their professional ratings and advance within the Air Force. They are currently in review to become joint certified.

Cyber 200 and 300 are part of the USAF cyber force development process for 17XX officers. However, students from other AFSCs—including intel, acquisition, and R&D—as well as from the civilian, Army, and joint world are also enrolled. Cyber 200, a three-week course for officers with about six to eight years of commission time, runs like a cyber Squadron Officer School. Cyber 300 is designed primarily for majors and lieutenant colonels. The focus shifts from tactical operational-level discussions toward policy, strategy, and the big picture. The two classes are normally taught in conjunction, and their students graduate at the same time. In a capstone course, students from both classes work together as part of a larger campaign plan. Another class that has been running is C-EDGE, a one-day class for colonels and above that typically has six to eight students. It addresses high-level awareness of the nature of cyber. AFIT/EN has been working with the AFIT Civil Engineer School to help develop short courses on cyber vulnerabilities and dependencies. It is also working with AFIT/LS (Logistics Systems), the Air Force Life Cycle Management Center, and Headquarters Air Force Materiel Command on short courses for cyber-dependent weapon systems.

Air University: Education at the Operational and Strategic Levels of Cyber Conflict

The teaching and research at AFIT are critical to the Air Force; however, it is not enough to have people who are technically proficient. The Air Force also requires individuals who can apply technology within a joint operational planning construct (e.g., JP 5-0, *Joint Operation Planning*, 11 August 2011) and use critical thinking in determining the impact of cyber on their mission. Every Air Force mission requires networked connectivity to some degree or another.[23] Additionally, every weapon system depends on data and signals both internally to accomplish its own mission and externally to connect and work with the rest of the forces. How do we establish a secure software/hardware environment if industry builds our platforms?

To assure our missions, the Air Force needs a cadre of mission planners who understand the effect of cyber dependencies. This cadre must also articulate mission requirements to the engineering community

(62Es) and other acquisition personnel who recognize a platform's reliance on cyber and know how to design security into key components of the cyber platform. Conceptualizing and articulating the specifications to be built into the hardware/software will increase the cost of success to the adversary but require 62Es and system engineers to document appropriate operational requirements in contracts. This practice can also be extended into mission planning during which teams of nontechnical mission planners relay to the technical cyber wizards the mission requirements and objectives.

The integration of cyberspace and military operations, however, is still a nascent capability. As a result, concepts of operations are still in their embryonic stage. There is no focal point that serves to bring together technical cyber operators and nontechnical mission planners, analysts, and operators for resolving issues related to integrating cyber into military operations. It is our determination that AU has an important role to play in allowing select students to blend operations and theory in the classroom and experiment with new ideas.[24] AU is ideally suited to fill this unmet need because it can combine the technical capabilities of AFIT with the political science aspects of the schools at Maxwell AFB. The area of focus at Maxwell should not be tactical since other schools (such as the USAF Weapons School at Nellis) address this area. AU's emphasis should be on operational-level issues and topics applicable to the broad Air Force audience. As of this writing, AU is standing up a Cyber and Electronic Warfare (EW) Research Task Force to help bridge the gap between operations and theory. The research team recommends that after one year of initial operating capability, the cyber/EW task force be evaluated for consideration to serve as the foundation for a new Consortium for Advanced Cyber Thinking and Strategy (C-ACTS) at AU. This center will provide thoughtful leadership to promote new ideas and concepts and to perform Air Force core missions (air and space superiority, ISR, rapid global mobility, global strike, command and control) in, through, and by means of cyberspace. As the Cyber/EW Task Force takes shape, the following existing cyber education initiatives at AU have contributed to cyber education at Maxwell AFB.

Air War College Cyber Horizons Research Elective

The Cyber Horizons Group Research two-term elective is taught by SMEs from the Air Force Research Institute, Air War College

(AWC), and the LeMay Center Directorate of Intelligence. It provides focused study and development of research projects that meet seminar requirements, supports student professional studies papers for AWC, and assists larger USAF requirements. The course is designed to make students, regardless of background, effective and credible within the cyber warfare community. Its purpose is to explore the organized use of cyber power for the state, with particular attention paid to the US government cyber community; allies, major partners, and global aspects in the conduct of cyber warfare; cyber vulnerabilities and threats; and operations, planning, and analysis of desired effects in the domain. The course objective is to cultivate students' ability to predict, deter, and prevent adversary actions and reactions in the cyber domain. Students leave this course with a clearer understanding of the larger context of cyber conflict; significant knowledge of vulnerabilities, threats, operations, mission planning, and analysis; an orientation to major policies and organizations in the cyber domain; increased literacy in strategic, policy, doctrinal, and technical aspects of cyber warfare; and an understanding of the adversary mind-set. Finally, through preparing their professional studies papers, students conduct research to address broader Air Force needs.

LeMay Center

Cyberspace Operations Executive Course. The COEC is a joint two-day USAF-owned course led by an experienced senior mentor and designed to provide senior USAF leadership with an understanding of network vulnerabilities, threat activity, and ongoing efforts to protect and operate within the cyberspace domain. Its objective is to broaden senior leaders' knowledge of cyberspace issues from a DOT-MLPF (doctrine, organization, training, materiel, leadership and education, personnel, and facilities) perspective so they can effectively influence national and strategic cyber policy. The long-term plan is for the COEC to transition to a joint course.

The COEC serves as the DOD's senior/intermediate general flag officer–level PCE course and is offered semiannually at two different levels. The first is the Senior COEC for three- and four-star flag officers and Tier 3 Senior Executive Service members. The second is Junior COEC for one- and two-star officers and civilian equivalents. Instruction for the course comes from national-level experts and leaders in industry, academia, and the military who offer senior perspectives on cyberspace issues and address topics such as definition of the cyberspace problem set, information assurance, legal implications, cyberspace integration, foreign policy, and national options.[25]

Senior Joint Information Operations Applications Course. The purpose of the SJIOAC is to prepare "selected general/flag officers and senior executive civilians to develop information operations (IO) into a warfighting core military competency that will enable combatant commanders to target adversary decision-making while protecting our own." SJIOAC's primary methodology is a "combination of informal lecture, interactive seminar discussion, demonstration, and case studies." Speakers include "senior national-level civilian and military leaders, representing national agencies and organizations, and combatant commands."[26]

Information Operations Fundamentals Application Course. The IOFAC educates intermediate leaders in the fundamental principles of IO in accordance with the LeMay Center's *Annex 3-13, Information Operations*. The course objective is "to provide students with a broad understanding of [IO] doctrine and insight into how [IO] is applied across the full spectrum of conflict from peace to war." It is taught through lectures, seminars, practical exercises, readings, and case studies.[27]

School of Advanced Air and Space Studies. SAASS currently requires students to take the 667 Information, Cyberspace, and Cyber Power course, which introduces basic cyber systems concepts to nontechnical students. The 20-day course examines "the fundamentals, development and evolution of information, cyber power, and intelligence. [It] intends to foster critical thinking about underlying concepts, strategies and issues that optimize information, cyber power, and intelligence as instruments of national power, and to advance the development of each student's personal theory of air, space and cyber power."[28]

One great hindrance to integrating "more cyber" into the AU curriculum is the Chairman of the Joint Chiefs of Staff Instruction (CJCSI) 1800.01E, *Officer Professional Military Education Policy [OPMEP]*, 29 May 2015. For ACSC and AWC, this instruction directs what must be taught. The research team believes that cyber is not included at the level that may be most appropriate to address the reality of this rapidly evolving domain. Currently, it is available only as an elective. If cyber is to be accepted and recognized for the operational domain it is, then the *OPMEP* must be updated and expanded for cyber.

In December 2005 the Air Force changed its mission statement to include cyberspace as an operational domain. Lt Gen Stephen Lorenz, the AU/CC, recognized in December 2006 that the PME school faculty lacked cyber expertise and direction on the cyber content to include at each level of PME.[29] At General Lorenz's direction, AFIT conducted a study of existing officer PME programs and developed a cyber-requirements document loosely modeled after the *OPMEP*. The idea was to produce something that each school could use to develop its own cyber curriculum that would best fit into its level of PME but not dictate course material.[30]

This approach was consistent with how the *OPMEP* works; in addition to service headquarters-level questions, CSAF guidance, CJCS/CSAF SEIs, and AETC guidance, the *OPMEP* simply states requirements for topics to be covered and leaves it up to the service schools to figure out how to implement the guidance within their own programs. The research team shared the final report for this study with all of the schools and briefed it to the AU/CC and his staff.[31] Although somewhat dated (2007), it remains useful since struggles with similar issues continue. For example, questions that arose at the time included how and by whom the content was developed and who sets the priorities for the content that comes out of the program to make room for cyber.

If the *OPMEP* drives the joint PME curriculum, then it appears that AU could influence PME programs by working proactively with the Military Education Coordination Council (MECC), the body that works the *OPMEP* requirements. In 2009 the MECC wanted to add "space as a contested environment" for inclusion into joint PME. The MECC tasked the National Security Space Institute (NSSI) to develop the coursework, which included five hours of instruction.[32] This coordination among PME/PCE institutions and MAJCOMs highlights a possible venue for cross-pollination between cyber operations and current joint PME. The potential thus exists for nesting the education under existing objectives rather than trying to add new objectives within the *OPMEP* (e.g., objectives that discuss how joint forces fight).

Toward an Air Force Cyber Operational History

Operational theory as it applies to cyber and EW "beyond poles and wires" is lagging technology, thus causing a significant problem for the Air Force and placing missions within the five core functions at risk of failure due to cyber disruptions.[33] We currently lack a historical context gleaned from lessons learned in cyber operations past. The generation and publication of a sufficiently rigorous and robust set of operational theory informed by cyber history can become the foundation on which to guide problem formulation. It can enable Airmen to leverage the opportunities of new, emerging computing and networking technologies while assuring missions against the vulnerabilities of adversary usage. However, the first step is for the USAF to recognize and be proud of its cyber heritage and instill a sense of cyber-mindedness in its Airmen.

The USAF has overinvested in capabilities and doctrine not guided by technological, operational, and strategic realities of cyber conflict as a result of lacking historical analysis of the domain. An initial effort to document these shortcomings is found in *A Fierce Domain*, an Air Force–centered cyber history book.[34] Without more efforts to codify unit histories and craft a formal Air Force cyber historical account that can then be integrated into its curriculum, the service is neglecting to integrate lessons learned from over 30 years of operational experience in the domain. The difficulty in assimilating cyber history into PME education is that the content of PME courses is specified by CJCSI 1800-01E, as described above. This instruction, under the purview of J7 (Joint Force Development), has a lengthy modification process, and the presidents of AU, Army War College, Navy War College, and National Defense University must agree to make any changes before starting this process with the MECC.

Simply finding that cyber history is not taught in PME is not enough; a systemic effort to collect and write the history of Air Force cyber should be conducted internally. Thus, the following actions are recommended:

- Commission the US Air Force Historical Research Agency to collect official cyber unit histories and oral histories of the pioneers of the Air Force cyber mission and to work closely with doctrinal authors to ensure continuity in cyber.
- Commission AU to use this material as the basis of a major study with appropriate lessons.
- Integrate cyber heritage and lessons into all PME.

Following these steps will ensure that cyber history begins to be taught and that we do not keep repeating the mistakes of lessons unlearned.

DOD Conference Policies' Negative Impact on Faculty and Curriculum Relevancy

Existing Air Force conference policies negatively affect faculty currency and credibility in a dynamic domain that relies on networks of personal relationships to facilitate information flow and foster professional development. Indeed, *Annex 1-1, Force Development*, that "educators should survey training methods outside of organizational bounds (other Services, government, and industry) to stay abreast of new training and education insights and best practices and adapt these methods to the programs for training and educating the force."[35] The current DOD and USAF restrictions for non-DOD conferences have rendered it virtually impossible for the USAF cyber force to operate within its doctrine and remain current with and relevant to the changes in cyber.

To be a leader in the emerging cyber profession requires not only immersion in technology but also participation in the forums of the communities of practice and professional societies.[36] If one is in the IT business, relationships with other IT leaders and professionals are critical. The field is complex, and faculty and researchers must be able to keep pace with changes to integrate the state of the art as it is being developed in the private sector into Air Force operations and curricula. Anecdotally, this study found that several senior Air Force leaders viewed their working relationships with Silicon Valley venture capitalists and industry leaders as crucial to their ability to succeed in the field. Thus, to grow these networks through interactions at workshops and conferences, it is critical that the Air Force amend its rules for faculty attending or presenting at such gatherings.

Training Cyber Forces

Although cyber force training was discussed in chapter 5, "Force Development," the focus here is on initial training for a handful of specialties. These include officers in the 17S-series (cyber warfare operations) and 14N-series (intelligence) cyber specialty codes as well as enlisted personnel in the 1B4X1 AFSC (cyber warfare operations—retrained from the 3DXX [cyberspace support specialty]) and, to a lesser extent, 1N4X1A—the fusion analyst / digital network analyst AFSC.[37] A research team interviewed leadership, staff, and students about cyber graduates at Keesler and Goodfellow AFBs and Hurlburt Field. Cyber training is a long process for 17S and 1B4X1 students. For those ultimately assigned to the national mission teams, the duration could be over 24 months. A comparison of the money and time allocated for training with the enlistment commitment or ADSC reveals that the return on investment can be quite low.[38]

Officer and enlisted students are exposed to a variety of theories and scenarios related to confronting threats to our national systems. Officers receive the broad overview of the systems and defenses, and enlisted students learn to operate the checklists to support and defend the networks. The initial course is roughly 90 to 95 percent theory and 5 to 10 percent hands-on experience, thus differing from some industry practices such as Google's, which advocates learning by doing rather than by studying.[39] It allows people to learn from their mistakes; emulating the cyber giant's hands-on approach is desirable. In follow-on courses for cyber Airmen, the hands-on time increases to 40 percent or more—more interactive and less book learning.

The Air Force's investment in producing these cyber Airmen is significant. To avoid squandering it, the service needs to examine its commitment and assignment processes for these officers and Airmen. Cyber Airmen should rotate less and have at least two consecutive cyber tours—a change that could alleviate additional training requirements while allowing the development of deeper cyber skills. Other cyber specialty training should also be more thoroughly reviewed, including that for positions such as civilians in the GS-2210 IT management series who acquire, manage, and maintain cyber systems. They should be key players in the procurement of cyber resources for the Air Force. The team discovered some additional training issues that bear mentioning.

Training Issues

Credit for Education and Experience

This study proposes evaluation of a test similar to the CLEP (used for student placement) for use in UCT to find individuals with the requisite skills. Students with either an educational foundation or previous work experience—commercial or military—could test out of certain portions of the curriculum. This test could also be applied to other cyber courses administered by the Air Force or the joint community. One professor mentioned that it was not a smart training model to repeat training for graduates in CS, CE, and EE at UCT just because other individuals are less familiar with cyberspace.[40]

This concept could also be used to grant mission equivalency based on previous experiences of students or to accommodate those returning to the cyber field (e.g., an AFSC 17D communications officer). Although this situation may apply to only a small number of students, they could be fast-tracked or given other experiential work, saving resources for the Air Force. Other alternative on-ramps should be available for individuals to enter the cyber field based on their educational or experiential backgrounds.

Facilities and Equipment

The USAF cyber force receives its training at underfunded and underdeveloped training locations. Initial training at Keesler—a cobbled-together, understaffed operation—nonetheless provides solid entry-level training to future cyber forces. Additional funding in 2014 allowed expanding existing and building new sensitive compartmented information facilities (SCIF) to handle an expected increased training load. The cyber range also underwent a $1.5 million upgrade.[41]

Despite increased funding, the Keesler team has no backup for its cyber range equipment. This range—built in-house with castoff and obsolete equipment—provides suboptimum and incomplete training. When a system technology must be refreshed, the school has to curtail training for that time. Training pauses are not feasible because of student production scheduling. A joint range could be used to satisfy training requirements, but the faculty believes it needs its own operating environment to better prepare students.

Although Air Force flying ranges are POM supported and championed, cyber ranges such as the one at Keesler have no funding line or advocates in the POM process. Cyber ranges are neither properly funded nor sustained to meet new mission challenges. The acquisition portion of this study states that funding programs reflect what a service values (see chap. 2). While the DOD will not keep pace with cyber-development cycles, the Air Force needs to stay in that ballpark with procurement. The service must find ways to make cyber training and education adaptive to the developments in the field (OPR: SAF/FM, AFSPC, AETC, 24th AF).[42]

Standardization and Jointness

Students in the cyber schoolhouses are meeting the initial qualifications for their given AFSCs. For example, the Business and Enterprise Systems Office believes that enlisted personnel (about 300 of the 3D0X4 programmers) arrive at Maxwell Gunter Annex well trained by the AETC system.[43] That said, they still require about one year of OJT before being completely trained and able to accomplish the mission. As with other AFSCs, manpower documents assume these Airmen to be fully productive upon arrival at their units; however, that assumption is untrue across most of the cyber enterprise.

For many Airmen, specific mission qualification training occurs in their units, as does their upgrade and continuity training. Unfortunately, as of this writing, many units have no credentialed instructors or valid syllabi to prepare those Airmen to meet mission-ready standards. For example, Airmen in the areas of cybersecurity and control systems, Air Force intranet control, and cyber defense analysis receive their "finishing" training in their units. Therefore, such training will not be standard across the Air Force. As with other specialties, such as pilots and missileers, recurring training for cyber Airmen is a must. Such training may also need to be conducted more often to keep up with the dynamics of the cyber domain, but it is absent, as is the standardization/evaluation process. Further, unlike their flying counterparts, many cyber units have no budget or manning for in-house training. It all comes from their existing funds. The result is a lack of standardization for students and an additional workload for unit members.

In a more standardized approach, the 39 IOS handles OJT and mission qualification for Airmen in the cyber warfare operations control center application; cyber vulnerability/hunt; Air Force cyber defense; and command, control, and communications mission system arenas. The 39th sends INWT instructors on temporary duty (TDY) with the recently graduated students to their gaining units. Once there, the 39th instructors conduct OJT / mission qualification instruction with students using the gaining units' systems for two to four weeks. This process completes the upgrade of the students to mission-ready status. The TDY cost is considerable, but the current belief is that this method not only is less expensive than establishing training systems for all students at Hurlburt but also creates a more uniform training result.

Standardized training has benefits for both the Air Force and the joint community. Joint ranges might become useful and cost effective, as could joint schoolhouses. The DOD continues to work more jointly, and joint training could facilitate the movement into joint cyber operations. As the DOD moves toward the NICE cybersecurity workforce standards for KSAs, curricula should conform to that common cybersecurity structure. Since Air Force career fields and training already closely track the NICE framework, it makes sense to capitalize on that training and open the door to train for the other services as well. A joint facility would help to fulfill the Air Force's needs, bring the DOD under one training regime, and save scarce training dollars.

Sustaining Materials and Skills

Maintaining up-to-date course materials and keeping Airmen's skills current is a challenge. Cyberspace is constantly changing, and keeping courses relevant is difficult—especially for those with a formal review process. TTPs in the cyber domain change on 90-day cycles, but some course updates take years to complete. Some curricula at the Keesler schoolhouse can be quickly adapted. However, much of the work is still done the old-fashioned way with a cumbersome curriculum review cycle. Even so, the team at Keesler frequently updates certain blocks of instruction. For example, the threats block is continually updated with the latest threat information regarding viruses and malware. The AETC curriculum review pipeline must be streamlined so that schoolhouses will be able to assure cyber curriculum relevance with the operational needs of the cyber force. Similarly, keeping course material current in a dynamic cyber training domain cannot be done with traditional print media. Continual updates through various digital media are essential to keep the cyber force current.[44] For the cadre at the 39 IOS, updating curriculum based on the Twenty-Fourth Air Force's task training list can take as little as one week, allowing for rapid adjustments as TTPs change.

The latest system configurations and equipment are not taught at Keesler, but they should be. Our student cyberspace warriors need robust training in the IPv6 framework. As IPv4 becomes saturated, the IPv6 framework will grow in use and operational significance (see the chap. 2 discussion on IPv6). AFSPC and Twenty-Fourth Air

Force should address this need with training tasking letters to the schoolhouses for incorporation into initial and follow-on courses.

Once trained, cyber warriors must maintain their currency, especially when they rotate to different positions. As with pilots transitioning back to the cockpit after a school tour, what would the transition back to the "cyber cockpit" involve? The dynamic cyberspace environment makes cyber skills highly perishable. One option for alleviating this problem is fewer moves for cyber warriors. Another might be to rotate them into positions in which they can maintain a level of currency, thereby reducing retraining time when they return to operational status.[45] Continuous learning is not optional in the cyber defense field. To that end, this study recommends that HAF A2/A3/A6 examine the possibility of a single cyberspace transition course or work with USCYBERCOM and the joint community to create a replacement training unit (RTU) or transition course (OPR: HAF A1/A6, 24th AF).

Update Process for AETC Undergraduate Cyber Training Curriculum

In discussion with operations units, the research team found that substantial manpower was devoted to training new accessions in cyber developments in areas that UCT could have addressed. Follow-on discussions with staff at AETC/A3 revealed that the curriculum revision timeline for UCT was incapable of keeping pace with the evolving technology of cyber. The undergraduate schoolhouse at Keesler generally operates with an 18-month lag over current practice. The gap is then covered by operational units when a new accession reports for operations duty and goes through unit-specific training.

The lag for the UCT curriculum is a product of risk mitigation strategies for a new curriculum—seeking to ensure that it is ready to be taught and instructors are properly trained. Attempting to speed up this timeline is risky from a curriculum development standpoint. AETC staff argued that the Instructional Systems Development (ISD) process takes considerable time.

This study finds that the ill-prepared nature of graduates from UCT can be remedied through a two-pronged effort, both parts of which are currently under way. First, in negotiations about the course content of UCT, AFSPC should insist that the course be monitored and, if necessary, modified to keep it current with emerging threats and technology. Second, AFSPC and AETC should establish a robust working relationship parallel to that between the 39 IOS and AFPC, whereby lesson plans are revised, through mutual effort, at least once every 180 days, with course sections on fundamental technologies revised at least annually. Doctrinally based courses are updated every 18 months. UCT instructors must be SMEs and should be personally responsible for their lesson plans.

Air Force developmental teams ensure that initial training and upgrade training create technically sound cyber members. In consultation with training stakeholders (e.g., HAF A2/A3/A6, AETC, and AFSPC), the teams make inputs to the utilization and training work groups and training planning teams. They assess and revise courses based on the ISD process, but developing education or training standards is time consuming. By the time all parties sign off on a standard, it may well have become obsolete. To overcome this problem, this study recommends reforming the ISD process to ensure timely cyber career field training attuned to the operational environment. Along these lines, HAF A3/A6 is reviewing the requirements document governing the UCT curriculum. By becoming less restrictive with its specifications, the subsequent requirements document will keep pace with the rapidly evolving cyber domain, allowing courses to maintain operational currency between triennial reviews.

As indicated, cyber training has many stakeholders, including the 17-series career field managers, 14N managers, AFSPC/A3D (which tracks 4Ns), and NSA/USCYBERCOM. The service branches and several national agencies have varied cyber training paths with no curriculum or course currency requirements standards. Consequently, levels of expertise will vary within the Air Force and across the DOD. Since the cyberspace domain is so pervasive and joint in nature, this study recommends mapping training to the NICE cybersecurity workforce framework for KSAs or NICE KSAs. This standard is a reasonably good one, appropriate not only for the Air Force but also for the other military branches and government agencies.

Cyber Instructors

Sufficient numbers of quality instructors are necessary for successful training. It takes two to six months to spin up a qualified officer or NCO to become an instructor, a time frame not unlike those of other institutions such as Squadron Officer College. The process includes shadowing an instructor in class, teaching under the supervision of a mentoring instructor, and, finally, independently teaching student cyber warriors. Instructors must remain current in the cyber discipline during the course of their teaching duties, both for instructional purposes and in preparation for their follow-on assignments. They do so by completing continuing-education short courses in the latest TTPs in use by friend and foe—at a minimum.

The Air Force cyber schoolhouses require more instructors with operational relevance—a desirable objective—but schoolhouse manning is always short. Releasing instructors for continuing education places even greater burdens on those who remain, especially since only 66 percent of the officer cyber instructor billets are filled.[46] The schoolhouses must also contend with a two-edged sword: They would like to keep instructors, especially the very good ones, for longer than the typical assignment period; however, even though continuity is desirable, staying in the schoolhouse too long hurts the member's career progression. Schoolhouse manning should be investigated to find ways to maintain adequate numbers of instructors while allowing for their proper continuing education and career progression (OPR: AETC/A1 [Manpower and Personnel]).

Summary

With the accelerating changes in the cyber domain, the cyber Airmen of today will differ from those of 2020. The Air Force has done a remarkably good job of laying a foundation for its cyber force and is ramping up to meet the challenge of producing hundreds more trained cyber warriors for the mission teams. Nonetheless, more needs to be done, especially in terms of educating the career field. Educating and training Air Force cyber warriors will require state-of-the-art equipment and facilities, expert faculty, and rapidly evolving curricula.

RECOMMENDATIONS SUMMARY

- To overcome the problem of obsolete standards, reform the ISD process to ensure timely cyber career field training attuned to the operational environment. Along these lines, HAF/A6SP is reviewing the requirements document governing the UCT curriculum. To keep pace with the rapidly evolving cyber domain, the subsequent requirements document will be less restrictive with its specifications, thus allowing courses to maintain operational currency between triennial reviews.

EDUCATING AND TRAINING CYBER FORCES | 185

RECOMMENDATIONS SUMMARY (*continued*)

- Since the cyberspace domain is so pervasive and joint in nature, map training to the NICE cybersecurity workforce framework for KSAs or NICE KSAs. This standard is a reasonably good one, appropriate not only for the Air Force but also for the other military services and government agencies.
- HAF A2/A3/A6 should examine the possibility of a single cyberspace transition course or work with USCYBERCOM and the joint community to create an RTU or transition course.
- Investigate schoolhouse manning to find ways to maintain adequate levels of instructors while allowing proper continuing education and career progression for instructors.
- The USAF must find ways to make cyber training and education adaptive to the developments in the field.
- The best way to increase interest in the 17-series AFSC is for USAFA customers to tell, and then prove to, cadets that the Air Force has good jobs for them. Knowing there are interesting jobs in the field will drive up interest.
- Creating a summer course for cadets would be useful as a means of enticing them into the career field. Currently, one does not exist (it was eliminated when the 110 course was updated and offered to all cadets in their first year.)
- Maintain steady ROTC budgets to hedge against the risk of OTS not producing adequate quality/quantity of 17D accessions when the economy picks up.
- The USAF should take a more focused look at how the two Cyber ACE programs can be better leveraged to help meet USAF cyber needs.
- To continue the trend of developing highly capable cyber operators, fully fund and expand the AFIT/AFRL distinct ACE programs. Fully fund, in POM, the AFRL/RI ACE program. Fully fund, in POM, the AFIT ACE program for ROTC.
- Mandate an AFIT name change to avoid confusion with the distinct AFRL/RI program. Re-recognize AFRL/RI ACE as a national asset and a CSAF special-interest item.

Notes

1. Kugelman, "Bloom's Taxonomy."
2. Beaver, "Five Network Security Lessons."
3. Verton, "Anthem Hack Reveals Limits."
4. Borrely, "To Certified Training."
5. Thomas, *Decoding the Virtual Dragon*, 152–57.
6. Ibid.
7. ICPC, "ICPC Fact Sheet," 1.
8. 27th International Olympiad in Informatics, "Call for Papers."
9. Air Force Personnel Center, Personnel Database.

10. The website Capture the Flag (CTF) time, which tracks cyber capture-the-flag competitions worldwide, lists some of the most relevant competitions to the Air Force cyber mission (although it does not list the National Collegiate Cyber Defense Competition, http://www.nationalccdc.org). Among competitors from around the world, in 2014 the USAFA placed 82d (http://www.ctftime.org/team/446, accessed September 2014). Although not a scientific analysis, this rating system does offer a compelling metric of the capabilities that the cyber range brings to students at the academy.

11. "National Centers of Academic Excellence."
12. House, National Defense Authorization Act for Fiscal Year 2010, 200.
13. Dr. Kamal Jaboor, telephone interview by research team, July 2014.
14. Dr. Yannakogeorgos is grateful to the professors and senior scientists at AFIT and AFRL who walked him through this timeline and provided much of the background information on the history of the two programs.
15. Data provided by Office of the Registrar, Holm Center, AU, March 2014.
16. Levine, *Economic Growth and the Unemployment Rate*, 1.
17. With p-value=0.018.
18. Bureau of Labor Statistics, "Labor Force Statistics."
19. Although this correlation does not necessarily imply causation, the likely negative consequences of assuming spurious correlation necessitate reaching this conclusion.
20. Air Force Personnel Center, Personnel Database.
21. LeMay Center, *Volume II, Leadership*, 42.
22. Respectively, the student output per year from 2007 until 2012 was 12, 5, 5, 12, 7, and 4.
23. Dr. Yannakogeorgos is indebted to Col William Young, the Air War College Cyber Chair, for sharing his thoughts that shaped this section of the study.
24. Fadok and Raines, "Driving towards Success in the Air Force Cyber Mission," 4–11.
25. LeMay Center, "Cyberspace Operations Executive Course."
26. LeMay Center, "Senior Joint Information Operations Applications Course."
27. LeMay Center, "Information Operations Fundamentals Application Course."
28. SAASS 667, Information, Cyberspace, and Cyber Power, course syllabus.
29. Mills, teleconference meeting minutes.
30. AU/AFIT faculty, interviews by research team, December 2013.
31. Mills, Raines, and Williams, *Developing Cyberspace Competencies*.
32. Andrus, teleconference meeting minutes.
33. Col William Young (director, AU Cyber/EW Research Task Force), interview by Dr. Yannakogeorgos, Maxwell AFB, AL, January 2015.
34. Healey, *Fierce Domain*.
35. LeMay Center, *Annex 1-1, Force Development*, 10.
36. Raduege, interview.
37. On 1 November 2014, the 17D cyberspace operations officer specialty was split into two AFSCs—a 17D network operations officer and a 17S cyber warfare operations officer.
38. Enlistment for 1B4X1 is four years; ADSC is four years. The USAF gets two years of "use."

39. Vint Cerf (vice president, Google), interview by research team, Washington, DC, February 2014.
40. Comment by senior USAFA professor in CS/CE.
41. Twenty-Fourth Air Force, vice-commander, briefing.
42. Cerf, interview.
43. Col Kjall GoPaul (AFLCMC/HIZ [chief, Operations Division, Business and Enterprise Systems Directorate, Air Force Life Cycle Management Center]), interview by Dr. John Geis (Air Force Research Institute), 11 June 2014, Gunter Annex, AL.
44. Raduege, interview.
45. US Army Cyber Command (ARCYBER), staff interview by research team, Fort Meade, MD, January 2014.
46. Further aggravating the manning situation is the fact that some of the 17S/D officers will be or have been caught in the reduction in force (RIF), which may affect the students as well. Each student represents an investment of $68,000 for training and 115 days of technical training. The RIF would allow only six months of operational duty.

Chapter 8

Concluding Thoughts

With cyberspace underpinning all of the Air Force's core missions, the cyber workforce will be vital to mission success. Every Air Force mission requires networked connectivity to some degree or another. Every weapon system depends on data and signals, both internally to ensure platform functionality to accomplish Air Force missions and externally to connect and work with the rest of the forces. Therefore, as this study found, our cyber workforce tasks are twofold: (1) recruit, educate, train, and sustain an educated workforce that understands the dependencies and risks that cyberspace may pose to a mission, and (2) develop Airmen in career fields outside cyber to apply cyber operational concepts and capabilities to actively engage, counter, and mitigate the cyber risks posed to their missions. Without addressing the first issue, the second will be problematic.

Regarding the first area, the Air Force is aware of the challenges in planning, developing, and managing a complex cyber operations workforce. However, debates are ongoing as to the kind of person who makes a good cyber operator. Rooted in the decision to migrate the 33S (communications) officers into the 17D (cyberspace officer) career field is the persistent perception that cyber means anything concerning IT. The conventional wisdom seems to be that IT personnel in DODIN roles are cyber operators when they are truly serving an important enabling function that overlaps with DCO. DODIN operators fulfill the roles of system administrators (responsible for patching), network administrators (responsible for monitoring), and security operations center analysts (responsible for collected observation analysis and correlation). They fall within the cyber warrior spectrum and obviously have a role in the defensive and, if engaged in active defense, the offensive side as well. Operators in this specialty have security functions in establishing and maintaining the network in accordance with best practices and standards. Since experience is critical in understanding the cyber domain, the rotation of cyber Airmen between DCO/OCO and DODIN ensures readiness.

As this study concludes, the management of IT differs from the conduct of cyber operations to meet commanders' intent to assure missions in support of national security. IT and OT have unique attributes.

Much of the IT paradigm is concerned with enforcing confidentiality versus integrity and availability of information systems. Military operations rely on platforms with OT embedded with them. They are thus much more focused on system integrity and availability. Compromises of these two elements can lead to immediate mission failure, whereas violations of confidentiality must be leveraged in conjunction with some other capability to produce mission failure as a second-order effect. We thus strongly encourage force planners not to equate traditional IT roles with mission assurance. As has been highlighted, military missions rely on the embedded processors, controllers, and other elements that comprise operational IT.

As of this writing, the USAF is beginning to move past the generalities and establish some definite tactical/operational requirements for cyber operators, one aspect of which is USCYBERCOM's Cyber Mission Force. CMF constructs deal mainly with what have typically been thought of as the DCO and OCO sides of cyber operations. The rest of DODIN ops (build, operate, maintain, and secure networks) is not in that construct. The DODIN is more related to what communication squadrons, and eventually the joint information environment, will tackle down to the base level. The CMF construct dictates three types of teams with Cyber Command: cyber protection teams, cyber mission teams, and national mission teams. The basic structure defines exactly what kinds of people should appear on each kind of team (17 series, 14N, 1B4, 1NXX). The Air Staff as the cyber force-development lead (A6S) and AFSPC/A3 (Directorate of Air, Space, and Information Operations) are doing the operational test and evaluation for that. The Airmen on those CPTs, CMTs, and NMTs that the Air Force provides will require training that has already started at the UCT, 39 IOS, and AFIT schoolhouses and that Twenty-Fourth Air Force has been influencing in conjunction with the Air Staff and AETC. As this study has reiterated, however, we still have a long way to go in ensuring an up-to-date curriculum and a training infrastructure at the schoolhouse—one that reflects operational challenges beyond just IP network operations.

The second area—developing Airmen outside cyber to recognize and mitigate cyber risks posed to their missions—is no less critical and perhaps the greater challenge. Technological solutions alone will not solve our cyber problems. Cyber operators, planners, and strategists must be developed at every level of education. The need will continue for creating and sustaining a cyber-aware workforce that can articulate the extent to which cyber puts missions at risk to commanders. A concurrent need will exist for fostering cyber-savvy commanders who grasp their mission's dependencies on the domain. Shrinking defense budgets and commitments to our core mission areas remain obstacles to achieving these objectives. Nonetheless, the foundation for these proficiencies is the education and research that enable the creation of innovative concepts to develop capabilities that meet a commander's mission needs and ensure effective operations with an extremely high level of certainty.

The Air Force is communicating that it places a low value on educating cyberspace professionals. At a minimum, the service is losing the battle of perceptions with the other services that have built or plan to build cyber research centers at their institutions of higher learning. The Military Academy, Naval Academy, Naval Postgraduate School, and Naval War College are all establishing cyber programs. Indeed, as of this writing in June 2015, Air University is establishing an Air Force Cyber College that will blend technology, operations, and strategy, and the Air Force Academy is establishing a Cyber Innovation Center. When the study was ongoing, a key recommendation was to take such action not only from an educational perspective but also from a recruitment standpoint. A prospective cadet or recruit interested in cyber would be prone to choose a military service based on the visible emphasis it puts on cyber. The Air Force must enhance these embryonic efforts with the appropriate funding and resources when it comes to cyber, or it will eventually suffer the consequences and potentially lose talent to other services. As this study has indicated, conveying an institutional commitment to cyber and developing cyber warriors are of utmost importance. The Air Force clearly displays its level of commitment through how it chooses to operationalize the domain, develop its human capital, and equip its cyber forces. We therefore strongly urge the establishment of a robust cyber capacity at Air University, where the art and science of cyber operations and strategy can be crafted to guide the force.

Continuous learning in cyberspace is also mandatory—analogous to the continuing training that a pilot receives. Like pilots, cyber operators cannot be away from operations for very long and retain currency. Maintaining a level of future awareness and an exposure to new ideas is necessary. Therefore, we need a cohort of quality Airmen who understand the domain and know how to operationalize it. Today the Air Force focuses on "poles and wires" in cyberspace. The result is that we have tactics masquerading as strategy and doctrine that lacks true utility. AU has a significant role in balancing the art and science of cyber conflict in a meaningful way to operationalize the cyber domain. In cyberspace, the USAF cannot simply develop its strategic approach based on past lessons from air and space strategy and then expect to sprinkle some "cyber" on it. Rather, the service needs to effectively blend air, space, and cyber power from the onset of campaign design to maximize the inherent advantages of each of the Air Force's five core mission areas and fuse them into an elegant whole that cannot be disaggregated. Doing so requires not only cyber operators but also mission planners who understand the risk to their operations in, through, and by means of cyber—an area we identified as a critical gap that AU is in a unique position to address.

The USAF needs to recognize the dynamics that will exist in the cyber domain and the ways they apply to a force structure. This study presented solutions for how the Air Force can develop cyber leaders while ensuring that it educates and trains cyber operators. Good cyber leaders need to be competent experts in the field. Offering a continuity of assignments will promote having leadership with the experience to operationalize the cyber domain. Cyber leaders should be able to fulfill the traditional leadership roles of mentoring and providing direction; they should also cultivate team resources (a process that includes developing individual skills, devising team approaches to development and operations, and managing human resources).

For retaining a quality cyber workforce, the government pay/grade structure as it stands today isn't competitive with that of the private sector. It will never be. However, salary is not the primary motivating factor with the incoming millennials. They want to be challenged, receive rapid feedback, and contribute through public service; moreover, they don't want to be dragged into too much administrivia. That said, there are hurdles to retention as the nationwide demand for cyber talent increases. The effect of the revolving door of military-to-contractor personnel exchanges on retention needs to be further explored, along with legal instruments such as noncompete clauses that would bar recruitment of USAF personnel from the operational floor by companies fulfilling contracts there.

We cannot solve every problem related to the application of cyber and electronic warfare across core functions. However, as the intellectual center of the Air Force, AU owes it to the service and the nation to conduct research necessary to begin the development of robust, rigorous, and scalable methodologies that enable Airmen both to frame and to solve institutional problems in a more useful manner. As a result, we must lead the development of theory necessary to secure the advantage enabled by effective integration of cyber advances into the Air Force's strategic, operational, tactical, technical, and policy decisions. The emergent operational concepts and strategic policies will allow the Air Force and the nation to mature and develop their cyber forces. We find that our Air Force is leading the nation down this very path today.

Appendix

Overall Recommendations and Status

APPENDIX | 197

KEY RECOMMENDATIONS

Organize	Educate/Train	Equip
Use economic indicators with existing manning and retention stats to adjust selective reenlist bonuses to mitigate manning crisis levels. (AFPC)	Examine/implement reforms to Instructional Systems Development (ISD) process with career field to ensure that education and training are attuned to the operational environment. (AETC/AFPSC)	Mandate IPv6 transition for the USAF's operational benefit. (HAF/A6/AFNIC)
Recognize cyber as a separate domain with separate language / social science requirements, and catalog personnel identified/recruited.	Map curriculum to National Initiative for Cybersecurity Education (NICE) knowledge, skills, and abilities (KSA) to ensure interagency relevance. Investigate use of cyber competitions for recruiting.	Actively contribute to Internet governance. (A6/AFRL/AU)
Incorporate Department of Homeland Security (DHS)-NICE framework across cyber career fields. (A6S)	Enhance the IPv6 networking and software programming in curriculum. (AFSPC/AETC)	Equip schools consistent with POMed (requested in program objective memorandum) lab/range equipment, including software/hardware.
Create electronic position description/tracking mechanism mapped to NICE. Investigate use of special experience identifiers (SEI) to track specialized cyber skills for assignments. (A1)	In lean years, give the 1B4 career field priority for tuition assistance and other like programs in cyber-related fields.	Integrate acquired systems to avoid a "patchwork quilt" of systems and software. (AFSPC, SAF/AQ, AFMC)
Mandate that cyber units code their billets for advanced academic degrees (AAD).	Fully fund the Air Force Institute of Technology (AFIT) / Air Force Research Laboratory (AFRL) distinct Advanced Cyber Education (ACE) programs (change AFIT program name); estimated cost is $1.6M.	Emphasize software assurance, and incentivize contractors to use best practices.
USAFA customers should create demand signal to cadets that there are good jobs for them as 17D/Ss. Create a summer course for cadets as a means of enticing them into the career field. (USAFA)	Ramp up cyber AAD production (including AFIT) to meet identified demand. Create a cyber hygiene curriculum for accessions programs. (AETC)	Develop technical cyber acquisition certification similar to that for engineering.

RECOMMENDATIONS: CONNECTING TECHNOLOGY AND POLICY (CHAP. 2)

	Recommendation	Implementation/Status
1	Manpower planners must account for the Joint Information Environment (JIE) and other systemic technological paradigm shifts as they assess their 5-to-10-year workforce requirements.	In Progress: HAF/A6SP
2	The DOD and USAF should document their roles and provide metrics on their participation and position with Internet governance bodies.	HAF/A6
3	The USAF chief information officer (CIO) should develop and establish enforcement mechanisms to ensure standard Air Force–wide information technology (IT) configurations, allowing better network integration and fewer base-specific failures with security/network defense tools.	HAF/A6P
4	The USAF should embed the life-cycle-management process as part of its cyber decision making.	In Progress: AFSPC, SAF/AQ, AFMC Air Force Business and Enterprise Systems (BES) Directorate, and SECAF initiated "Bending the Cost Curve Program"
5	The USAF should increasingly rely on its enlisted programmers to supply the talent to perform many software assurance activities. Although civilians and officers can perform these functions admirably, they are often considerably more expensive to obtain and retain.	AFPC
6	The DOD and Air Force should provide adequate incentives for secure programming that far exceeds the level necessary to avoid liability.	SAF/AQ Research on methodology in progress: AU
7	The USAF should examine holding vendors financially liable for inept software designs and/or coding that leaves systems vulnerable.	SAF/AQ Research on methodology in progress: AU
8	Incorporate the DHS's NICE framework across cyberspace career fields.	In Progress: HAF/A6SP
9	Create electronic professional development tracking mechanism (such as SEIs) mapped to NICE.	HAF/A1, SAF/A6SP, AFPC
10	Recognize cyberspace as a domain with language and social science requirements, and catalog personnel.	HAF/A1/A2, AFPC
11	Mandate a firm transition date to IPv6 utilizing DOD acquisition policies and the JIE.	CSAF
12	The USAF needs to ensure that adequate training exists on cyberspace ranges within IPv6 environments for cyberspace operators. All current operators need to be proficient in IPv6 now.	A6SF, 24th AF, AETC/AFSPC

APPENDIX | 199

Recommendations: Connecting Technology and Policy (Chap. 2) (continued)

	Recommendation	Implementation/Status
13	The DOD, particularly the USAF, should take a more active role in the development of the cyberspace infrastructure and the standards and norms of Internet governance mirroring its actions in the domain of space at International Telecommunication Union (ITU)-Radiocommunications.	HAF/A6, AETC/AU, AFSPC
14	The USAF should develop and implement proprietary protocols designed to be mathematically secure.	Development in Progress: AFRL/RI Implementation A6P
15	Broadband mobility provides opportunities to engage with target audiences; social scientists and linguists will be critical to do so effectively. The USAF needs to ensure that it has an adequate number of linguists and social scientists educated / trained / experienced in cyberspace operations.	A1
16	Develop formal partnerships between the engineering communities, which understand operational IT, and the cybersecurity communities, which understand network IT, to mitigate vulnerabilities and manage risk to critical infrastructure.	In Progress: HAF/A6WW "Cybersecurity Taskforce"
17	Bring together a core group of programmers who can disseminate best practices throughout the Air Force.	
18	Ensure a baseline level of quality is achieved in the implemented software. Toward that end, the Air Force should devote sufficient resources to this important task since doing so is certainly preferable to continuation of the recent hacking of weapon systems data.	
19	Big-data analytics will require greater emphasis in the future, and the USAF and DOD will need to be able to recruit, train, and track analysts capable of manipulating big-data sets. Examine the need for big data analysts, establish formal requirements to address these needs, and work to establish a mechanism to identify and track expertise.	24th AF/25th AF, HAF/A1
20	Cultivate a culture of understanding the differences between IT and OT to serve as a foundation for discussion of the cyber dependencies of core Air Force missions.	AU

RECOMMENDATIONS: RECRUIT, RETAIN, REGAIN (CHAP. 3)

	Recommendation	Implementation/Status
21	Examine ways to give opportunities to Airmen in other career fields to transfer into 17X/1B4/3D or cyber-related civilian career fields.	HAF/A1
22	The cyber test could be one way to allow Airmen from other Air Force specialty codes (AFSC) who have an interest in cyber or have computer science (CS), computer engineering (CE), or electrical engineering (EE) degrees to demonstrate their aptitude to be cyber warriors.	In Progress: AFRL/711HPW, AETC/A1
23	The USAF should not put national security missions at risk by actively seeking to recruit from the destructive hacker pool. Instead, leverage games and competitions to serve as an outlet for people with inquisitive hacking skills and instill our core values into those who aspire to join the ranks of the "good guys" defending the nation in the role or capacity they choose.	Ongoing: AFRS
24	The USAF should explore the legalities of including noncompete clauses within contractor agreements so contractors are prohibited from recruiting or hiring current USAF employees who are not retiring within one year.	HAF/A1, SAF/AQ
25	Recruit cyber-educated Airmen from the 1B4, 1NX, and 3D career fields.	
26	Offer tuition assistance—especially in CE or EE—to Airmen in the 1B4, 1NX, and 3D specialties to enhance their education in cyber fields.	
27	Continue to produce a portion of cyber operators from the arts, humanities, and social sciences to assure that cyber professions include a cadre of creative thinkers.	

RECOMMENDATIONS: UNDERSTANDING THE IMPACT OF MILLENIALS ON THE CYBER WORKFORCE (CHAP. 4)

	Recommendation	Implementation/Status
28	The USAF should highlight its health-care benefits and high promotion potential as it attempts to recruit from a smaller pool of qualified 18-to-24-year-old millennials.	AFRS
29	The USAF can improve its millennial recruiting by appealing to the desire of young Americans to promote peace and security more broadly and their role in performing that function as a USAF member. Given its technical focus, the USAF is particularly well positioned to appeal to this desire.	AFRS

RECOMMENDATIONS: UNDERSTANDING THE IMPACT OF MILLENIALS ON THE CYBER WORKFORCE (CHAP. 4) (continued)

	Recommendation	Implementation/Status
30	In many respects, the highly skilled jobs that are the hallmark of the USAF are one of its greatest recruiting tools. The unique DOD mission set (Title 10) is attractive and should be leveraged in recruitment campaigns.	AFRS
31	Include a short course in cyber hygiene that achieves analysis-level learning objectives in cyber information assurance operations as part of all accessions programs: Basic Military Training (BMT), Officer Training School (OTS), US Air Force Academy (USAFA), and Reserve Officer Training Corps (ROTC).	AETC, USAFA, AF-CIO
32	Follow-on studies should look closely at the cyber intelligence collection field (1N2) and examine the enlisted 3DXX career field set more thoroughly.	HAF/A1/A2
33	Although the USAF should continue to work with the DHS in implementing the NICE framework, it should not undertake wholesale changes to the 2210 civilian occupational specialty until the framework is finalized. The Office of Personnel Management (OPM) will not complete reclassification of the cyber civilian workforce until at least 2018.	HAF/A6S
34	Build a robust 14XX website for the 14N career field, maintained by HQ AFPC, and clearly communicate that website's location to the field.	In Progress: HAF/A2, AFPC
35	The functional manager for the 14XX career field should consolidate all documents and management of the career field at the corporate USAF level and work with AFPC to publish the appropriate USAF-level guidance.	In progress: HAF/A2, AFPC
36	The intelligence community, including Twenty-Fifth Air Force, should reexamine the Intelligence Officer Course to determine if recent events in cyberspace warrant adjustment of course content and reallocation of time across the various intelligence disciplines and competencies.	In progress: 17 TW, AETC/A3, 25th AF, HAF/A2
37	Cyberspace 14Ns should be assigned a minimum of two—preferably three—back-to-back cyberspace tours before career broadening into other areas to reduce the training demand and create more highly experienced cyberspace intelligence officers.	HAF/A2

RECOMMENDATIONS: FORCE DEVELOPMENT (CHAP. 5)

	Recommendation	Implementation/Status
38	Because the career-path tool is not currently in active use at AFPC, give 14Ns an SEI that tracks their specialized expertise and makes it easier for the assignment system to manage them as the specialized resource they are.	In progress: HAF/A2, 25th AF, and AFPC
39	Economic trends should be monitored closely, and the personnel community should stand ready on short notice to implement retention and accessions incentives should these trends appear and/or grow worse.	HAF/A1 with offices of collateral responsibility (OCR) A6SP, AFSPC, 24th AF
40	Develop a cyber College Level Examination Program (CLEP) exam for Undergraduate Cyber Training (UCT) for personnel with deeper cyber education or experience. This test would create additional on-ramps for individuals to enter the program and potentially help avoid repeated training for officers with technical degrees, such as CS, CE, and EE. Those time savings could shorten the pipeline for some, leaving the UCT course for others without the requisite education or experience.	AETC
41	Due to the need for stable accessions of technically savvy officers in the cyber domain and the stability that ROTC and the USAFA confer in officer accessions, we recommend that for the time frame of this study the Air Force plan to access all its cyberspace officers entirely through the USAFA and ROTC.	HAF/A1D, AU, USAFA, SAF/FM, AETC
42	Establish a formal transition course for operators on the national mission teams (NMT), national support teams, cyber mission teams (CMT), cyber support teams, and cyber protection teams (CPT). This course should be critical, as is true in the rated force, for those who spend more than 12 months but fewer than 48 months away from the operations floor. Beyond a 48-month absence, this study recommends attainment of full mission requalification.	AETC, 24th AF
43	Make all cyberspace training ranges (including those at Keesler AFB and Hurlburt Field) formal programs embedded within the POM process in the same manner as the training ranges in the air domain. The POM process should be used for maintenance, operations, and upgrade of the facilities on a planned rather than ad hoc basis.	AETC, AFSPC, SAF/FM
44	Prioritize the 1B4 career field for allocation of tuition assistance and other academic programs in those fiscal years when resources are tight.	HAF/A1

Recommendations: Force Development
(Chap. 5) (continued)

	Recommendation	Implementation/Status
45	The A1 should make deliberate use of the Conference Board's Leading Economic Index (often called the index of leading economic indicators) in combination with existing manning and retention statistics to adjust selective reenlistment bonuses and other retention incentives to curb adverse manpower trends before manning reaches crisis levels.	HAF/A1
46	Because language is developing into a greater cyber enabler, Air Forces Cyber (AFCYBER) should evaluate the various languages in which programming is currently found and establish the requirements for programming-proficient foreign linguists. Once these requirements are established, it should conduct an analysis of alternatives to determine whether this need—often episodic—is best met by military, civilian, or contract personnel and whether physical or virtual availability is sufficient.	24th AF
47	DOD senior language authority should initiate planning for a Defense Language Proficiency Test (DLPT) writing test using the existing American Council on the Teaching of Foreign Languages (ACTFL) 2012 Writing Proficiency Test as a guide.	DOD senior language authority
48	Add a computer coding component to this linguistic testing to identify potential cyberspace linguistic analysts. Once individuals with these skills are identified, establish a special cyber experience identifier for cyber linguists to enable tracking them in the various personnel databases.	HAF/A2
49	Since the ability to read programming language in a foreign tongue is not a skill for which all linguists are suited, manage those who develop this skill similarly to their 1N4X1A counterparts, with an emphasis on—but not necessarily exclusive use of—service in cyberspace roles and missions.	HAF/A1 (USAF Senior Language Authority), AFPC's 14NB Cyber Operations Assignment Team, and the assignment manager for airborne cryptanalysts (1A8X1 assignments)
50	Until the new cyber linguist cohort is fully established, use Guard and Reserve assets to address any short-term manning shortfalls. As the cyber linguist mission matures, Guard and Reserve support in this area may also grow. To fill this role, these components will need to implement tracking procedures for foreign language expertise as indicated above.	HAF/A1D (USAF Senior Language Authority)

Recommendations: Force Development (Chap. 5) *(continued)*

	Recommendation	Implementation/Status
51	Maintain a tracking system of this expertise on all operational cyberspace floors to ensure that, when needed, these experts can be called upon in a short period of time—a condition analogous to quick-reaction alert status.	AFPC
52	Due to the rapidly changing nature of the cyber domain, AFCYBER should review these language requirements and their tracking mechanism no less than once every two years as part of the formal POM cycle.	AFCYBER
53	Because cyberspace-specific skills overlap several specialties, examine the prospects of establishing a single cyberspace transition course for all personnel returning to the cyberspace field after lengthy periods away or working with US Cyber Command (USCYBERCOM) and the associated joint community to create such a course.	HAF/A2, A6SP
54	AFCYBER and Twenty-Fifth Air Force should collectively and comprehensively examine the needs for big-data analysts, establish formal requirements to address these needs, and then work with A1 to create a mechanism for the identification and tracking of this specialized expertise within the Air Force personnel system.	AFCYBER, A1

Recommendations: The Air National Guard, the Air Force Reserve, and Cyber (Chap. 6)

	Recommendation	Implementation/Status
55	Reassess the cost of active duty "when not activated," and recalculate Reserve Component (RC) costs upon activation.	HAF/A1
56	Clarify missions that the Guard and Reserve are currently performing by providing categories of cyber work, including combat communications, for each RC unit.	AF/RE, AFRC/A1, ANGRC, 25th AF/A1
57	Discontinue the use of the term *computer network attack* (as well as any other terms associated with offensive cyber missions) to describe a cyber mission. Explicitly define those missions within cyber (computer network defense, etc.) that can be performed by Guard and Reserve personnel. In particular, clearly define what functions Guard personnel can perform in Title 32 or state active duty (SAD) status.	HAF/A1, AF/RE, ANGRC

RECOMMENDATIONS: THE AIR NATIONAL GUARD, THE AIR FORCE RESERVE, AND CYBER (CHAP. 6) (continued)

	Recommendation	Implementation/Status
58	Collocate CPTs at each Federal Emergency Management Agency (FEMA) regional headquarters—all located in highly populated urban areas—to aid in recruiting a trained cyber workforce and help mitigate sourcing problems.	HAF/A1, AF/RE, ANGRC
59	Increase training funds to assure cyber reservist currency.	HAF
60	The National Security Agency (NSA) and USCYBERCOM should clearly articulate in formal planning documents the Guard and Reserve cyber missions. In the interim, designate projected CPTs as Guard units (per the Council of Governors) for each FEMA region. Otherwise, halt further expansion until formal planning is accomplished.	NSA, USCYBERCOM
61	The DHS should fund the Guard's cyber accessions in support of the DHS. Use the Office of National Drug Control Policy (ONDCP) counterdrug funding example as a guide.	SAF/FMB
62	Recruiting for cyber units should not focus exclusively on employees from the computer / cyber security industry. They may have the proper background, but conflicts of interest could inhibit their full utilization in an emergency.	AFRC, ANGRC

RECOMMENDATIONS: EDUCATING AND TRAINING CYBER FORCES (CHAP. 7)

	Recommendation	Implementation/Status
63	To overcome the problem of obsolete standards, reform the ISD process to ensure timely cyber career field training attuned to the operational environment. Along these lines, HAF/A6SP is reviewing the requirements document governing the UCT curriculum. To keep pace with the rapidly evolving cyber domain, the subsequent requirements document will be less restrictive with its specifications, thus allowing courses to maintain operational currency between triennial reviews.	In Progress: HAF/A6SP, AETC
64	Since the cyberspace domain is so pervasive and joint in nature, map training to the NICE cybersecurity workforce framework for KSAs or NICE KSAs. This standard is a reasonably good one, appropriate not only for the Air Force but also for the other military services and government agencies.	In Progress: HAF/A6SP

Recommendations: Educating and Training Cyber Forces (Chap. 7) (continued)

	Recommendation	Implementation/Status
65	HAF A2/A3/A6 should examine the possibility of a single cyberspace transition course or work with USCYBERCOM and the joint community to create a replacement training unit (RTU) or transition course.	HAF/A1/A6, 24th AF
66	Investigate schoolhouse manning to find ways to maintain adequate levels of instructors while allowing proper instructor continuing education and career progression.	AFSPC, AETC/A1
67	The USAF must find ways to make cyber training and education adaptive to the developments in the field.	SAF/FM, AFSPC, AETC, 24th AF
68	The best way to increase interest in the 17-series AFSC is for USAFA customers to tell, and then prove to, cadets that the Air Force has good jobs for them. Knowing there are interesting jobs in the field will drive up interest.	USAFA, 24th AF, NSA
69	Creating a summer course for cadets would be useful as a means of enticing them into the career field. Currently, one does not exist (it was eliminated when the 110 course was updated and offered to all cadets in their first year).	USAFA
70	Maintain steady ROTC budgets to hedge against the risk of OTS not producing adequate quality/quantity of 17D accessions when the economy picks up.	AETC/AU
71	The USAF should take a more focused look at how the two Cyber ACE programs can be better leveraged to help meet USAF cyber needs.	AU/CC
72	To continue the trend of developing highly capable cyber operators, fully fund and expand the AFIT/AFRL distinct ACE programs. Fully fund, in POM, the AFRL/RI ACE program. Fully fund, in POM, the AFIT ACE program for ROTC.	SAF/FM
73	Mandate an AFIT name change to avoid confusion with the distinct AFRL/RI program. Re-recognize AFRL/RI ACE as a national asset and a CSAF special-interest item.	AU/CC

Abbreviations

AAD	advanced academic degree
ABET	Accreditation Board for Engineering and Technology
AC	active component
ACC	Air Combat Command
ACE	Advanced Course in Engineering
ACSC	Air Command and Staff College
ACTFL	American Council on the Teaching of Foreign Languages
ADSC	active duty service commitment
AETC	Air Education and Training Command
AFA	Air Force Association
AFCYBER	Air Forces Cyber
AFDD	Air Force doctrine document
AFERB	Air Force Education Requirements Board
AFISRA	Air Force Intelligence, Surveillance, and Reconnaissance Agency
AFIT	Air Force Institute of Technology
AFIT/EN	Air Force Institute of Technology/Graduate School of Engineering and Management
AFNIC	Air Force Networking Integration Center
AFOQT	Air Force Officer Qualifying Test
AFPC	Air Force Personnel Center
AFR	Air Force Reserve
AFRC	Air Force Reserve Command
AFRI	Air Force Research Institute
AFRL	Air Force Research Laboratory
AFRL/RI	Air Force Research Laboratory/Information Directorate
AFSC	Air Force specialty code
AFSPC	Air Force Space Command

AGR	Active Guard and Reserve
altDNS	alternative domain name system
ANG	Air National Guard
ASVAB	Armed Services Vocational Aptitude Battery
AU	Air University
AWC	Air War College
BCS	building control system
BMT	Basic Military Training
C-ACTS	Consortium for Advanced Cyber Thinking and Strategy
CAG	Cyber Advisory Group
CCAF	Community College of the Air Force
CDC	career development course
CE	computer engineering
CFETP	career field education and training plan
CIFTU	Cyber Intelligence Follow-on Training Unit (course)
CIO	chief information officer
CIPP	Career Intermission Pilot Program
CLEP	College Level Examination Program
CMF	Cyber Mission Force
CMSgt	chief master sergeant
CMT	cyber mission team
CNCI	Comprehensive National Cybersecurity Initiative
CNODP	Computer Network Operations Development Program
CNS	computer and network security
COEC	Cyberspace Operations Executive Course
COS	civilian occupational specialty
CPT	cyber protection team
CS	computer science
CSAF	chief of staff of the Air Force

CST	combat mission direct support team
DAF	Department of the Air Force
DARPA	Defense Advanced Research Projects Agency
DCO	defensive cyberspace operations
DHS	Department of Homeland Security
DISA	Defense Information Systems Agency
DLPT	Defense Language Proficiency Test
DNS	Domain Name System
DOD	Department of Defense
DODIN	Department of Defense Information Network
DODNIC	Department of Defense Network Integration Center
DSCA	Defense Support to Civil Authorities
ECSS	Expeditionary Combat Support System
EE	electrical engineering
EW	electronic warfare
FAPSI	Federal Agency for Government Communications and Information (Russia)
FedVTE	Federal Virtual Training Environment
FEMA	Federal Emergency Management Agency
FLPP	foreign language proficiency pay
FM	Financial Management
FTP	file transfer protocol
FTU	follow-on training unit
FY	fiscal year
gTLD	generic top-level domain name
HAF	Headquarters Air Force
HAF/A1	Headquarters Air Force/Deputy Chief of Staff for Personnel
HAF/A2	Headquarters Air Force/Intelligence
HQ	headquarters
HTTP	hypertext transfer protocol

IADS	integrated air defense system
ICANN	Internet Corporation for Assigned Names and Numbers
ICS	industrial control system
IDA	Institute for Defense Analyses
IDE	intermediate developmental education
IDS	intrusion detection system
IMA	individual mobilization augmentee
INWT	Intermediate Network Warfare Training
IO	information operations
IOFAC	Information Operations Fundamentals Application Course
IOS	information operations squadron
iOS	iPhone Operating System
IP	Internet Protocol
IPTV	Internet Protocol television
IPv4	Internet Protocol version 4
IPv6	Internet Protocol version 6
IQT	initial qualification training
ISD	Instructional Systems Development
ISR	intelligence, surveillance, and reconnaissance
IT	information technology
ITU	International Telecommunication Union
IW	intelligence wing
JAG	judge advocate general
JCAC	Joint Cyber Analysis Course
JIE	Joint Information Environment
JP	joint publication
KSA	knowledge, skill, and ability
LAN	local area network
LTE	long-term evolution
MAJCOM	major command

MECC	Military Education Coordination Council
NAF	numbered Air Force
NCO	noncommissioned officer
NCOIC	noncommissioned officer in charge
NCSAF	National Commission on the Structure of the Air Force
NDAA	National Defense Authorization Act
NICE	National Initiative for Cybersecurity Education
NIST	National Institute of Standards and Technology
NMT	national mission team
NSA	National Security Agency
NSSI	National Security Space Institute
OCO	offensive cyberspace operations
OCR	office of collateral responsibility
OJT	on-the-job training
OMB	Office of Management and Budget
ONDCP	Office of National Drug Control Policy
OPM	Office of Personnel Management
OPR	office of primary responsibility
OT	operational technology
OTS	Officer Training School
PCE	professional continuing education
PLC	programmable logic controller
PM	program management
PME	professional military education
POM	program objective memorandum
POTS	plain old telephone system
R&D	research and development
RAM	random access memory
RC	Reserve Component

RFPB	Reserve Forces Policy Board
RNET	reserve network
ROTC	Reserve Officer Training Corps
RTU	replacement training unit
SAASS	School of Advanced Air and Space Studies
SAD	state active duty
SAF/CIO/A3C/A6C	Air Force Secretariat/Cyberspace Ops and Warfighting Integration Directorate
SAF/CIO/A6	Air Force Secretariat/Office of Information Dominance and Chief Information Officer
SAF/CIO/A6S	Air Force Secretariat/Cyberspace Strategy and Policy Directorate
SCADA	supervisory control and data acquisition
SCI	sensitive compartmented information
SE	systems engineering
SEC	US Securities and Exchange Commission
SECAF	secretary of the Air Force
SEI	special experience identifier
SFITS	Federal Information and Telecommunications System (Russia)
SIGINT	signals intelligence
SJIOAC	Senior Joint Information Operations Applications Course
SMART	Science, Mathematics, and Research for Transformation
SME	subject matter expert
SMS	short message service
SMSgt	senior master sergeant
STEAM	science, technology, engineering, arts, and mathematics
STEM	science, technology, engineering, and mathematics
TCP	transmission-control protocol

TDY	temporary duty
TOR	The Onion Router
TS	Top Secret
TTP	tactics, techniques, and procedures
TW	training wing
UCT	Undergraduate Cyber Training
USAFA	United States Air Force Academy
USCYBERCOM	United States Cyber Command
WO	warrant officer
WWW	World Wide Web

Bibliography

Aguilar, Luis A., commissioner, US Securities and Exchange Commission. "Boards of Directors, Corporate Governance and Cyber-Risks: Sharpening the Focus." Speech. "Cyber Risks and the Boardroom" Conference. New York Stock Exchange, 10 June 2014. http://www.sec.gov/News/Speech/Detail/Speech/1370542057946.

Air Force Association. *CyberPatriot VII: National Youth Cyber Defense Competition Rules and Procedures*. Arlington, VA: CyberPatriot Program Office, Air Force Association, October 2014. https://www.uscyberpatriot.org/competition/rules-book.

Air Force Institute of Technology. Graduate School for Engineering and Management. Advanced Cyber Education (ACE). "Course Information." Accessed 20 May 2015. http://www.afit.edu/ace.

Air Force Instruction 36-2605. *Air Force Military Personnel Testing System*, 24 September 2008 (incorporating change 1, 26 January 2015).

Air Force Personnel Center. Personnel Database. Extracts of Officer Data, 1995–2014.

Air Force Research Laboratory, Information Directorate. *ACE Information Assurance*. Air Education and Training Command (AETC) pamphlet 2014-0668. http://www.wpafb.af.mil/afrl/ri/.

Air Force Space Command. "Air Force Space Command Cyberspace Intelligence, Surveillance and Reconnaissance Force Development Roadmap." Peterson AFB, CO: Air Force Space Command, 7 January 2013.

"Airman Leadership School." 42d Force Support Squadron. Accessed August 2015. http://42fss.us/airmanleadershipschool.html.

Alsop, Ron. *The Trophy Kids Grow Up*. New York: Jossey-Bass, 2008.

Anand, LCDR A. "Threats to India's Information Environment." In *Information Technology: The Future Warfare Weapon*, by LCDR A. Anand, 56–62. New Delhi, India: Ocean Books, 2000.

Andrus, Paul. Consortium for Advanced Cyber Thinking and Strategy. Teleconference Meeting Minutes, 26 February 2014.

Bailey, Lt Col Stephen G., HAF A3C/A6C (Cyberspace Ops and Warfighting Integration). Presentation. Air Force Research Institute (AFRI) Cyber Advisory Group. Maxwell AFB, AL, 15 July 2014.

Barbie, Barrie. "Air Force Facing Shortage of Researchers due to Retirements." *Knoxville News*, 20 May 2014. http://www.knoxnews.com/news/2014/may/20/air-force-facing-shortage-of-researchers-due-to/?partner=RSS.

Beaver, Kevin. "Five Network Security Lessons Learned from the Sony Pictures Hack." Accessed August 2015. http://searchsecurity.techtarget.com/tip/Five-network-security-lessons-learned-from-the-Sony-Pictures-hack.

"Benefits Summary." Science, Mathematics and Research for Transformation. Accessed August 2015. http://smart.asee.org/about/benefits.

Bensahel, Nora. *Beyond the QDR: Key Issues Facing the National Defense Panel*. Policy brief. Washington, DC: Center for a New American Security, May 2014.

Berners-Lee, Tim. "Linked Data." From Design Issues: Architectural and Philosophical Points [on Web Architecture] website, 27 July 2006. http://www.w3.org/DesignIssues/LinkedData.

Binsalleeh, Hamad, Thomas Ormerod, Amine Boukhtouta, Prosenjit Sinha, Amr Youssef, Mourad Debbabi, and Lingyu Wang. "On the Analysis of the Zeus Botnet Crimeware Toolkit." In *2010 Eighth Annual International Conference on Privacy, Security and Trust*, 31–38. Red Hook, NY: Institute of Electrical and Electronics Engineers (IEEE), Curran Associates, Inc., November 2010.

Biros, David P., and Todd Eppich. "Human Element Key to Intrusion Detection." *Signal*, August 2001. http://www.afcea.org/content/?q=human-element-key-intrusion-detection.

Bloom, Benjamin S., and D. R. Krathwohl. *Taxonomy of Educational Objectives: The Classification of Educational Goals, Handbook I: Cognitive Domain*. New York: David McKay Company, 1956.

Bobko, Philip, Alex J. Barelka, and Leanne M. Hirshfield. "The Construct of State-Level Suspicion: A Model and Research Agenda for Automated and Information Technology (IT) Contexts." *Human Factors: The Journal of the Human Factors and Ergonomics Society* 56, no. 3 (May 2014): 489–508.

Boeing. "KC-46A Pegasus Customer." Accessed August 2015. http://www.boeing.com/defense/kc-46a-pegasus-tanker#/facts.

Borges, Nicole J., R. Stephen Manuel, Carol L. Elam, and Bonnie J. Jones. "Differences in Motives between Millennial and Generation X Medical Students." *Medical Education* 44, no. 6 (2010): 570–76.

Borrely, Maj Pierre Arnaut. "To Certified Training by a Post Master-Master's Degree." Presentation. Baltic Defence College Workshops on Cyber Education, Tallinn, Estonia, 4 April 2014.

Breznitz, Dan, and Michael Murphree. "The Rise of China in Technology Standards: New Norms in Old Institutions." Research report prepared on behalf of the US-China Economic and Security Review Commission, 16 January 2013. http://origin.www.uscc.gov/sites/default/files/Research/RiseofChinainTechnologyStandards.pdf.

Broadhurst, Roderic G., and Alan N. Chantler. "Cybercrime Update: Trends and Developments." Final draft, 27 June 2006. In "Expert Group Meeting on the Development of Virtual Forum against Cybercrime," 21–56. Unpublished report. Conference hosted by the Korean Institute of Criminal Justice Policy in collaboration with the United Nations Office on Drugs and Crime. Seoul, Korea, 28–30 June 2006. QUT ePrints. http://eprints.qut.edu.au/4690/.

Brokaw, Scott C., JCS/J1 (Joint Staff, Manpower and Personnel). To John Conway, AFRI. E-mail. Subject: Follow Up on Air Force Cyber Linguist Positions, 18 April 2014.

Brown, Cheryl, and Laura Czerniewicz. "Debunking the 'Digital Native': Beyond Digital Apartheid, towards Digital Democracy." *Journal of Computer Assisted Learning* 26, no. 5 (2010): 357–69.

Buckley, Sean. "AT&T Officially Endorses G.hn Home Networking Standards." *Fierce Telecom*, 2 June 2011. http://www.fiercetelecom.com/story/att-officially-endorses-ghn-home-networking-standard/2011-06-02.

Bureau of Labor Statistics. "Labor Force Statistics from the Current Population Survey: Seasonally Adjusted Unemployment Rate—LNS14000000, 2004–14." Accessed September 2014. http://data.bls.gov/timeseries/LNS14000000.

Burleigh, Scott, Adrian Hooke, Leigh Torgerson, Kevin Fall, Vint Cerf, Bob Durst, Keith Scott, and Howard Weiss. "Delay-Tolerant Networking: An Approach to Interplanetary Internet." *IEEE Communications Magazine* 41, no. 6 (2003): 128–36.

Calabresi, Massimo, and Zeke J. Miller, "Up in Smoke: FBI Won't Change Rules on Pot Smoking Recruits," *Time*, 21 May 2014. http://time.com/107525/up-in-smoke-fbi-wont-change-rules-on-pot-smoking-recruits.

Callander, Bruce D. "The In-Betweeners." *Air Force Magazine* 74, no. 11 (November 1991). http://www.airforcemag.com/Magazine Archive /Pages/1991/November%201991/1191between.aspx.

CareerBuilder. "2015 U.S. Job Forecast," 1 January 2015. http://ca reerbuildercommunications.com/pdf/careerbuilder-q1-2015-fore cast.pdf.

Cashell, Brian, William D. Jackson, Mark Jickling, and Baird Webel. *The Economic Impact of Cyber-Attacks*. Washington, DC: Congressional Research Service, 1 April 2004.

Chairman of the Joint Chiefs of Staff Instruction (CJCSI) 1800.01E. *Officer Professional Military Education Policy*, 29 May 2015. http://www.dtic.mil/cjcs_directives/cdata/unlimit/1800_01a .pdf.

Chander, Anupam, and Uyen P. Le. "Data Nationalism." *Emory Law Journal* 64, no. 3 (2015): 677–739.

Chesney, Robert. "Military-Intelligence Convergence and the Law of Title 10 / Title 50 Debate." *Journal of National Security Law and Policy* 5 (2012). University of Texas Law. Public Law Research Paper No. 212, 541, 580–81, and 607–8. http://papers.ssrn.com /sol3/papers.cfm?abstract_id=1945392.

Clark, William A. V. *Life Course Events and Residential Change: Unpacking Age Effects on the Probability of Moving*. Los Angeles: California Center for Population Research, 2012.

Codrington, Graeme. *Detailed Introduction to Generation Theory*. London: Tomorrow Today, 2008.

Coleman, Liv. "Next Generation Internet Policy in Japan, China and India." *Asia and the Pacific Policy Studies* 1, no. 3 (September 2014): 497–512.

Comprehensive National Cybersecurity Initiative (CNCI). Accessed August 2015. http://www.whitehouse.gov/issues/foreign-policy /cybersecurity/national-initiative.

Conference Board. Leading Economic Index. Accessed August 2015. https://www.conference-board.org/data/bcicountry.cfm?cid=1.

Cook, Brian J., AFISRA/A6S (Air Force Intelligence, Surveillance, and Reconnaissance Agency, Reserve Affairs / Cyberspace Strategy and Policy). Briefing. Subject: Cyber ISR Workforce Development. To Air Force Research Institute research team. AFISRA Headquarters, Joint Base San Antonio, TX, 3 March 2014.

Corrin, Amber. "Is There a Cybersecurity Workforce Crisis?" *Federal Computer Week*, 15 October 2013. http://fcw.com/articles/2013/10/15/cybersecurity-workforce-crisis.aspx.

Council of Europe. Convention on Cybercrime. European Treaty Series (ETS) No. 185. Budapest, 23 November 2001.

Creswell, John. *Qualitative Inquiry and Research Design*. Thousand Oaks, CA: Sage Publishing, 2007.

Currie, Karen, John Conway, Scott Johnson, Brian Landry, and Adam Lowther. *Air Force Leadership Study: The Need for Deliberate Development*. Air Force Research Institute Paper 2012-1. Maxwell AFB, AL: Air University Press, February 2012.

Curtis E. LeMay Center for Doctrine Development and Education. *Annex 1-1, Force Development*, 15 December 2014. https://doctrine.af.mil/DTM/dtmforcedevelopment.htm.

———. *Annex 3-12, Cyberspace Operations*, 30 November 2011. https://doctrine.af.mil/download.jsp?filename=3-12-Annex-CYBERSPACE-OPS.pdf.

———. "Information Operations Fundamentals Application Course." Accessed 26 August 2015. http://www.au.af.mil/au/lemay/content/iofac.htm.

———. "Senior Joint Information Operations Applications Course." Accessed 26 August 2015. http://www.au.af.mil/au/lemay/content/sjioac.htm.

———. *Volume II, Leadership*, 4 November 2011. https://doctrine.af.mil/download.jsp?filename=Volume-2-Leadership.pdf.

"CyberCorps: Scholarship for Service." Accessed August 2015. US Office of Personnel Management. https://www.sfs.opm.gov.

Cyberspace Advisory Group Meeting. Hosted by Air Force Research Institute. Maxwell AFB, AL, 15–16 July 2014.

Dacus, Chad, and Panayotis Yannakogeorgos. "Designing Cybersecurity into Defense Systems: An Information Economics Approach." *IEEE Security and Privacy* (forthcoming, 2016).

Dalkey, Norman, and Olaf Helmer. "An Experimental Application of the Delphi Method to the Use of Experts." *Management Science* 9, no. 3 (1963): 458–67.

Defense Acquisition University. *2014 Course Catalog*. Fort Belvoir, VA: Defense Acquisition University, 2014. http://icatalog.dau.mil/onlinecatalog/doc/2014Catalog_Online.pdf.

Demchak, Chris C., and Peter Dombrowski. "Rise of a Cybered Westphalian Age." *Strategic Studies Quarterly* 5, no. 1 (Spring 2011): 32–61.

Department of Defense (DOD). *Department of Defense Cyberspace Workforce Strategy*. Washington, DC: DOD, 4 December 2013. http://dodcio.defense.gov/Portals/0/Documents/DoD%20Cyberspace%20Workforce%20Strategy_signed(final).pdf.

———. *Department of Defense Strategy for Operating in Cyberspace*. Washington, DC: DOD, July 2011.

Department of Homeland Security (DHS). *National Strategy to Secure Cyberspace*. Washington, DC: DHS, February 2003. http://permanent.access.gpo.gov/lps28730/cyberspace_strategy.pdf.

———. "Workforce Development Initiatives: Building America's Future Homeland Security Science and Engineering Workforce." Accessed August 2015. http://www.dhs.gov/science-and-technology/workforce-development-initiatives.

Department of the Air Force. *Air Force Specialty Code 14NX Intelligence Officer Career Field Education and Training Plan*, 13 February 2013.

———. *Air Force Specialty Code 1N0X1 Operations Intelligence Career Field Education and Training Plan*, 1 January 2013.

Doidge, Norman. *The Brain That Changes Itself*. New York: Viking Press, 2007.

Dowd, Alan W. "World War 2.0." *American Legion Magazine*, 1 January 2010, 34–37.

Dutt, Varun, Young-Suk Ahn, and Cleotilde Gonzalez. "Cyber Situation Awareness Modeling Detection of Cyber Attacks with Instance-Based Learning Theory." *Human Factors: The Journal of the Human Factors and Ergonomics Society* 55, no. 3 (2013): 605–18.

———. "Cyber Situation Awareness: Modeling the Security Analyst in a Cyber-Attack Scenario through Instance-Based Learning." In *Data and Applications Security and Privacy XXV: 25th Annual IFIP WG 11.3 Conference, DBSec 2011, Richmond, VA, July 2011 Proceedings*, 280–92. New York: Springer, 2011.

81st Training Wing Plan of Instruction. Undergraduate Cyber Training (Phase I). E3OQR17D1 0A1A, 22 October 2012.

81st Training Wing Tentative Plan of Instruction. Cyber Defense Operations. E3ALR1B431 0A1A, 7 November 2013.

Espinoza, Chip, Mick Ukleja, and Craig Rusch. *Managing the Millennials*. New York: Wiley, 2010.

Executive Office of the President. *Administration Strategy for Mitigating the Theft of U.S. Trade Secrets*. Washington, DC: Executive Office of the President of the United States, February 2013.

———. *Cyberspace Policy Review: Assuring a Trusted and Resilient Information and Communications Infrastructure*. Washington, DC: Executive Office of the President of the United States, 2009.

Executive Order (EO) 13636. Improving Critical Infrastructure Cybersecurity. *Federal Register* 78, no. 33 (12 February 2013): 11739.

Fadok, David S., and Richard A. Raines. "Driving towards Success in the Air Force Cyber Mission: Leveraging Our Heritage to Shape Our Future." *Air and Space Power Journal* 26, no. 5 (September–October 2012): 4–11.

"*Federal Acquisition Regulation*; FAR Case 2005–041, Internet Protocol Version 6 (IPv6)." In *Federal Register* 74, no. 236 (10 December 2009): 65605. http://www.gpo.gov/fdsys/pkg/FR-2009-12-10/pdf/E9-28931.pdf.

50 USC. War and National Defense. *United States Code*, 2011 edition. US Government Printing Office. http://www.gpo.gov/fdsys/pkg/USCODE-2011-title50/html/USCODE-2011-title50.htm.

Frankel, Sheila E., Richard Graveman, John Pearce, and Mark Rooks. *Guidelines for the Secure Deployment of IPv6*. Washington, DC: National Institute of Standards and Technology, 29 December 2010.

French Ministry of Foreign Affairs and International Development. "The Status of French in the World," 2015. http://www.diplomatie.gouv.fr/en/french-foreign-policy-1/francophony-1113/the-status-of-french-in-the-world.

Fritz, Jason. "How China Will Use Cyber Warfare to Leapfrog in Military Competitiveness." *Culture Mandala* 8, no. 1 (October 2008): 28–80.

Gallaher, M. P., and B. Rowe (RTI International) for National Institute of Standards and Technology (NIST). *IPv6 Economic Impact Assessment: Final Report*. Research Triangle Park, NC: RTI International, October 2005. http://www.nist.gov/director/planning/upload/report05-2.pdf.

Geis, John P., II, Grant T. Hammond, Harry A. Foster, and Theodore C. Hailes. *Blue Horizons IV: Deterrence in the Age of Surprise*. Occasional Paper no. 70. Center for Strategy and Technology. Air War College. Maxwell AFB, AL: Air University Press, January 2014.

General Accounting Office. *Cybersecurity for Critical Infrastructure Protection*. Washington, DC: GAO, 2004.

George, Alexander L., and Andrew Bennett. *Case Studies and Theory Development in the Social Sciences*. Cambridge, MA: MIT Press, 2005.

"Ghost Route Hunter: IPv6, DFP [Default Free Prefix] Visibility." SixXS. Accessed 28 March 2015. http://www.sixxs.net/tools/grh/dfp.

Gildea, Debbie. "45 AFSCs Removed from SRB List as AF Gets Leaner, Smaller." *U.S. Air Force News*, 26 November 2013. http://www.af.mil/News/ArticleDisplay/tabid/223/Article/467611/45-afscs-removed-from-srb-list-as-af-gets-leaner-smaller.aspx.

Gopaul, Kjall. "IT [Information Technology] vs. PM [Program Management] Track." Defense Acquisition Workforce Improvement Act (DAWIA) Comparison Brief, 29 May 2014. Gopaul. To Pano Yannakogeorgos. E-mail, May 2014.

Gorman, Siobhan, Yochi J. Dreazen, and August Cole. "Insurgents Hack U.S. Drones." *Wall Street Journal*, 17 December 2009. http://www.wsj.com/articles/SB126102247889095011.

Grandstaff, Mark R. *Foundation of the Force: Air Force Enlisted Personnel Policy, 1907–1956*. Washington, DC: Government Printing Office (GPO), 1996.

———. "Neither Fish nor Fowl: The Demise of the USAF's Warrant Officer Program." *Air Power History* 42, no.1 (Spring 1995): 40–51.

Green, C. Shawn, and Daphne Bavelier. "Action Video Games Modify Visual Attention." *Nature* 423 (2003): 534–37.

Hailes, Theodore C., and John Geis. "Observer Warrior: An Unwanted Necessity." In *Crosscutting Issues in International Transformation: Interactions and Innovations among People, Organizations, Processes and Technology*, edited by Derrick Neal, Henrik Friman, Ralph Doughty, and Linton Wells, 147–66. Washington, DC: National Defense University Press, 2009.

Halpin, John, and Karl Agne. *The Political Ideology of the Millennial Generation*. Washington, DC: Center for American Progress, 2009.

Hart, Kim. "Longtime Battle Lines Are Recast in Russia and Georgia's Cyberwar." *Washington Post*, 14 August 2008.

Headquarters Air Force (HAF). *America's Air Force: A Call to the Future*. Washington, DC: HAF, July 2014. http://airman.dodlive.mil/files/2014/07/AF_30_Year_Strategy_2.pdf.

———. A6. To Air Force Research Institute cyber research team. E-mail, March 2014.

———. A3C/A6C. "Career Field Snapshot—17D Cyberspace Operations." Slide presentation, updated 11 February 2014, current as of 23 April 2014.

———. CSAF Strategic Studies Group (HAF/CK). On behalf of CSAF. To AFRI/CL (Director). Memorandum, 18 March 2013.

———. Personnel Center / Directorate of Personnel Services (DPSIC). *Air Force Officer Classification Directory: The Official Guide to the Air Force Classification Codes*. Washington, DC: Headquarters US Air Force, 30 April 2013. Headquarters Air Force Space Command / A3 (Operations). Briefing. Subject: AFRI Cyberspace Development Questions. To AFRI research team. Peterson AFB, CO, 3 March 2014.

Healey, Jason, ed. *A Fierce Domain: Conflict in Cyberspace, 1986 to 2012*. Arlington, VA: Cyber Conflict Studies Association, 2013.

Heikkinen, Christine, AFISRA/A1R. To John Conway, Air Force Research Institute. E-mails, May–September 2014.

Homeyer, Jane, Margaret Maxon, and John Mills. "Introduction to NICE Cybersecurity Workforce Framework." Briefing slides from videocast. NICE Conference, Gaithersburg, MD, 21 September 2011. http://csrc.nist.gov/nice/Sept2011-workshop/presentations/NICE-%20Agenda-Presentation_Ver2.pdf.

Hoogerheide, J., F. Rempt, and W. P. H. Hoogenboom. "Acquired Myopia in Young Pilots." *Ophthalmologica* 163, no. 4 (1971): 209–15.

House. National Defense Authorization Act for Fiscal Year 2006. Public Law 109-163, sec. 221. H. R. 1815. 109th Cong., 1st sess., 6 January 2006. Washington, DC: GPO, 2006. http://www.gpo.gov/fdsys/pkg/PLAW-109publ163/html/PLAW-109publ163.htm.

———. *National Defense Authorization Act for Fiscal Year 2010: Report of the Committee on Armed Services of the House of Representatives on H. R. 2647*. Report 111-166. 111th Cong., 1st sess. Washington, DC: GPO, 2009. http://www.gpo.gov/fdsys/pkg/CRPT-111hrpt166/pdf/CRPT-111hrpt166.pdf.

———. National Defense Authorization Act for Fiscal Year 2013. Public Law 112-239, 2 January 2013. Sec. 933. 112th Cong., 2d sess. Washington, DC: GPO, 2013. http://www.gpo.gov/fdsys/pkg/PLAW-112publ239/pdf/PLAW-112publ239.pdf.

———. National Defense Authorization Act for Fiscal Year 2014. H. R. 3304. Public Law 113-66, 26 December 2013. Sec. 933. 113th

Cong., 1st sess. Washington, DC: GPO, 2013. http://www.gpo.gov/fdsys/pkg/PLAW-113publ66/pdf/PLAW-113publ66.pdf.

Hultquist, John. "Update on Sandworm Team Targeting SCADA Systems," 21 October 2014. isight Partners. http://www.isightpartners.com/2014/10/sandworm-team-targeting-scada-systems.

"Information Assurance (IA) Development Programs." National Security Agency (NSA) / Central Security Service, May 2014. https://www.nsa.gov/careers/career_fields/ia2.shtml.

International Collegiate Programming Contest (ICPC). "ICPC Fact Sheet," 28 April 2015. http://icpc.baylor.edu.

Internet Corporation for Assigned Names and Numbers. "Internationalized Domain Names." Accessed August 2015. http://www.icann.org/en/resources/idn.

———. "Montevideo Statement on the Future of Internet Cooperation," 7 October 2013. https://www.icann.org/news/announcement-2013-10-07-en.

Jabbour, Kamal, and Sarah Muccio. "On Mission Assurance." In *Conflict and Cooperation in Cyberspace: The Challenge to National Security*, edited by Panayotis A. Yannakogeorgos and Adam B. Lowther, 127–60. Boca Raton, FL: Taylor and Francis Group, 2014.

Jackson, CMSgt Robert, Air Force 3DXXX career field manager. To Dr. John P. Geis II, AFRI. E-mails, March, April, and May 2014.

Joint Chiefs of Staff. *Joint Information Environment*. White paper. Washington, DC: Department of Defense, 22 January 2013.

Kikukawa, Azusa, Shoichi Tachibana, and Shigeyuki Yagura. "G-Related Musculoskeletal Spine Symptoms in Japan Air Self Defense Force F-15 Pilots." *Aviation, Space, and Environmental Medicine* 66, no. 3 (March 1995): 269–72.

Knott, Benjamin A., Vincent F. Mancuso, Kevin Bennett, Victor Finomore, Michael McNeese, Jennifer A. McKneely, and Maria Beecher. "Human Factors in Cyber Warfare Alternative Perspectives." *Proceedings of the Human Factors and Ergonomics Society Annual Meeting* 57, no. 1 (September 2013): 399–403.

Kreft, Elizabeth. "Senate Report: Air Force 'Systematically Failed' with Billion Dollar Software Acquisition." *Blaze*, 8 July 2014.

Kugelman, Francie. "Bloom's Taxonomy Cheat Sheet." Accessed 15 May 2015. http://www.bloomstaxonomy.org.

Lacks, SMSgt Christopher, HAF/A2DFM (Headquarters Air Force, Deputy Chief of Staff, Intelligence, Surveillance and Reconnaissance, functional manager). Bullet background paper. Subject:

Presenting Enlisted ISR [Intelligence, Surveillance, and Reconnaissance] to CMF [Cyber Mission Force] Teams, 1 August 2013.
Lancaster, Lynne, and David Stillman. *The M-Factor: How the Millennial Generation Is Rocking the Workplace*. New York: Harper, 2010.
Lancaster, Lynne C., and David Stillman. *When Generations Collide*. New York: Collins Business, 2002.
Lawson, Stephen. "IPv6 Can Boost Mobile Performance, Battery Life, Proponents Say." *Computer World*, 11 January 2013.
LeMay Center. "Cyberspace Operations Executive Course," 19 March 2015. http://www.au.af.mil/au/lemay/content/coec.htm.
———. "Information Operations Fundamental Application Course," 19 March 2015. http://www.au.af.mil/au/lemay/content/iofac.htm.
———. "Senior Joint Information Operations Applications Course," 19 March 2015. http://www.au.af.mil/au/lemay/content/sjioac.htm.
Levine, Linda. *Economic Growth and the Unemployment Rate*. Washington, DC: Congressional Research Service, 28 October 2011.
Libicki, Martin C. "Cyberspace Is Not a Warfighting Domain." *I/S: A Journal of Law and Policy for the Information Society* 8, no. 2 (Fall 2012): 325–40.
Losey, Stephen. "Air Force to Offer 3 Years Off for Airmen to Start Families." *Air Force Times*, 15 May 2014. http://www.airforcetimes.com/article/20140515/CAREERS/305150044/Air-Force-offer-3-years-off-airmen-start-families.
Lowther, Adam B. "The Post-9/11 American Serviceman." *Joint Force Quarterly* 58, no. 3 (Fall 2010): 76–84.
———. "Rise of the Millennials: How They Will Impact the Cyber Workforce." *International Affairs Forum* 5, no. 2 (July 2014): 97–105.
Lurie, Orit, Yehuda Zadik, Shmuel Einy, Ricardo Tarrasch, Gil Raviv, and Liav Goldstein. "Bruxism in Military Pilots and Non-Pilots: Tooth Wear and Psychological Stress." *Aviation, Space, and Environmental Medicine* 78, no. 2 (February 2007): 137–39.
Mansfield, Ian. "Huawei Conducts World's First Commercial Network LTE Category 4 Trial." *Cellular News*, 9 May 2012. http://www.cellular-news.com/story/54329.php.
Markoff, John. "Georgia Takes a Beating in the Cyberwar with Russia." *New York Times*, 11 August 2008.
McCullagh, Declan. "US Was Warned of Predator Drone Hacking." *CBS News*, 17 December 2009. http://www.cbsnews.com/blogs/2009/12/17/taking_liberties/entry5988978.shtml.

McGarry, Brendan. "Air Force to Introduce New Bonuses for Nuke Force." *Military.com News*, 18 June 2014. http://www.military.com/daily-news/2014/06/18/air-force-to-introduce-new-bonuses-for-nuke-force.html.

McKinney, Lt Col Maurice M. "A National Solution: Rethinking the Employment of Air National Guard Title 32 Status Citizen-Airmen to Defend the Nation's Cyberspace Infrastructure." Unpublished research paper. Air War College. Maxwell AFB, AL, 14 February 2013.

McNeese, Michael, Nancy J. Cooke, Anita D'Amico, Mica R. Endsley, Cleotilde Gonzalez, Emilie Roth, and Eduardo Salas. "Perspectives on the Role of Cognition in Cyber Security." *Proceedings of the Human Factors and Ergonomics Society Annual Meeting* 56, no. 1 (2012): 268–71.

Mell, Peter, and Timothy Grance. *The NIST Definition of Cloud Computing*. NIST Special Publication 800-145. Gaithersburg, MD: National Institute of Standards and Technology, September 2011.

Military Pay Act of 1958. Public Law 85-422, 20 May 1958. http://www.ncohistory.com/documents/1958-085-0422a.pdf.

"Millennials in Adulthood: Detached from Institutions, Networked with Friends." Pew Research Center, 7 March 2014. http://www.pewsocialtrends.org/2014/03/07/millennials-in-adulthood.

Miller, Drew, Daniel B. Levine, and Stanley A. Horowitz. *A New Approach to Force-Mix Analysis: A Case Study Comparing Air Force Active and Reserve Forces Conducting Cyber Missions*. IDA Paper P-4986. Alexandria, VA: Institute for Defense Analysis, September 2013.

Mills, Robert F. Consortium for Advanced Cyber Thinking and Strategy. Teleconference Meeting Minutes, 26 February 2014.

Mills, Robert F., Richard A. Raines, and Paul D. Williams. *Developing Cyberspace Competencies for Air Force Professional Military Education*. Wright-Patterson AFB, OH: Air Force Institute of Technology, Center for Cyberspace Research, 2007. http://www.dtic.mil/dtic/tr/fulltext/u2/a486832.pdf.

Nakishima, Ellen. "Confidential Report Lists U.S. Weapon System Designs Compromised by Chinese Cyberspies." *Washington Post*, 27 May 2013.

"National Centers of Academic Excellence—Cyber Operations." NSA/Central Security Service. Accessed August 2015. https://www.nsa.gov/academia/nat_cae_cyber_ops.

National Commission on the Structure of the Air Force. *Report to the President and the Congress of the United States*. Arlington, VA: National Commission on the Structure of the Air Force, 30 January 2014.
National Guard Association of the United States. "It's Official: Guard a Bargain." News release, 31 December 2012. http://www.ngaus.org/newsroom/news/its-official-guard-bargain.
National Initiative for Cybersecurity Careers and Studies. "Cyber Competitions." Accessed August 2015. http://niccs.us-cert.gov/training/tc/search/cmp/new.
———. "Cybersecurity Workforce Planning Diagnostic." Accessed August 2015. https://niccs.us-cert.gov/research/cybersecurity-workforce-planning-diagnostic.
———. "Federal Virtual Training Environment (FedVTE), The." Accessed August 2015. http://niccs.us-cert.gov/training/fedvte.
National Initiative for Cybersecurity Education. "National Cybersecurity Workforce Framework," March 2013. http://csrc.nist.gov/nice/framework.
National Institute of Standards and Technology. "Update on the Cybersecurity Framework," 31 July 2014. http://www.nist.gov/cyberframework/upload/NIST-Cybersecurity-Framework-update-073114.pdf.
National Security Council. *International Strategy for Cyberspace: Prosperity, Security, and Openness in a Networked World*. Washington, DC: Executive Office of the President of the United States, May 2011.
National Transportation Safety Board (NTSB). *Pacific Gas and Electric Company Natural Gas Transmission Pipeline Rupture and Fire, San Bruno, California, September 9, 2010*. Pipeline Accident Report NTSB/PAR-11/01. Washington, DC: NTSB, 30 August 2011. http://www.ntsb.gov/investigations/AccidentReports/Reports/PAR1101.pdf.
Nurse, Jason R. C., Oliver Buckley, Philip A. Legg, Michael Goldsmith, Sadie Creese, Gordon R. T. Wright, and Monica Whitty. "Understanding Insider Threat: A Framework for Characterising Attacks." In *Proceedings of the 2014 Workshop on Research for Insider Threat (WRIT), IEEE* [Institute of Electrical and Electronics Engineers] *Computer Society Security and Privacy Workshops*, 214–28. Held in San Jose, CA, 18 May 2014. Los Alamitos, CA:

IEEE Computer Society. http://www.ieee-security.org/TC/SPW20 14/papers/5103a251.PDF.
Office of Personnel Management (OPM). *Handbook of Occupational Groups and Families.* Washington, DC: OPM, May 2009.
Office of the Chairman of the Joint Chiefs of Staff. *The National Military Strategy for Cyberspace Operations.* Washington, DC: DOD, JCS, 2006.
"14XX Intelligence: Applicable to Active Duty." Air Force myPers Web portal. Accessed August 2015. https://gum-crm.csd.disa.mil /app/answers/detail/a_id/13747/kw/14N%20career%20manage ment/p/8%2C9.
Organisation Internationale de la Francophonie. "Benchmarks." Accessed 7 May 2015. http://www.francophonie.org/Welcome-to-the -International.html.
Paulsen, Celia, Ernest McDuffie, William Newhouse, and Patricia Toth. "NICE: Creating a Cybersecurity Workforce and Aware Public." *IEEE Security and Privacy* 10, no. 3 (May–June 2012): 76–79.
Peng, H. "Research on IPv6 Environment Support of Web Application Systems in Chinese Campus Networks." In *Advances in Communication Technology and Application,* edited by P. Lorenz, 345–52. Ashurst Lodge, UK: WIT Press, 2015.
Pilkington, Ed. "China Winning Cyber War, Congress Warned." *Guardian,* 20 November 2008. http://www.theguardian.com/tech nology/2008/nov/20/china-us-military-hacking.
"Post-Graduation Employment Placement." Science, Mathematics and Research for Transformation. Accessed August 2015. http:// smart.asee.org/about/benefits/post_graduation_employment _placement.
Punaro, Maj Gen Arnold, US Marine Corps, retired. Testimony to the National Commission on the Structure of the Air Force. Open hearing. Minutes, 26 June 2013. http://afcommission.whs.mil /public/docs/meetings/20130626/FINAL%20Minutes%20for%20 June%2026%202013%20NCSAF%20Meeting.pdf.
Raytheon. *Preparing Millennials to Lead in Cyberspace.* Sterling, VA: Raytheon, 2013.
Reserve Forces Policy Board. *Eliminating Major Gaps in DoD Data on the Fully-Burdened and Life-Cycle Cost of Military Personnel: Cost Elements Should Be Mandated by Policy.* Final report to the secretary of defense. RFPB Report FY 13-02. Falls Church, VA: Reserve Forces Policy Board, 7 January 2013. http://www.ngaus.org/sites

/default/files/RFPB_Cost_Methodology_Final_Report_7Jan13.pdf.

———. *Reserve Component Use, Balance, Cost and Savings: A Response to Questions from the Secretary of Defense*. Final report to the secretary of Defense. RFPB Report FY 14-02. Falls Church, VA: Reserve Forces Policy Board, 11 February 2014.

Rhoads, Christopher, and Farnaz Fassihi. "Iran Vows to Unplug Internet." *Wall Street Journal*, 28 May 2011.

Richtel, Matt. "Digital Devices Deprive Brain of Needed Downtime." *New York Times*, 24 August 2010. http://www.nytimes.com/2010/08/25/technology/25brain.html?_r=0.

Riley, M. W. "On the Significance of Age in Sociology." *American Sociological Review* 52, no. 1 (Winter 1987): 1–14.

Sanders, CMSgt John, HAF/A6S. To Dr. John P. Geis II, Air Force Research Institute. E-mails, 1 May 2014.

Schmitt, Michael N., ed. *Tallinn Manual on the International Law Applicable to Cyber Warfare*. New York: Cambridge University Press, 2013.

School of Advanced Air and Space Studies 667. Information, Cyberspace, and Cyber Power. Course syllabus. Accessed 26 August 2015. http://www.au.af.mil/au/aul/school/saass/saass667_AY13-14.htm.

Secretary of the Air Force, Public Affairs. "Rise of the Cyber Wingman: 10 Principles Airmen Must Know," 12 November 2009.

"Selective Reenlistment Bonus Program Applicable to Active Duty." myPers, Air Force Personnel Center website. Accessed August 2014. https://gum-crm.csd.disa.mil/app/answers/detail/a_id13829.

Senate. *Department of Defense Authorization of Appropriations for Fiscal Year 2015 and the Future Years Defense Program: Hearings before the Armed Services Committee on the National Commission on the Structure of the Air Force*, 29 April 2014. 113th Cong., 2d sess. http://www.armed-services.senate.gov/download/14-42_-4-29-14pdf.

———. Permanent Subcommittee on Investigations, Committee on Homeland Security and Government Affairs. "The Air Force's Expeditionary Combat Support System (ECSS): A Cautionary Tale on the Need for Business Process Reengineering and Complying with Acquisition Best Practices." Staff report, 7 July 2014. http://www.hsgac.senate.gov/download/?id=DEB00A15-DA26-4174-A997-53BB4AE752F4.

Senior Language Authority Roundtable. National Security Agency, Fort Meade, MD, 11 March 2014.

17D Officer Assignment Team. Cyberspace Operations "Spread the Word" briefing, 9–11 April 2014. Lt Col Ross Morrell, 17D assignments chief, HAF Personnel Center. To Dr. John P. Geis II, AFRI. E-mail, 22 April 2014.

17th Training Group/CC. Memorandum. Subject: Intelligence Officer Student Assignment Selection Process, 17 July 2013.

17th Training Wing. 14N Course Chart/Schedule, 9 September 2013. (FOUO; information used is unclassified) Obtained by John Conway through discussion with Maj James Davitch, HAF/A2, functional manager for the 14N career field, 9 October 2014.

———. Intelligence Officer Course Syllabus, 3 December 2012. (FOUO; information used is unclassified)

Shadbolt, Nigel, Wendy Hall, and Tim Berners-Lee. "The Semantic Web Revisited." *IEEE Intelligent Systems* 21, no. 3 (May/June 2006): 96–101.

Shulenberger, Eric, and Janet Olsonbaker. *Solving the Shortage of STEM [Science, Technology, Engineering, and Mathematics] Personnel in Navy Laboratories: Strategic Plan for Navy Investments in STEM Education Targeted at the "Navy after Next."* Seattle: University of Washington Applied Physics Lab, 2009.

Skibell, Reid. "Cybercrime and Misdemeanors: A Reevaluation of the Computer Fraud and Abuse Act." *Berkeley Tech. LJ* 18 (2003): 909.

Smith, Craig. "By the Numbers: 100+ Interesting Instagram Statistics," 14 December 2014. http://www.expandedramblings.com/index.php/important-instagram-stats.

Spiegel, Diane. *The Gen Y Handbook*. New York: Select Books, 2013.

Stafford, Tom. "Does the Internet Rewire Your Brain?" *BBC*, 24 April 2012. http://www.bbc.com/future/story/20120424-does-the-internet-rewire-brains.

Stenbit, John P., DOD chief information officer. To secretaries of military departments et al. Memorandum. Subject: Internet Protocol version 6 (IPv6), 9 June 2003. http://www.defense.gov/news/Jun2003/d20030609nii.pdf.

Stouffer, Keith, Joe Falco, and Karen Scarfone. "Guide to Industrial Control Systems (ICS) Security: Recommendations of the National Institute of Standards and Technology." NIST Special Publication 800-82. Gaithersburg, MD: NIST, June 2011.

Strategy and Planning Committee, Federal Chief Information Officers Council. "Planning Guide/Roadmap toward IPv6 Adoption with the U.S. Government." Ver. 2.0, July 2012. https://cio.gov/wp-content/uploads/downloads/2012/09/2012_IPv6_Road map_FINAL_ 20120712.pdf.

StreetAuthority. "The Economy Is Finally Approaching Lift-Off—4 Sectors to Target." NASdaq.com, 23 April 2014. http://www.nasdaq.com/article/the-economy-is-finally-approaching-lift-off-4-sectors-to-target-cm346655.

Sujansky, Joanne, and Jan Ferri-Reed. *Keeping the Millennials: Why Companies Are Losing Billions in Turnover to This Generation and What to Do about It*. New York: Wiley, 2009.

Summers, Ann. "A Theoretical Analysis of Leadership Style Preferences among Millennial Generation Company-Grade Officers." PhD diss., University of Maryland, 2011.

Svan, Jennifer H. "Air Force to Test Sabbatical Program for Limited Number of Airmen." *Stars and Stripes*, 16 May 2014. http://www.stripes.com/news/air-force-to-test-sabbatical-program-for-limited-number-of-airmen-1.283424.

Tapscott, Don. *Grown Up Digital*. New York: McGraw Hill, 2009.

10 USC. Sec. 571, "Warrant Officers: Grades." Subtitle A, pt. 2, chap. 33A. *United States Code*. Title 10 – Armed Forces. 2006 ed., supp. 4, 2010. US Government Publishing Office. http://www.gpo.gov/fdsys/pkg/USCODE-2010-title10/pdf/USCODE-2010-title10-subtitleA-partII-chap33A-sec571.pdf.

———. Sec. 10216, "Military Technicians (Dual Status)." Subtitle E, pt. 1, chap. 1007. *United States Code*. Title 10 – Armed Forces. 2013 ed. US Government Publishing Office. http://www.gpo.gov/fdsys/pkg/USCODE-2013-title10/pdf/USCODE-2013-title10-subtitleE-partI-chap1007-sec10216.pdf.

39th Information Operations Squadron (IOS). Intermediate Network Warfare Training (INTW). IOS-INWT 001. PDS CODE 06S. Initial Qualification Training. Ver. 1.2, February 2014.

Thomas, Timothy L. *Decoding the Virtual Dragon*. Fort Leavenworth, KS: Foreign Military Studies Office, 2007.

———. "Russian View on Information Based Warfare." *Airpower Journal* 10 (Special edition, 1996): 28.

Thurman, Susan. *Emerging Workforce, The: Generational Trends*. Atlanta: National Society of High School Scholars, 2013.

———. *NSHSS Scholar 2013 Millennial Career Survey Results: The Emerging Workforce: Generational Trends*. Atlanta: NSHSS, 2013.

Trippe, D. Matthew, Karen O. Moriarty, Teresa L. Russell, Thomas R. Carretta, and Adam S. Beatty. "Development of a Cyber / Information Technology Knowledge Test for Military Enlisted Technical Training Qualification." *Military Psychology* 26, no. 3 (May 2014): 182–98.

Tulgan, Bruce. *Not Everyone Gets a Trophy: How to Manage Generation Y*. San Francisco: Jossey-Bass, 2009.

Twenty-Fourth Air Force, vice-commander. Briefing. To Air Force Research Institute research team. San Antonio, TX, 5 March 2014.

27th International Olympiad in Informatics. "Call for Papers." 2015 competition, Kazakhstan. Accessed August 2015. http://www.ioinformatics.org/index.shtml.

Ungerleider, Neal. "Iran Cracking Down Online with 'Halal Internet.'" *Fast Company*, 18 April 2011. http://www.fastcompany.com/1748123/iran-cracking-down-online-halal-internet.

US Air Force Chief Scientist. *Cyber Vision 2025: United States Air Force Cyberspace Science and Technology Vision 2012–2025*. AF/ST TR 12-01. Washington, DC: Office of the Chief Scientist, United States Air Force, 13 December 2012.

US-China Economic and Security Review Commission. "The National Security Implication of Investments and Products from the People's Republic of China in the Telecommunications Sector." Staff report, January 2011.

"USCYBERCOM Cyber Mission Force." Briefing slides. Scott C. Brokaw, JCS/J1. To John Conway, Air Force Research Institute. E-mail, 18 April 2014.

US Marine Corps Training Command. "Joint Cyber Analysis Course." Accessed August 2015. http://www.trngcmd.marines.mil/Units/Southeast/MATSG21/MARDETCorryStation.

Vanderbeek, Rodger D. "Period Prevalence of Acute Neck Injury in US Air Force Pilots Exposed to High G Forces." *Aviation, Space, and Environmental Medicine* 59, no. 12 (December 1988): 1176–80.

Van Evera, Stephen. *Guide to Methods for Students of Political Science*. Ithaca, NY: Cornell University Press, 1997.

Vautrinot, Maj Gen Suzanne. Briefing. Subject: AFCYBER (Air Forces Cyber). To Air War College, Maxwell AFB, AL, 21 February 2012.

"VC-25—Air Force One." USAF fact sheet, 1 July 2003. http://www .af.mil/AboutUs/FactSheets/Display/tabid/224/Article/104588 /vc-25-air-force-one.aspx.

Verton, Dan. "Anthem Hack Reveals Limits of Voluntary Cyber Frameworks." *Information Week*, 5 February 2015. http://fedscoop.com /anthem-hack-reveals-inadequacy-of-voluntary-cybersecurity -frameworks.

Warrant Officer Act of 1954. Public Law 379. H. R. 6374, 29 May 1954. http://www.gpo.gov/fdsys/pkg/STATUTE-68/pdf/STATUTE -68-Pg157.pdf.

Watkins, Steve. "Federal Big Data Spending to Increase despite Sequester." *C4ISR and Networks*, 8 May 2014. http://www.c4isrnet.com/ar ticle/20140508/C4ISRNET14/305080003/Federal-Big-Data -spending-increase-despite-sequester.

Watson, CMSgt Adam, functional manager, 1NXXX career fields, HAF/A2, Pentagon. To Dr. John P. Geis II, Air Force Research Institute. E-mail, 7 May 2014.

Welsh, Gen Mark A., III. "Global Vigilance, Global Reach, Global Power for America: The World's Greatest Air Force—Powered by Airmen, Fueled by Innovation." *Air and Space Power Journal* 28, no. 2 (March–April 2014): 4–10.

West, Joe. "Last Known Warrant (Officer) Retires." *Air Force Times*, 30 November 1992.

White House. "Comprehensive National Cybersecurity Initiative." Accessed August 2015. https://www.whitehouse.gov/issues/foreign -policy/cybersecurity/national-initiative.

———. "Cybersecurity—Executive Order 13636." Accessed 18 August 2015. https://www.whitehouse.gov/issues/foreign-policy/cybersec urity/eo-13636#.

———. *National Security Strategy*. Washington, DC: Executive Office of the President, February 2015. http://www.whitehouse.gov/sites /default/files/docs/2015_national_security_strategy_2.pdf.

[Yannakogeorgos, Panayotis A]. "Command and Control of Cyber Operations." In *Air Force Command and Control: The Need for Increased Adaptability*. AFRI Paper 2012-5 by Jeffrey Hukill (team leader), Larry Carter, Scott Johnson, Jennifer Lizzol, Edward Redman, and Panayotis Yannakogeorgos. Maxwell AFB, AL: Air Force Research Institute, Air University Press, 2012, 96–108.

———. "The Rise of IPv6: Benefits and Costs of Transforming Military Cyberspace." *Air and Space Power Journal* 29, no. 2 (March–

April 2015): 103–28. http://www.airpower.maxwell.af.mil/article.asp?id=261.

———. "USAF Cyber Education." Presentation. Baltic Defence College Workshops on Cyber Education, Tallinn, Estonia, 7 April 2014.

Yardley, Jim. "Panic Seizes India as a Region's Strife Radiates." *New York Times*, 17 August 2012.

Zhong, Chen, Deepak S. Kirubakaran, John Yen, Peng Liu, Steve Hutchinson, and Hasan Cam. "How to Use Experience in Cyber Analysis: An Analytical Reasoning Support System." In *Proceedings of the 2013 IEEE International Conference on Intelligence and Security Informatics*, edited by Kristin Glass et al., 263–65. Hoboken, NJ: IEEE Press, 2013.

Zuehlke, Maj Gen Sheila, mobilization assistant to the commander, US Cyber Command. To John Conway, Air Force Research Institute. E-mail, 24 July 2014.

About the Contributors

Col John L. Conway III, USAF, retired, is a military defense analyst at the Air Force Research Institute, Maxwell AFB, Alabama. During his more than 30 years in the Air Force, he served as an intelligence officer with major assignments at Headquarters Air Intelligence Agency, North American Aerospace Defense Command, and the National Security Agency. He was the senior intelligence officer at Headquarters Air Force Reserve Command (AFRC), Robins AFB, Georgia, and held several wing and squadron intelligence assignments, including a combat tour at the II Direct Air Support Center in Pleiku Province, Republic of Vietnam, and a term as chief of the Counterdrug Support Division, Headquarters AFRC. After retiring from active duty in 2001, Colonel Conway was a civilian adviser to the commander, Gordon Regional Security Operations Center, Fort Gordon, Georgia, following 9/11. From 2002 to 2004, he was a systems engineering and technical assistance contractor in the U-2 Directorate at the Warner Robins Air Logistics Center, Robins AFB, Georgia. He is the author of several articles published in the *Air and Space Power Journal* on diverse topics such as the C-27 beddown issue, Total Force matters, foreign language capabilities, disaster preparedness, and High North search and rescue. Colonel Conway earned a bachelor of arts and a master of arts degree at the University of Alabama.

Chad Dacus is a research professor and economist at the Air Force Research Institute and an adjunct professor at Air University, Maxwell AFB, Alabama. His current research interests include defense acquisition, economics and strategy, and cyberspace risk modeling. Before joining the Air Force Research Institute, Dr. Dacus worked as a field representative for the Center for Naval Analyses. He holds a PhD in economics from Rice University, a master of science degree in statistics from Texas A&M University, and a bachelor of science in engineering management with highest honors from Missouri University of Science and Technology.

Lt Col Steven Drinnon, USAF, is the chief of professional journals at the Air Force Research Institute, Maxwell AFB, Alabama. Colonel Drinnon served as a T-1A instructor pilot (IP) with the 14th Flying Training Wing, Columbus AFB, Mississippi, where he also held the positions of line pilot, assistant director of operations (ADO) for training, and chief of the Commander's Action Group; he also was ADO of the 14th Student Squadron. At Squadron Officer School, Maxwell AFB, Colonel Drinnon held the positions of flight commander, assistant operations officer, and academic department chair. He served as a KC-135R/T pilot and IP for two assignments (350th and 99th Air Refueling Squadrons), where his positions included chief of squadron mobility and chief of training. He is a senior pilot with over 2,600 hours, including 400-plus combat hours in Operations Enduring Freedom and Iraqi Freedom. Colonel Drinnon has deployed to Africa, Asia, and the Middle East. In 2004 he was selected as the Cargo/Tanker Pilot of the Year by the Air Force Association's Carl Vinson Chapter. He holds a bachelor of science degree from Valdosta State University, where he received his commission from the Air Force Reserve Officer Training Corps.

Col John P. Geis II, USAF, retired, is the director of research at the Air Force Research Institute, Maxwell AFB, Alabama. Dr. Geis's Air Force career included training and combat operations flying the T-37, the AT-38B, the T-43, two variants of the F-111, and the AC-130H special operations gunship. He also served as the director of long-range planning for all US Air Force special forces and served for eight years as the director of the Air Force Center for Strategy and Technology, where he provided advice to national leadership on the strategic implications of emerging technologies. Dr. Geis holds a bachelor's degree in meteorology and a master's degree in political science from the University of Wisconsin, a master's degree in political science from Auburn University, a master's degree in strategic studies from Air University, and a PhD in political science from the University of Wisconsin.

Col Stephen Hagel, USAF, retired, served as a researcher and analyst at the Air Force Research Institute, Maxwell AFB, Alabama, until his retirement from civil service in August 2015. His research interests there included defense logistics, acquisition, and strategic planning. Prior to joining the Air Force Research Institute, he served on the Air War College faculty, teaching courses in the Warfighting Department. In addition, he created and taught the Logistics, Total Force, and J8-directed Planning electives. He has served at the base, major command, center, joint, and Headquarters Air Force levels as a logistics planner, logistics researcher, combat-support battle staff director and team chief, war gamer, and strategy and doctrine developer.

He has also served as a senior reliability analyst and process improvement specialist at FedEx Corporation and has taught logistics and business courses at two universities. He holds a bachelor of arts degree in history from South Dakota State University and a master of science in logistics from the Air Force Institute of Technology, where he did research in logistics war gaming.

Adam B. Lowther is director of the School for Advanced Nuclear Deterrence Studies (SANDS) at Kirtland AFB, New Mexico. He previously served as a research professor and director of the Center for Academic and Professional Journals at the Air Force Research Institute, Maxwell AFB, Alabama. His principal research interests include deterrence, airpower diplomacy, and the Asia-Pacific. Dr. Lowther is the author or editor of five books and has published in the *New York Times, Boston Globe, Joint Force Quarterly, Strategic Studies Quarterly*, and a variety of other journals and outlets. Formerly, Dr. Lowther was on the faculty of two universities, where he taught courses in international relations, political economy, security studies, and comparative politics. Early in his career, he served in the US Navy aboard the USS *Ramage* (DDG-61). He also spent time at CINCUSNAVEUR–London and with Naval Marine Construction Battalion 17. He holds a PhD from the University of Alabama and a bachelor of arts degree and master of arts degree from Arizona State University.

Panayotis "Pano" A. Yannakogeorgos is dean of the Air Force Cyber College, Maxwell AFB, Alabama. His expertise includes the intersection of cyber power, national security, and military operations; international cyber policy; cyber arms control; global cyber norms; and Eastern Mediterranean security. He recently authored *Strategies for Resolving the Cyber Attribution Challenge* and coedited the book *Conflict and Cooperation in Cyberspace*. His published work has also appeared in the *National Interest, CNN Online*, the *Atlantic*, the *Diplomat, Strategic Studies Quarterly*, the *Journal of Information Warfare and Terrorism, Crime and Terrorism Risk: Studies in Criminology and Criminal Justice* (Routledge), and *Global Norms: American Sponsorship and the Emerging Pattern of World Politics* (Palgrave). Dr. Yannakogeorgos was formerly a member of the faculty at Rutgers University's Division of Global Affairs and has served as an adviser with the United Nations Security Council on issues related to nuclear nonproliferation, the Middle East, al-Qaeda, and Internet misuse. He holds a PhD and a master of science degree in global affairs from Rutgers University and a bachelor of liberal arts degree in philosophy from Harvard University.